Eisenhower: Captive Hero

Eisenhower: Captive Hero

A Critical Study of the General and the President

Marquis William Childs

Harcourt, Brace & World, Inc. New York

The publisher and the author acknowledge permission from the following to reprint material from the sources listed:
A. D. Peters, London, "Earth shall be fair" by Clifford Bax
Doubleday & Company, Inc., *Crusade in Europe* by Dwight D. Eisenhower; *Man from Abilene* by Kevin McCann, copyright 1952 by The Defiance College, copyright 1952 by New York *Herald Tribune*
Henry Holt and Company, Inc., *A Soldier's Story* by Omar N. Bradley
Little, Brown & Company, *Melville Goodwin, U.S.A.*, copyright 1951 by John P. Marquand
McGraw-Hill Book Co. Inc., *Watching the World* by Raymond Clapper
New York *Herald Tribune* and Walter Lippmann, "The Problem of Sincerity" by Walter Lippmann, Dec. 26, 1957
G. P. Putnam's Sons, *Arms and Men*, copyright 1956 by Walter Millis
Simon and Schuster, Inc., *My Three Years with Eisenhower*, © 1946, by Harry C. Butcher

For Malissa Childs Redfield

A Note on Sources

The Eisenhower literature is small. For the most part it consists of books and articles that have the strong stamp of official approval. A note of worshipfulness runs through it.

Two books have been most helpful. One is *Soldier of Democracy* by Kenneth S. Davis, which is a serious effort to present the Eisenhower background. The other is *Eisenhower: The Inside Story* by Robert J. Donovan, first-rate reporting based on a privileged view of the files of the administration in the first term. Merriman Smith's *Meet Mister Eisenhower* contains interesting anecdotes of the President's early years in the White House. Richard Rovere's *Affairs of State: The Eisenhower Years* looks more deeply below the smooth surface of the first term.

Aside from these sources, I have drawn chiefly on my own knowledge of the events that marked the rise of an obscure Army officer to a position of world fame. My deepest debt is to my daughter, Mrs. Redfield, who with unfailing patience has done so much in so many ways to help me in the preparation of this book.

Contents

Cartoons

Eisenhower:
Captive Hero

Introduction

Between the reputation of a great man at the summit of his career and the judgment ultimately passed upon him there is invariably a discrepancy. Often the contemporary verdict is too harsh, as in the instance of Andrew Johnson, who succeeded to the presidency in an era of savage reprisal following a long civil war. But in our own time, with the techniques of the publicist applied to the media of mass communication, we are more likely to discover that reputations have been grossly inflated.

This is where biography and history have their burrow. In the neutral zone between the purple glory of great achievement, or what passes at the moment for achievement, and the steel-gray judgment of the long view, the appraisers, the searchers, the compilers of records dig and delve. Nearly two thousand books are now devoted to Abraham Lincoln, and the lengthening shadow of his lonely greatness falls across the years. Already nearly fifty books have been written about Franklin Roosevelt, although he has been dead scarcely more than a decade. Many were written by hostile critics determined to pull down what seemed to them Roosevelt's vastly overrated reputation; others by men who believe him the greatest man of our time. Historians think that within three or four decades the library of Rooseveltiana will be larger than that of Lincolniana.

While it is too early for any summary estimation of Dwight Eisenhower, a useful purpose may be served by trying now to put in somewhat clearer perspective the relation between the man and his exalted reputation. Taking the reputation at its face value, accepting the legend in full, has been a grave disservice. The President has himself tried on several occasions to say that the American people should not look to him to solve all their problems. He said so frequently in response to the speculation about a second term in the months leading up to his heart attack in September of 1955.

Before the loud hosannas of innumerable Republican jubilees the President protested that the party, the people, must work their own way out of the wilderness. If he has seemed reluctant to wear the mantle of personal authority, and it may well be a genuine reluctance, it is one of the ironies of his extraordinary career that this was one way to insure that the American people would insist on giving him such authority. If a Caesar returned victorious from the foreign wars was what popular opinion wanted, then Eisenhower was a timid and hesitant one. He agreed to go for the ride on the tiger, but he has never ceased to look back nervously.

Eisenhower has, however, worn an outward smile of confidence, a smile that is increasingly hard to maintain. With the greater part of his second term still to run, the inevitable discrepancy between his reputation and his performance is becoming more and more painfully apparent. This cruel process has undermined other great men in our national life, as it did Woodrow Wilson in the tragic aftermath of that earlier world war. Who can deny that something like this might have happened to Lincoln, also, had he lived on into the reconstruction era. Often by the mischance of events or by their own miscalculation, heroes set up in the national pantheon have been angrily dashed to earth while they were still living. The higher they ride, the harder they fall. If we enjoy creating the heroic image, building it big, we also delight in shattering it.

What happened to Lieutenant Colonel Eisenhower after 1941 has no parallel in our history. It is a little like the story of Ulysses S. Grant. But it is Grant magnified a thousand times, magnified to world dimensions, magnified by the scope of America's fantastic power. Eisenhower was shot out of a cannon from complete obscurity to a position at the very top, where he spoke as an equal with kings and prime ministers and presidents. The trajectory went from the drowsy Indian posts, from Fort Lewis, Fort Leavenworth, Jefferson Barracks—where he had spent nearly thirty years of his life as part of an unknown caste—to Paris, London, Algiers, to the center of the stage of a vast struggle for world power. He was a professional soldier before December 10, 1941, that is to say, a museum piece. Overnight he was given authority on a scale exercised by few human beings in recorded history. The transition itself might well have been expected to overwhelm most men.

In the first year of the war we had a desperate need for a hero. One might almost say a guilty need. We had for so long neglected, if not ignored, our destiny. Eisenhower was chosen to be that hero, to be the symbol of a warmhearted, friendly, simple America, personifying the mighty rush, the Niagara, of American power coming into being.

It might not have come off. General Eisenhower himself had serious doubts in those early months. During the fluctuating fortunes of the Battle of the Kasserine Pass in North Africa, Eisenhower, consumed by every kind of tension and uncertainty, commuted between his command headquarters in Algiers and the front. Harry Hop-

"Rough, eh, Soldier?"

Mauldin in the St. Louis *Post-Dispatch*   May 4, 1958

kins had sent word that if he succeeded, if his armies could sweep on to take Tunisia, he would become one of the greatest generals, one of the greatest heroes, of all time. Hopkins did not add what General Eisenhower knew well enough in those weeks of uncertainty—if he failed he would very likely go home in defeat to obscurity again.

He did not fail. The symbol grew until it towered above the dark and bloody horizon of the war; the earnest, patient, good general in there pitching for all of us, making sure that American boys had everything they needed so they could fight and win. The symbol owed its strength in part to the vast military information system, in part to the Office of War Information. But to ascribe the growth of the symbol to "propaganda" alone would be naïve. The need, the deep inner necessity, for a symbol, was there in a whole people who had found themselves, in a state of shock, in the midst of a war for which they were unprepared.

Other generals might have done as well. But as symbol, as the apotheosis of America forced to carry the leadership of an unwanted war, Eisenhower seems, at least in hindsight, to have been the inevitable choice. He is, above all, adaptable, capable of being what he is expected to be. This is not to say that he consciously plays a role. It is, rather, that he has a high degree of empathy. He has long antennae that vibrate in response to the signals around him.

This has been both his strength and his weakness. "Ike," the great hero of the war, responded intuitively to the demands of a vast new public. There were skillful handlers in the background, a growing corps of friendly experts, looking out for his reputation. But as some of them have testified, his own sense of the proper conduct of a hero was often better than theirs. Yet the same intuition has led him far too often to compromise in response to popular clamor.

Eisenhower held a conviction that most of us wanted to share: the conviction that we could get along with our allies, perhaps even with Soviet Russia. This was the conviction of a professional soldier who had always found war repugnant and who was convinced, after World War II, that another war would mean mass suicide. He spoke of this eloquently both in public and in private. Surely one who had been the supreme commander of a combined war effort would know how to get along with allies, most Americans thought wistfully.

Only three years after the end of the war, the Democrats, or a considerable segment of the Democratic party, made a serious and determined effort to draft Eisenhower as their candidate for president. This was proof, if any proof was needed, of the enormous power of the legend that had grown up around him. No one doubted that he could win. His name was magic. These Democrats seemed to be confessing the political bankruptcy of their party, and even, in a sense, the bankruptcy of the system itself, though the candidate whom they had wanted to reject, Harry S. Truman, was to win in an old-fashioned campaign that carried the fight to the enemy.

The lesson was not lost on the Republicans. In 1952 they "drafted" the hero. The time was even more propitious for him than it was in 1948. Peace had not come to America. The war in Korea was a festering wound. Who better than a hero-general could bring an end to the conflict and make matters right with America's allies once again? It was a time of petulance and irritation, with the errors of a party long in power magnified by a hostile press. And just as he had done in 1943, so again Eisenhower could lead us. If Adlai Stevenson had

"Settled"

Hesse in the St. Louis *Globe-Democrat*   July 13, 1952

"And I Still Say, 'Who Could Ever Fill Your Shoes?'"

Hugh Haynie in the Greensboro *Daily News*   August 9, 1957

expected to conduct a political dialogue, he was doomed
from the first to disappointment. A great many Americans
wanted to believe again in the lucky general.

He was our hostage against ill fortune, our warranty
that all would be well. Whether he lent himself to this
role willingly or only after long doubt and earnest persuasion was irrelevant—just as the real nature of the
man and his equipment, or lack of it, for the highest
office were also irrelevant. Foremost among the prizes
brought home by victorious armies in the ancient past
were living symbols of triumph, a captive prince or king
whose existence among the victors insured the peace
and the well-being that must go with peace. Something
of this same hope was invested in Eisenhower. He was
our captive hero.

Some of those who could not make themselves heard
above the roar of "We like Ike" put the whole thing
down to a monstrous conspiracy. Their frustration was
almost comic. This simple-minded general was the tool
of big business and the militarists, who would elect and
use him for their own sinister ends. He was a Hindenburg
who would prepare the way for fascism in America. No
doubt there were men who hoped to "use" Eisenhower
once he was in the presidency. And the benefits he has
conferred on business have been taken as confirmation
of this "plot." But it is a naïve devil theory that overlooks
the larger facts of life. If there was to be a two-party system, and if the opposition party was to take power after
twenty years out of office, Eisenhower appeared to be
almost the only candidate with a chance. He seemed
virtually the only "Republican" who could be elected.
Again and again he spoke the right lines, the words so
many of us wanted to believe. It was not a conspiracy;
it seemed more like destiny.

His great victory at the polls in 1952 carried all but

nine states in the Union. He was the wonder-worker, the man who had done it in war and would now do it in peace. It was so much easier to believe in Eisenhower the hero than to face up to the fearful complications of a time of troubles. We could put our trust in Ike and Mamie.

The larger victory of 1956 was taken as proof that the President's reputation had, if anything, grown. Even with the series of misfortunes that began in the fall of 1957, his popularity did not suffer an immediate and disastrous decline. His party and the members of his administration were to blame for the calamities that befell us. Having invested so heavily in Eisenhower the hero the American people seemed reluctant to reject him and take their losses. Possibly he would escape an ordeal that would put his reputation to the ultimate test. Something very like this happened to Grant, who, overwhelmed by personal tragedy in the trials of his second term, continued, nevertheless, to hold a high place in the public mind.

But surely it is possible now to make at least a tentative examination of Eisenhower the man against Eisenhower the almost legendary hero and hostage. He himself has resented the shrine. Surely it is time to try to look with some realism at what has happened to him and to us. As the President has so often said, our political life can have no solid base in the wishful reliance on a hero, a savior. That is not representative government. In the aftermath of a great war it may have been a natural recourse. But the phase of the hero has ended. It is time to ask what Eisenhower has meant to us, where we have come with him, and where we may be going.

One

Abilene, Kansas

For most men in public life fame is achieved by slow stages. There are rings of growth, each one larger in circumference, until finally the circle encompasses the nation and the world. The man and his time come gradually to an understanding. Dwight Eisenhower, however, grew not in measured stages, but suddenly—and surprisingly. At one moment he was an obscure lieutenant colonel in the United States Army with a record good but not distinguished. The next moment he was a national hero, symbol of the hope and resolution we needed in our pitiful unpreparedness to assume the leadership in a global war against a ruthless and formidable enemy.

This transfiguration occurred with such astonishing suddenness that the hero stood before the world without a past. He was catapulted from the wings to the center of the greatest drama of our time, but he was, after all, fifty-two years old, and he had, after all, a past. It became necessary at once to discover it.

It turned out to be a story that could not have been better had Frank Merriwell lived it or Horatio Alger written it. The hero's background had all the elements of the classic American legend of poor but proud: the boy who takes obstacles as a challenge and wins through to success. These are the elements that we have treasured,

the components of the story of the triumph over a continent: the devout, hard-working mother, the wrong side
of the tracks, the victory over the town bully, working
nights and summers to help pay for a brother's education. Those who prospected Eisenhower's past in a kind
of journalistic gold rush fell upon this treasure with cries
of delight. If they had set out to invent a myth to enhance
the magic of his name, they could not have improved it.

That there seemed to be no shadows and no depths
was for the moment unimportant. What his countrymen
desired, what they so passionately wanted to believe in,
was just this classic legend of the boy from the heart of
America who would lead the free world to victory. There
are some signs that he resisted the process, in the initial
phase at least, but even if he had wished to stop it he
would have been powerless. He was in his person the
myth, the image, of the crusader, an image almost as
important to the America of late 1942 and early 1943
as the tanks, planes, and ships we were beginning to
produce with a flood of energy. Letters he had written
to his mother and to other members of his family were
discovered and syndicated in newspapers across the
country. General Eisenhower reacted with anger. This
was his private life, and who were these interlopers who
dared to intrude on it? But the process went on, each
nugget quarried out of the native rock.

We discovered that he was born in Denison, Texas.
When he was only a few months old the family settled
permanently in Abilene, Kansas. Abilene, Kansas! What
if he had grown up in Brooklyn? Impossible! Santa Barbara, California? It would never do. Abilene was so right
that no novelist would have ventured to put him there.
Abilene: a small town, set only a few miles from the
geographic heart of America, so solid, so far removed

from the uncertain complexities of the sophisticated coastal cities, a town to be identified with America's most enduring native qualities. But it was a town with a history, a dramatic past—still recent and vivid in Eisenhower's childhood. Abilene had been an important outpost on the western frontier, the very model, for a few years, of the lawless western cowtown made so familiar by television and the movies. While the frontier moved on with the opening of the Far West, Abilene remained in spirit a frontier town. In this environment Dwight Eisenhower grew up; perhaps more than anything else, Abilene may have shaped his character and purpose.

When the first Eisenhowers arrived in 1878 to establish farms nearby, Abilene had been settled for scarcely two decades and had only recently become a comparatively quiet and ordered community. For four years after the Kansas-Pacific Railroad reached Abilene in 1867 the town was a principal cattle market, destination of millions of Texas cattle driven up the Chisholm Trail. Until the railroad pushed farther west, the cattle trade brought in a wild, lawless element—cowboys, gamblers, prostitutes, gunmen. The town became notorious. One of the legendary heroes of the old West helped make Abilene more respectable: Wild Bill (James Butler) Hickok, famous as a dead shot, was town marshal in the early seventies.

The Eisenhowers found a country both harsh and richly promising. The fierce climate ranged between the scorching heat of dry, dusty summers and the bitter cold of snowbound winters. From the reasonable, rolling vistas of Pennsylvania to the lonely sweep of the prairies and the endless sky was a psychological journey. But the land they farmed, in the valley of the Smoky Hill River in Dickinson County, proved remarkably fertile; its deep alluvial soil was ideal for the raising of varied and abundant crops.

Jacob Eisenhower and his wife, Rebecca, their four children, and Jacob's old father had prospered on their land back in Elizabethville, Pennsylvania. Theirs was the thrifty yet bountiful Pennsylvania Dutch tradition, and the property they sold before going west testified to its success: a nine-room brick house, a generous barn, a hundred acres of land with a vineyard, orchards, beehives. This had been the tradition for a hundred and fifty years, since the first Eisenhowers came to America and settled in Pennsylvania, a tradition of hard work, temperance, self-denial, simple living, a life ordered with a fundamental, almost Biblical simplicity.

The Eisenhowers brought with them to America the faith of their German forebears, which had in it something of the rigors of the Old Testament. They were members of an American Mennonite sect, the River Brethren, later known as the Church of the Brethren in Christ. Far more than most Protestant sects, the church exercised a comprehensive and immediate influence on the lives of its adherents. But at the same time it made for the development of strong individual character. At the core of the faith of the River Brethren was the conviction that no organized priesthood, no church hierarchy, had any intermediate authority between man and God; every individual soul, guided and informed by the Bible, confronted God alone. Sharing this exacting belief, the River Brethren were a deeply committed, close-knit religious community which declined to conform with customs and requirements of the rest of society that were not its own. This nonconformity was evident in their strong pacifism; Jacob Eisenhower, a minister of his church, was an uncompromising man of peace. Many

of the River Brethren in and around Abilene were paci-
fists in World War II. They gave the local draft board a
great deal of trouble.

But for all their unworldliness, the River Brethren
regarded material prosperity as a sign of God's favor.
They were by no means indifferent to economic opportunity. This was apparently the principal reason why a
substantial group, including the Eisenhowers, moved to
Kansas. Although things had gone well with them in
Pennsylvania, they believed they would do even better
in the West. They were responding to the widespread
restlessness inspired by the beckoning frontier, the great
American itch to get up and move on. For the River
Brethren it was a community venture, carefully, provi-
dently planned. Advance reports assured them of the
desirability of their new location, and they arrived fully
prepared to re-establish their lives, ready to begin farm-
ing and worshiping again.

Jacob and Rebecca Eisenhower, with Hannah Amanda,
David, Abraham, and Ira, settled on a farm of one hundred and sixty acres. There Jacob soon built, we are told,
a typical Pennsylvania Dutch barn and windmill and a
sizable house where Sunday services were conducted
before the church was built. Theirs was the image of
the Biblical family with flocks and herds, working hard
on the land and flourishing with the blessing of God.
Jacob was able to accumulate sufficient capital to invest,
over the years, in a small bank in the nearby village of
Hope, and he provided his children with a generous start
on their own lives. When Amanda married a neighboring
farmer in 1884, she received a farm of one hundred and
sixty acres and two thousand dollars in cash, a substantial dowry for the time.

As David came of age, he broke with the Biblical past.
He did not want to be a farmer. By temperament he was

quiet, reflective, unaggressive. Not quite sure what he did want to do, he persuaded his rather reluctant father to send him to a small, church-run school in Lecompton, Kansas, called Lane University. There he studied mechanics and the general academic course. He had already demonstrated a certain mechanical ability and thought he might become an engineer. This is so much in the American tradition, so much a part of the time, that it is hard to realize how radical a break with the centuries it was and how hesitant and unsure of himself David must have felt in leaving the well-worn family path. After two years at Lane, whatever larger ambitions he may have cherished and such modest intellectual stimulation as he was receiving were put aside in favor of marriage to a fellow student, Ida Elizabeth Stover. Their wedding took place on September 23, 1885.

Ida Eisenhower is a classic figure in the American success story, a woman of extraordinary strength of character and will. Her presence at Lane, in an era when higher education for women was still rare, testified to the resoluteness, the indomitable quality, that were to have such a formative effect on her marriage and her family. Her lively, outgoing, decisive nature was in sharp contrast to her husband's, but in its fundamentals her background was similar, and she devoutly shared the faith of the River Brethren. Born in Virginia and orphaned as a young girl, she had used her parents' small legacy to go to Kansas, where her brothers were living, for two years' study at Lane. The inheritance also provided an ebony piano that was to be a prized possession and a parlor ornament, a sign of aspiration and ambition, all her life.

With a partner to provide some experience, David Eisenhower put up the capital to start a general merchandise store in the village of Hope. His father's wedding present—like Amanda's, a one-hundred-and-sixty-acre farm and two thousand dollars—made the venture possible, and David raised an additional two thousand dollars on the farm. The beginning was encouraging, but apparently a combination of inattention and inexperience weakened a promising business. The store's situation became steadily more precarious until, in the fall of 1888, everything was lost—the store, the mortgaged farm, everything but a few household items, and the ebony piano.

In his shame and humiliation David chose to leave the scene of his defeat and took a badly paid railroad job in Denison, Texas. One child, Arthur, had been born in 1886, and another was on the way. After the birth of Edgar in January 1889, Ida joined her husband in Denison. And there, in a small frame house facing the railroad tracks, their third son, David Dwight, was born on October 14, 1890. The following spring David took the family back to Abilene, where he had accepted a job as mechanic with the Belle Springs Creamery, a prosperous concern owned and operated by the River Brethren. The job paid less than fifty dollars a month—only a little more than he had made with the railroad—and during his twenty years at the creamery his wage was scarcely doubled.

The cycle of the business failure, the stay in Denison, and the return to Abilene determined the content of the legendary themes woven through future accounts of Dwight Eisenhower's boyhood, as it also determined the major bent of the boy's character. A novelist would have hesitated to make so explicit the incentives that were to spur the Eisenhower boys on as they grew up.

David Eisenhower, who was naturally quiet and gentle, never really recovered from the blow to his self-confidence of that early failure. But Ida Eisenhower was

stimulated by the disaster to bring all her energy and
drive to bear on making the best of the situation. She
carried through her life a determination never to admit
defeat or betray disappointment or sorrow. This was the
stamp she put on her sons. Show a brave face to the
world, smiling, cheerful; never let anyone know if you
feel anxious or despondent. During the Denison years
it was Ida Eisenhower who assumed all but nominal
command of the family, setting a pattern of tireless, disciplined activity. The religious beliefs of husband and
wife, which had evolved in the Denison period of sorrow
and humiliation into a highly personal kind of mysticism,
gave a special strength and certitude to the rigorous
standards she set for herself and the children, although
the beliefs themselves were to be discarded by the boys
as they grew up.

They were among the poorest people in town. Abilene
had the classic geography of the American small town:
a "right" side and a "wrong" side of the railroad tracks.
The Union Pacific and Santa Fe tracks were the great
divide, separating the affluent and the assured on the
North Side from the poor and hard-working on the South.
The Eisenhower boys were keenly aware that they lived
on the South Side. Their contemporaries found them to
be resentful and contemptuous of North Side snobbishness.
With Dwight Eisenhower this sometimes took the form
of bravado, a certain defiance of the standards of the
other side. You might want to be like the banker, the
merchant, the doctor, but it was a matter of pride not
to let anyone know it.

For several years after the return to Abilene, the Eisenhowers lived in a small, inadequate house on South East
Second Street. Here Roy was born in 1892, a son named
Paul, who died after a few months, in 1894, and Earl
in 1898. In 1899 their last child, Milton, was born, a few

months after they had moved to the two-story white frame house on South East Fourth Street that was to be their permanent home. Today it is preserved exactly as it was when the family lived there. Although far from a spacious dwelling for the parents, six boys, and David's old father, Jacob, who lived with them until his death in 1906, the house had definite advantages for the family's comfort, and, much more important, for their economic welfare. On the three-acre lot they had room for a vegetable garden, a strawberry patch, grapevines, and fruit trees. In a large barn on the property they kept a horse, cows, chickens, and other livestock, and the feed for all the stock could be grown on the place. They even had a smokehouse and cured their own meat.

The emphasis was on self-reliance. Ida Eisenhower and her family stored away in the summer and fall much of the food they would consume in the winter. Meats were salted and dried. Root vegetables were stored in a root cellar, while other vegetables and fruits were preserved in jars. The small town of that earlier America seemed to be complete in itself, as did the family unit in the town. This was the spirit of the frontier in the small-town, Midwestern America of fifty years ago, and it left an indelible imprint on the Eisenhower boys. They were to carry over into a complex and compartmentalized age the habits of thought of that time and place in which individual initiative and enterprise counted for everything.

The Eisenhower family economy, maintained on a very small income, required the most careful management and constant labor, and the boys were expected from their earliest years to carry their share of the load. Under no circumstances were the chores assigned to them to be shirked: tending the stock, caring for the garden in the summer, bringing in scuttles of coal for the kitchen range and coal stoves in the winter. Their most hateful task was selling surplus vegetables from the garden to the prosperous families on the North Side. Loading up the buggy or a coaster wagon with peas, beans, lettuce, corn, they would start out to show their wares from door to door and sometimes to take well-remembered rebuffs. As soon as he was old enough, each boy brought in additional income from odd jobs at the Belle Springs Creamery.

It was a healthy, rigorous, active life. The boys were constantly busy at work or vigorous play. They learned early to accept responsibility and discipline and to adjust readily to people and circumstances; to be adaptable, in short. Adaptability was, through all his life, to be one of Dwight Eisenhower's prime characteristics.

At no time is there any record of intellectual curiosity, the thirst of the young Lincoln for knowledge. The personal qualities that were to stand Eisenhower in good stead later, as well as those that were not so useful, were being formed, but it is impossible to find the future hero in the boy. His biographers, most notably Kenneth S. Davis, who developed the earliest years in the greatest detail in *Soldier of Democracy,* have set down countless incidents and anecdotes of the young Eisenhower. But they could almost all be told of any boy growing up in similar circumstances at that time.

As a schoolboy, both at elementary and high school, Ike, as he was called, was generally regarded as an average student, although most of his high-school grades, particularly in mathematics and history, were respectably above average. To have been marked as a conspicuously brilliant or conscientious scholar would have been out of character for a boy who was so much a "regular fellow," even something of a tough guy. It was on the athletic field and in the outdoor life generally that he was happiest. A mainstay of the high-school football and baseball teams, in his senior year he took the lead in establishing an athletic association to win financial support for the teams, which the school did not at that time provide. He was a physically daring and venturesome boy, and accounts of his play outside the school are full of episodes in the Tom Sawyer vein—adventures on the river and long expeditions into the countryside. In that town "Wild West" games were naturally a particular childhood favorite.

A youngster of unusual warmth, good humor, and charm, in the memory of his contemporaries and teachers, Ike had, nevertheless, a highly inflammable temper. One fist fight in particular has taken on with its telling and retelling a heroic quality. His opponent was the North Side champion, later billed as the "town bully." Wesley Merrifield was a heavier, stronger, far more experienced fighter than thirteen-year-old Ike. A crowd gathered around the two on a vacant lot at Third and Broadway across from the city hall. Soon Ike seemed beaten. His face was a pulp, both eyes almost closed. But he would not yield. Not until two hours later, when the boys could barely stand, and Merrifield gasped out that he couldn't lick Ike, did the battle end.

Fights were an almost daily occurrence between Big Ike—Edgar—and Little Ike—Dwight—with the latter, two years younger, usually the furious underdog. But the two were also boon companions and made common cause against any outside threat. When Dwight, at fourteen, skinned his knee and blood poisoning developed, the family doctor announced that the only way to save his life was to amputate the leg. Terrible as the pain was, the boy said he would never permit it. Committed to a concept of life based on the fullest physical participation, he would rather die than be crippled. He extracted a promise from Edgar that if he went into a delirium

Edgar would prevent the operation. For two days, while death seemed certain and the doctor tried to convince his troubled parents that the operation was essential, Edgar was on guard outside his brother's door. Miraculously, Ike recovered, after the doctor had long since given him up.

He was a strong, healthy, outgoing boy whose boundless vitality carried him through a strenuous schedule of work, school, and play. Whatever his differences with the North Side, he had no trouble making a circle of friends, and he was generally very much at home in life as he found it. He was ready for whatever might come along. Whether it was partly fatalism or partly indifference, his was the cheerful opportunism of the American who waits for something to turn up.

Edgar and Dwight graduated from high school together in the spring of 1909. According to the class prophet, Edgar was going to become president of the United States and serve for two terms; Dwight would be a history professor at Yale. Edgar's own ambition was to be a lawyer, and he had already decided to enter the University of Michigan Law School. Dwight, with a vague desire to get some more education, proposed that he spend the following year working to help pay Edgar's college expenses, and the year after that they would reverse the roles. So Edgar went off that fall to college while Dwight took a full-time job at the creamery.

Working hard at his job, knocking around with his old friends, having casual dates with girls, he spent the better part of the next year without settling on any long-term goal. What finally happened was pure chance, the sort of accidental opportunity that seemed to mark so many stages of his career from then on. A North Side boy named Swede Hazlett, became a close friend in the

summer of 1910. Swede was getting ready to take the
entrance examination for Annapolis and during that
summer interested Ike in applying, too. At first he had
doubts, mainly on the score of his parents' religious opposition to war and militarism. But this was at least a
definite course of action; he decided to try for an appointment.

He was recommended by a local newspaper editor and
other townspeople to the senator with appointments
available and passed a preliminary examination in the
fall, indicating that he would take either Annapolis or
West Point. The choice was made for him when he discovered that at twenty he was overage for Annapolis.
In January he passed the West Point entrance examina-
tions with a high grade. As he had anticipated, his plans
did not please his mother and father, but they believed,
in accord with their faith, that it was a matter for his own
conscience. Ida Eisenhower never let him see, even on
the day he left home, the grief she felt. This was part of
her discipline, the discipline she had imposed on the son
who was in some ways so much like her.

For the purposes of the legend, for the image of the
hero, all of this background was nearly perfect. It conveyed at the time of its discovery exactly what we wanted
to know: that out of the simplest American origins a
leader of world armies could come. It was the most reassuring discovery: the famous general was just a small-
town boy from Kansas! It has only been later, when viewed
against the awesome complexity of the presidency in a
time of world crisis, that this record has seemed to have
an almost implausible simplicity. The boyhood image
had a formless quality; it was so typical as to be almost
meaningless. This is the dilemma of those who want to
comprehend Eisenhower and to make him come alive

"Opening Chorus"
Fitzpatrick in the St. Louis *Post-Dispatch*   June 5, 1952

in relation to the awful responsibility that is his. The boy from Abilene, the cheerful, smiling, self-confident, all-around American boy, obscures the man.

One clue emerges. It is the young Eisenhower's reluctance to commit himself completely to any course of action. The strong imprint of his mother was on him; the desire to make good, to show them on the other side of the tracks that you were as good as they. But his biographers make plain that there were reservations and that he did not altogether subscribe to the credo of the time and the place. This suggests a dualism that comes to light in his later career: a part of himself he withheld as detached spectator, the onlooker viewing, from the vantage point of his own self-esteem, events on the outcome of which he had risked something less than his entire fortune.

Two

The Iron Mold

When the invasion of Sicily was being launched, with North Africa in the immediate background and D day still to come, General Eisenhower turned to an aide to ask whether anyone could tell him what in his education could possibly have prepared him for the task of supreme commander of an allied army, navy, and air force. The answer to his rhetorical question was, of course, nothing. The complexity of that command, with all its technical, political, and psychological ramifications, could not by the wildest stretch of the imagination have been foreseen by the authors of the textbooks that Dwight Eisenhower studied at West Point. It was, nevertheless, a poignant question that a great many Americans were asking about their own education as they found themselves at war in alien lands.

West Point in the early years of the century evoked a gratifying vision of young American manhood deeply disciplined, schooled in honor, wearing a uniform that was the handsome heritage of a past when military men dressed up for the part. It was a romantic image, treasured perhaps because it satisfied our desire for martial splendor without intruding unnecessarily on the pacific present. Graduates of West Point were officers and gentlemen, following in the glorious tradition of Grant and Lee. If we had to have soldiers, and we were not sure we did,

28

because we did not believe in war or professional military fuss and feathers, this was the kind of soldier that we preferred. They were chosen democratically from every state in the Union. To be sure, politics entered in; you had to get a congressman or senator to sponsor you. But still, anyone—the boy next door, if he was smart enough —could get into West Point, and he might one day become a general. This was a far cry from a military caste system, the system that many Americans or their forebears had fled across the ocean to escape.

We knew, of course, that life at West Point was rugged: those hours of marching, standing at attention, walking guard duty, policing your room and your person to be ready for inspection at any moment. But this was part of the hardening process, and if a young man could stand up under it he came out of it stronger and more valiant. Football was an important part of the image of West Point, and the Army team in good years and bad was a national institution. In the extensive boys' literature of the time all this had a quality of innocent national pride.

Changed but little since the War of 1812, West Point was in fact a rigorous technical training school with iron disciplines intended to press raw American youth into the soldier's mold. The academic curriculum consisted almost entirely of technical subjects: civil and military engineering, physics, chemistry, mineralogy, geology, technical drawing, signaling and telegraphy, ordnance and gunnery, and military hygiene. The goal of a technical education in a frame of rigid discipline had been laid down nearly a hundred years before by Sylvanus Thayer, the "Father of the Academy." The standard of technical education at the Point was, on the whole, a high one.

The study of the humanities was confined to a single one-year course of four or five periods a week given by a joint English and history department for fourth-class men.

In history the cadet was to become acquainted with political, social, and economic developments since the end of the Middle Ages, typical forms of modern national and municipal governments, and the fundamental principles of government, with special reference to the United States. This was simple textbook civics scarcely above the high-school level. The study of English embraced the entire history of English literature and language as well as "rhetoric"—written and oral composition—including personal and official correspondence. The history texts in use were standard for the era: *A Political History of Modern Europe* by Ferdinand Schevill and *The Development of Modern Europe* by James Robinson and Charles Beard. Palgrave's *Golden Treasury,* Shakespeare, Tennyson's *Idylls of the King,* and selections from several historical writers made up the reading list in English. There was no program of assigned outside reading. Each cadet was required to study both French and Spanish, with about the same time allotted to each language as to the English and history course.

The faculty consisted primarily of young Academy graduates, three to five years out, whose teaching assignments were rarely longer than three or four years. They received no special training as teachers, and they were not likely to know much more about their respective fields than they themselves had learned as cadets. While outside lecturers were occasionally brought in, there was nothing then like the effort initiated between the two world wars to bring to the cadet an awareness of what was happening beyond the walls of the Point.

As a green youth right off the Kansas prairie, Eisenhower came to the Point in the early summer of 1911. He had passed a fairly stiff competitive examination to get the appointment, demonstrating the capacity he has shown repeatedly to buckle down and master a subject. He was probably no greener and rawer than the rest of the 265 who became plebes in what was the largest class West Point had admitted up to that time. In many ways he was well equipped for the ordeal of the Point. Physically tough, a good athlete, accustomed to long hours of hard work, he could adjust temperamentally to the unceasing discipline.

The trait he had brought out of Abilene was, above all, adaptability. You could adapt yourself to the Point in one of two ways. You could be a grind or a roughneck. Eisenhower was a roughneck. With the same defiance that had led him to caper on the very peak of the big barn back home on South East Fourth Street, he broke the rules at the Point just as often as he dared. Law-abiding classmates were shocked at his daring. On the long list of his demerits for 1912, the following were typical: "late at 9:30 gym formation; shoes under bed dirty; failed to execute 'right into line' properly; in room in improper uniform 1:50 p.m.; alcove not in order; late at breakfast; late to dinner; absent at retreat formation." The story is told of his standing in the dormitory corridor and blowing smoke into the room of one of the very best-behaved young men in the class, who implored him to go away before disaster should befall them both. The boy from the wrong side of the tracks was defying the code and yet managing by his resourcefulness to live within it.

Out of that remarkable class of 1915 were to come fifty-six generals. One of Ike's friends was a cadet from Missouri, Omar Bradley, the homeliest man in the class. The son of a poor itinerant schoolteacher, Bradley was in many ways Ike's opposite. In a graduating class of 164, he stood sixth for conduct while Eisenhower was ninety-fifth. Bradley was serious, quiet-spoken, always thoughtful of others. But the two, Brad and Ike, became friends, and they were to find their careers closely linked in some of the most dramatic moments of World War II. Another good friend in the class was Joe Swing, like Ike a roughneck. As president, Eisenhower was to make Major General Swing his Commissioner of Immigration, and in that office, in the good old scrounging Army style, Swing was to get himself into almost as much hot water as he had at the Point.

What meant most of all to Eisenhower at West Point was football. Playing with some distinction on the plebe team, he started with a tremendous rush in his second year as a halfback on the Army team. He replaced a star of the previous season injured in an early game and began to make a reputation for himself throughout the East. His name and his picture were on all the sports pages. When Army played the Carlisle Indians, Ike came up against Big Jim Thorpe, already a legendary figure. This was the West Point of the schoolboy's dream.

An injury to his knee in the last game of the season seemed minor. But the stubbornness of a riding master who ordered Cadet Eisenhower to mount and dismount for a whole afternoon, contrary to doctor's orders, finished off the knee. In this incident, as recounted by Kenneth Davis, Eisenhower's own stubbornness and pride came to light. He was too proud to tell the riding master he had been warned against putting undue strain on the knee. Hospitalizing him for many weeks, the injury, as recorded on his fitness report, nearly disqualified him from serving in the Army at all. In his last year he helped coach the plebe football squad, and this was some compensation for being out of the game himself. The class yearbook, *The Howitzer*, refers to a jovial, friendly roughneck who was on his way to being a spectacular football player when bad luck overtook him.

In the class of 1915 he stood sixty-first. There was nothing distinguished about his record. A trained military technician, he had very little knowledge outside his specialty. In high school he had been good in mathematics and history, and he was to continue to interest himself sporadically in military history. But this was the beginning and the end of his intellectual interests. Today for pleasure he reads only Westerns, consuming them voraciously for relaxation.

To the graduating class of 1915 Secretary of War Lindley M. Garrison spoke brave words about the call of a grim duty that might lie ahead for the long gray line of young men who had just filed past him. But the war in Europe was still very far off. To most Americans it seemed a little unreal. Even after the United States entered the conflict in April of 1917 it had the look, except for those who participated in it, of a set piece enacted on a distant stage. The Europeans had got themselves into a characteristic mess, and they had called on us to come over and help them end it. What is more, they had begun to interfere with our inalienable rights on the high seas. So we had to go in and put down the Hun. "Over there, over there," we sang, "the Yanks are coming, and we won't come home 'til it's over over there." We would come home as quickly as possible after we had set Europe to rights again.

On a summer of leave in Abilene, with the old friends, the old life, something of a hero to the town, the war might have been happening on another planet. As his first assignment after graduation, Eisenhower had expected to be sent to the Philippines, and in his optimism—one of the strongest traits in his developing character—he had even bought a white dress uniform. Instead, he was ordered to the 19th Infantry at Fort Sam Houston, near San Antonio, Texas.

A gentleman and an officer, a cocky young shavetail, Eisenhower, from all accounts, had at this time the at-

tractiveness and warmth of personality that would count
for so much throughout his career. Ingratiating is hardly
the word, since this implies servility, and there was nothing servile about the young second lieutenant. He was a
strong, vigorous male with a ready smile (and an almost
equally quick temper) who naturally drew people to him.
To use an overworked contemporary word, he was about
as complete an extrovert as one could be, or this, at any
rate, was the surface impression he gave. His temper
passed quickly, and when, rarely, he was despondent, this,
too, was a transitory mood. He had many of his mother's
traits—above all, thanks to discipline or to temperament,
or perhaps a combination of both, the capacity to put
aside disappointments and rebuffs and present a cheerful
and confident face to the world.

At Fort Sam Houston the young lieutenant in his
smartly tailored uniform and boots shining like polished
brass won his first victory. He had fallen in love with the
belle of the post, Mamie Geneva Doud, who was rushed
off her feet by officers of higher rank with much more to
offer than young Eisenhower. The Douds "wintered" in
San Antonio because the Doud girls had had more than
their share of ill-health. Although they came from a far
more prosperous background and could make greater
claims to social status, they had much in common with the
Eisenhowers. They were hearty, friendly Middle West-
erners. John Doud, a retired packing-house owner from
Boone, Iowa, was a successful man who, like all American
fathers, wanted his daughters to have every advantage in
life. They were a close-knit family, and Ike is said to have
made his way with the other members before he finally
won Mamie. They were married at the Doud family
house in Denver at 750 Lafayette Street on July 1, 1916.
The groom gave his bride a pair of seed-pearl earrings
which are today in the Eisenhower museum. Mamie wore

white lace, and Ike wore the starched white uniform that he had bought when he thought he was going to the Philippines. On their wedding day he received his promotion to first lieutenant.

They went to live in what had been Ike's bachelor quarters at Fort Sam Houston. The pattern of their life through the years was established from the first. They both needed people around them, and there was a constant coming and going in the small, one-bedroom apartment. They both liked card games. Eisenhower had begun to develop the card sense that was to be one of his resources in his Army career. Their friends found them gay and attractive, never at a loss for a comeback in the quick give and take of conversation. It was the Army life, with good old Joe or good old Pinky or good old Al just in from Fort Lewis or Fort Ord, so there was another party and then another party until good old Joe and his wife were a part of the gang.

Mamie quickly learned about the long separations that are a part of Army life both in peacetime and in war. She went back to her family's house in San Antonio when Eisenhower was sent as regimental supply officer of the 57th Infantry to Leon Springs, thirty miles away. America was at last in the war, and Leon Springs was the center of a rough, swiftly expanding Army camp, no place for a wife who was about to have a child. Mamie had told him the news shortly before he went away.

That assignment was the first of a series of bitter frustrations for the young temporary captain, who went from one training post to another. When their son was born in September 1917, Ike was at Fort Oglethorpe in Georgia as an instructor in the officers' training camp there. He was next ordered to report on December 12, 1917, to the Army Service School at Fort Leavenworth to serve as instructor. In February of the following year he reported to

Camp Meade in Maryland to expedite the organization of
the 65th Battalion Engineers. In March he was assigned
to Camp Colt at Gettysburg, Pennsylvania, as commander
of the Tank Training Center.

There the unreality of the war as Americans at home
saw it was painfully evident. Camp Colt was a tank
school without a tank. It was, in fact, a shambles, lacking
not only tanks but facilities of every kind. Something of
Eisenhower's drive and organizational ability began to be
apparent there. He exerted all of his tremendous energy
and his stern, often harsh way with subordinates to try to
whip Camp Colt into shape. Here one has the first glimpse
of the promise of his military career. Having decided at
his wife's insistence against a contemplated transfer to the
Air Corps, he had gone into tanks and had begun the
study of the new mobile warfare that was in an early re-
hearsal stage on the battlefields of France. For his work
at Camp Colt he was to receive, ten years later, the Distinguished Service Medal, and on this tour he achieved
the temporary wartime rank of lieutenant colonel.

But Camp Colt was not France. Classmates, friends,
and friends-to-be were over there in the thick of it.
Battle experience was what would count in future years
in your 201 file, the official career record that weighs so
heavily in promotions and assignments. If he was really
to go places in the Army he should be in France. George
Patton was over there as an aide to General Pershing and
at the same time as field commander of a tank unit.
Patton, of course, had come out of the Point nine years
ahead of Ike. The headlines were full of the exploits of the
Rainbow Division and its commander, Brigadier General
Douglas MacArthur. Eisenhower exulted when he finally
got orders to report to Camp Dix preparatory to overseas
duty. But the Armistice came on November 11; he had
been ordered to report on November 18.

The mood of America was to forget the war as quickly as possible now that it was over, to sweep out of sight such childish things as guns and tanks and uniforms. We wanted to believe that it had all been a bad dream. Certainly there would never be another war. America lived in a strange interlude between the wars. Having quickly reverted to the isolation of the past, behind the ocean barriers that we still believed to be secure, we wanted none of the military or their trappings. They were banished to the old Indian posts, to Jefferson Barracks, to Fort Lewis, to Fort Leavenworth, somnolent stations that had long since outlived their geographical usefulness. But they furnished business for nearby towns or cities, and if you tried to abolish them you immediately stirred up a congressional hornet's nest. It would be difficult to comprehend the folly of this indifference and neglect if it were not that many of the same symptoms of complacence reappeared, with far less justification, after World War II.

In the face of this studied neglect, the military became a kind of fraternity for self-preservation. They lived quite outside the main stream of American life, touched by it only when sharp fluctuations in the economy threatened military appropriations. One of the few penetrating records of this separate little world is in John P. Marquand's brilliant novel *Melville Goodwin, U.S.A.* Marquand conveys with a perceptivity that military men themselves have admired what the conditioning, beginning with the rugged indoctrination of West Point, does to the individual. The narrator in the Marquand novel tells the cynical magazine writer and his research girl, who are doing a profile of General Goodwin: "You can't put him into any ordinary category. Don't you see he's a hero. It's the power and the glory. Now you and I wanted to be heroes once, and Myra wanted to be Joan of Arc and we've all got over it, but Goodwin still has the virus.

It's catching around there at West Point. I don't say that I approve of heroes. I don't say they look so well in peacetime but he's a hero and he can't help it." This says a great deal about the men who were suddenly discovered to be heroes when America stood so desperately in need of them.

If you were the athletic type, and most Army men were, you could have a good life, with golf, tennis, hunting, even polo readily at hand. Because it was a small fraternity you knew everyone else, personally or by reputation, everyone who counted for anything, at any rate. And the bond was close since, as a vanishing species, you were determined to protect the last reservation. The malcontents, among them some of the sharper and more inquiring minds, got out. But the indoctrination of the Point had been strong, and what was remarkable when the test came was that so many men of ability were available to assume the leadership.

Not long after the tragedy of the loss of their first son, who died in 1921 of scarlet fever while they were stationed at Camp Meade, Maryland, Eisenhower was assigned to Camp Gaillard on the Panama Canal. A permanent major now, he went as executive officer to the 42nd Infantry, the only regiment activated with the 20th Brigade, at the request of General Fox Connor. General Connor, whom Eisenhower had first met at Camp Meade, was to exert a telling influence on the young man's career.

Connor was a rare figure in that army which in 1920 was headed for the museum. He had had wide experience overseas and at home and was a man of exceptional intellectual ability. As a student of history, he believed that a second world war was inevitable. Futhermore, he was convinced that in that war mobility, with the tank as the supreme weapon, would be decisive. Connor was impressed with Eisenhower and talked his ideas to him by the hour, often late into the night on the broad veranda of the Eisenhower quarters. The younger man was intensely admiring, the older man taken with the ability and the sincerity of the officer whom he came to regard as his protégé.

We are told that Connor guided Eisenhower's military reading. Under his tutelage the young major became engrossed in the philosophers of military strategy, Clausewitz, Mahan, and the others. Connor's own hero was George Catlett Marshall, who had served under him in World War I, and his highest praise for Eisenhower was to compare him to Marshall. Major Eisenhower shook up the regiment in a way that delighted his mentor, although it seems to have offended the junior officers, who suffered from the exec's intensive stress on spit and polish in that debilitating climate.

Eisenhower's biographers, looking back to try to find the qualities that would single him out for greatness, cite two or three episodes that set him apart from his fellow officers in the long years of waiting for promotions that never seemed to come. In 1925, while stationed at Fort Logan, just outside of Denver, he was notified that, thanks to Fox Connor, he had been selected for the Command and General Staff School at Fort Leavenworth. The sorting and sifting process at Leavenworth was essential to further advancement. In his year at the staff school Eisenhower showed again his capacity to absorb knowledge and give it back. It was the custom then to post publicly at the end of the school year the final rating of each officer, and so intense was the competitive strain that it was not infrequent for a man to break under it. Out of a class of 275 Eisenhower was number one. That would count heavily in the years ahead.

Although it seemed at the time a dull and fruitless assignment, what came a little later was to prove another break. Major Eisenhower was recommended by General Connor, then Deputy Chief of Staff in Washington, for the job of preparing a guidebook to the American battle-fields in Europe from material put together by the American Battle Monuments Commission. It was the kind of task for which most Regular Army officers were singularly ill-equipped. There was also the hazard that it would identify an officer as the brainy, office type, and this was to be avoided in the Army between the wars like the plague. The goal of almost every officer was to be with troops, to get a field command, and one of Eisenhower's chief frustrations in these years was that he was being stamped as a staff man. This meant the unrewarding desk assignments.

His wife urged him to take on the guidebook, and they went to live in Washington early in 1927. Perhaps one reason for his accepting the assignment was the presence of his brother Milton, who was moving rapidly up in the ranks of government. As proof of his skill in climbing the bureaucratic ladder, he was to stay on as right-hand man to a succession of Republican secretaries of agriculture and then to serve the New Deal's Henry A. Wallace. The close relationship between Milton and Dwight is an important element in the President's career. The youngest of the six brothers, Milton had little of the extrovert vigor of the rest of the family. He was considered frail, partly as the result of a serious illness in his childhood, and his interests were always more on the intellectual side. He had announced at a fairly tender age that he wanted to be a journalist. The two brothers, perhaps because they were so unlike in temperament, were closer than others in the family. Milton, more cautious and deliberate, was to counsel his brother at critical moments in his career. Eisenhower gratefully acknowledged in a copy inscribed to Milton the help Milton supplied in the preparation of the battlefield guidebook.

The project was completed with conspicuous success, drawing a commendatory letter from General Pershing himself. During that period the hospitable Eisenhowers began to know their way around in civilian Washington. Through Milton they became close friends of Harry C. Butcher, a personable young Middle Westerner then rising rapidly in the Columbia Broadcasting System to eventually become head of the CBS office in the capital, and of his wife, Ruth. This was part of the reputation that Eisenhower began to establish as being knowledgeable in the public-relations field. He knew his way around. He was a clever, attractive officer who understood something more than just squads right and squads left.

After graduation, on June 20, 1928, from the Army War College, one of the hierarchy of schools that an officer attends in his upward progress, Eisenhower was offered an assignment in Paris to make an extensive revision of the guidebook based on firsthand knowledge of the terrain of World War I. Again his wife's influence is said to have persuaded him in favor of Paris rather than a General Staff assignment. He visited every American battlefield during this tour of duty. Their life in Paris, where they had an apartment on the Rue d'Auteuil, was almost entirely circumscribed by their fellow Americans. The smattering of French he learned at West Point had long since been forgotten. Once again they enjoyed the gregarious Army life, with friends and acquaintances from the States coming and

"Views of Ike According to . . ."
Green in the Providence *Journal*

going in a steady procession. It was the caste life almost
as completely enclosed as though they had been living
on an Army post back home.

In Washington again in the fall of 1929, serving in the
office of the Assistant Secretary of War, Eisenhower attracted the attention of the most remarkable man in the
Army of the United States. Fifty at the time of his appointment in 1930, General Douglas MacArthur was the
youngest chief of staff in history. He was quite unlike
the average West Point graduate of modest background,
considering himself an aristocrat and a man with a mission. His father had been General Arthur MacArthur, one
of the conspicuous greats in the Army's annals, and the
son had set his sights even higher. With unquestioned
brilliance of intellect, MacArthur had an imperious bear-
ing and a regal temperament that impressed some but
annoyed many others. He was on stage every waking
moment of his life, with a conviction of his own destiny

May 30, 1952

in every word that he spoke. If he was not born with the posture of a great man, he acquired it very early.

Much about the relationship between MacArthur and Eisenhower is obscure and ambiguous. On MacArthur's part it has become corroded with an almost obsessive jealousy and resentment. In recent years the mildest form of denunciation that he has applied to his former subordinate is "the apotheosis of mediocrity." But in February 1933 MacArthur must have thought well of Ike to take him on his staff and assign him to an office next door to his own, which meant that they worked closely together from day to day. Word had gotten around that Eisenhower was skillful in public relations, and this may have been one of the reasons he was chosen by the Chief of Staff. Not long before, in driving out the bonus marchers encamped along Pennsylvania Avenue in Washington, MacArthur had appeared in person, resplendent in full regalia, as though directing a major field operation. The storm of angry criticism that followed indicated that the Chief of Staff could well use some good advice on how to get along with the public.

Frequently, during these Washington years, Eisenhower experienced a great sense of futility and was tempted at times to resign from the service. Still a major at forty-five, his life seemed to have come to a standstill. His brothers were forging ahead, successful in the terms in which America understood success. They were rising in their respective fields, making money, living in bigger and more comfortable houses, while he looked on from the small, isolated world that was the professional military establishment. And a small world it was: with the Depression and the economy it inspired in Congress, there were fewer than 120,000 men in the Army, and a sweeping reduction by Congress in the number of Regular officers had only narrowly been averted. Eisenhower worked on annual reports and public statements that bravely anticipated new weapons and a bold new strategy when in point of fact the Army had become scarcely more than a token force.

As in the earlier instance of Panama, it was in a sense an escape when MacArthur asked him to go with him to the Philippines to help create a military establishment for the islands, a part of the process of readying them for independence eleven years later. The opportunity for adventure and change in the Philippines was very welcome. In the fall of 1935 he sailed alone for Manila. Mamie and John, the son born to them in 1922, followed a year later, after John had finished junior high school.

The long-awaited promotion to lieutenant colonel at last came through in 1936. The four years in the Philippines were to confirm in the Eisenhower record the traits for which he had already become known in the service.

He was to enhance his reputation for getting along with people. The Filipinos liked him, and he worked whole-heartedly, with no sense of condescension, at starting a military academy modeled after West Point and at estab-lishing a reserve system. His biographers speak of this phase as enlarging his capacity as a diplomat. But it may have been merely that he was a natural, friendly Ameri-can, with a generous good will toward almost everyone. And always the contrast with MacArthur and his gran-diose view of himself and the world around him was in Ike's favor. Eisenhower became a friend of President Manuel Quezon, and during his frequent weekends on the presidential yacht, the *Casiana*, his skill at bridge and poker stood him in good stead.

But just as in the United States, military funds were so meager that at times it seemed almost as though the Americans were playing soldier with the friendly brown people who had been their wards since the turn of the century. A plan existed on paper to provide a sufficient military establishment so that the Philippine government could eventually safeguard its own independence. But only slowly, and by halting and uncertain stages, was the plan being executed, and as drawn up under the authority of Quezon and MacArthur it overlooked many realities.

Above all, the plan ignored the growing military might of Japan. Granted that military intelligence was then virtually nonexistent and that therefore the details of that might were unknown, it seems incredible, nevertheless, that Japan's militant intentions and her swift expansion in Asia did not serve as a warning. Perhaps MacArthur was merely putting up a brave front to encourage the Filipinos. Or his own indomitable sense of mission, his supercharged will, may have obscured the reality of Japan's deadly preparation for conquest. In any event, the statements he issued, right up to the time his planes were destroyed on the ground at Clark Field after Pearl Harbor, breathed an intrepid confidence.

While the job had its frustrations, there was always the interior life of the fraternity, the caste. In Manila it was a good life, a gay life. Money went farther, servants were plentiful, and the white man, even though he was now friend and collaborator rather than conqueror, still had a special place in the sun. The Eisenhowers lived pleasantly in the Manila Hotel with its splendid view across the bay. This closed world of the fraternity had conspicuous compensations in this tropical station where the Army had always run a good show.

In addition to the sports that he had always vigorously enjoyed, Eisenhower found a new outlet for his restless nature. He learned to fly a plane. For a man with his strong feeling for physical accomplishment this was a real joy. He was forty-eight years old when he got his pilot's license.

Obviously this was not an overly demanding life. A man operated in a rigid framework of rank, promotion, protocol, and in the chain of command his own responsibility was fixed within narrow limits. So long as he stayed in line and kept within those limits, so long as he didn't stick his neck out, he could not get into too much trouble. It had its compensations, even though in the interval between the wars the escalator of promotion seemed all but stationary.

This was Eisenhower's conditioning, this special, separate life, so far from the experience of most Americans. The boom of the twenties and the bust of the thirties seemed to affect him only as the rise and fall of the economy altered the attitude of Congress toward military appropriations. While he may have longed from time to time to break out of the closed world of the Army, he would not have known where to go. The entire conditioning of his past had made for acceptance; reluctant acceptance, perhaps, even grumbling acceptance at times, but acquiescence nevertheless. His temperament, it is fairly clear, is a passive one. The outward geniality, the eager good will conceal a caution that has made it excessively difficult for him to make decisions. He is moved by forces; he does not undertake to move them himself.

Three

Fort Sam Houston
to
Downing Street

It would have seemed logical to suppose that Eisenhower would remain on the staff of General MacArthur in the Philippines. The two had had a close relationship, and MacArthur had given every sign that he valued the services of the younger man. Why Eisenhower left in mid-December of 1939 is not clear. Or it may be more accurate to say that there are several explanations.

The Eisenhower biographers who put together his life story toward the end of World War II say that Mrs. Eisenhower was in poor health. The Philippines was only a temporary assignment, and Eisenhower felt it was time to return. The war in Europe had broken out three months before, and while it was still in the "phony" phase, reports from the States told of a great upheaval in the service. MacArthur cannot have been an easy commander to serve under for anyone unwilling to give him complete idolatry. To Eisenhower, so different in temperament and outlook, various comments have been attributed. "Oh yes, I studied dramatics under MacArthur in the Philippines for four years," he is supposed to have said.

Loyal members of MacArthur's staff tell a story of a bitter break over a personal matter. MacArthur's worshipful biographers maintain a studied reticence on the relationship. His principal Boswell, Major General Charles A.

Willoughby, merely says that Eisenhower "by the flip of a coin might have remained in the Orient." The animosity of MacArthur and all those around him might be explained by the feud that developed during World War II, with the Pacific command cherishing a sullen and ever-growing resentment for those directing the over-all strategy in Washington and Europe. But the feeling seems to have had an earlier origin in Eisenhower's case.

Whatever the reason, whether he was asked to leave or whether he went of his own accord, it was a piece of fantastic good fortune that was to change his life completely. The Eisenhowers left Manila in style. Regardless of any personal feeling that may have existed, MacArthur and his wife came down to the boat for the gala farewell for Mamie, Ike, and John. The day before, President Quezon had awarded Eisenhower the Distinguished Service Cross of the Philippines. At Quezon's request, Mrs. Eisenhower had pinned the decoration on her husband's tunic.

How much history was in the making at that moment, when the boat sailed away from the dock and moved out into Manila Bay for the long journey home. A flip of the coin! What a tragic irony that Eisenhower, scarcely more than two years later, reached the official conclusion that it was hopeless to try to supply the Philippines for further resistance, leaving nothing for the little band on Corregidor but surrender and the ordeal that came after surrender. MacArthur was to be frustrated by the Europe-first strategy executed by Eisenhower, with the press and public concentrating on the war against the Nazis and on Eisenhower. For a man of MacArthur's temperament and sense of mission this was a cruel fate. He was forever after to smolder like a great, half-ruined volcano, sending up columns of wrathful smoke and occasionally belching a little fire.

Eisenhower experienced something of the old sense of being trapped in a dead end on his return. He was sent to Fort Ord in California as executive officer of the 15th Infantry, and in March of 1940 went with the 15th to Fort Lewis in Washington. He liked being with troops, and yet, convinced of the certainty of America's participation in the war, he was disturbed, or so his biographers say, by the remarkable complacency of most of his fellow officers. In the spring, as Hitler's Panzer divisions overran all of Europe in the new war of movement, any remaining complacency was quickly swept away.

He believed that the United States would soon be in the fighting and wanted desperately to get a command of his own. It was unfair that he should be typed as a staff man. To everyone who might help him he sent urgent appeals. His letters, as printed by Kevin McCann in *Man from Abilene,* one of the most adulatory studies of the General, sound like those of a schoolboy pleading for a chance in the big game. In the fall of 1940 the future supreme commander was writing to Mark Clark in the War Department:

. . . It is perfectly okay with me if the personnel section . . . is aware of the fact that I have an ambition to command one of the next armored regiments to be formed. They will probably think me a conceited individual, but I see no objection to setting your sights high. . . . I do hope to avoid Staff and to stay on troop duty for some time to come. And since I notice that in the original assignments they gave one of the armored regiments to a lieutenant colonel, I will hope that they might think that much of me also.

With the Army in the upheaval of a vast expansion, an obscure lieutenant colonel had little chance of being heard. He was working hard, harder, perhaps, than at any time since 1918. In November he became chief of staff for Major General Charles F. Thompson, commander of the Third Division, which included the 15th Infantry. In March of the following year he achieved his lifelong ambition: he became a full colonel. From the beginning, he had said that if he could ever make "chicken" colonel he would be satisfied. Kenneth Davis stresses the great elation he felt at this promotion. It was the pinnacle of his hopes. And when a friend suggested that probably he would very soon be moving another rung up the promotional ladder Eisenhower was indignant. Weren't they content to let a man enjoy what he had hardly dared to hope he would finally get? His reaction was a measure of the long stagnation of the twenties and thirties. The rank was temporary, but then so was everything else in the America of that strange interlude.

Following the war news more closely than most of those around him, he was aware of the magnitude of the events that were so soon to draw America into the cataclysm of a global war. In the summer he was chosen as chief of staff for Lieutenant General Walter Kreuger, commander of the Third Army. High efficiency ratings had gone into his 201 file, and he had been personally selected by General Clark, whom General Marshall had assigned to survey all of the available officer material in the higher ranks.

In June the Eisenhowers went to Fort Sam Houston, headquarters for the Third Army. It was both a homecoming and a brief pause on the threshold of fame. Eisenhower began assembling the cast of characters who were later to move with him out onto the world stage. He asked a reserve officer, Ernest R. ("Tex") Lee, a former insurance salesman, to be his executive officer. Private First Class Michael J. McKeogh, who had been a bellhop at the Plaza Hotel in New York before he was drafted, became his orderly.

In August Eisenhower went off with Kreuger and the

Third Army to the Battle of Louisiana, the biggest peace-time maneuvers in the nation's history. The Second and Third Armies were to fight it out in warfare made as real as possible despite grave deficiencies in weapons and training. If they demonstrated nothing else, the Louisiana maneuvers revealed what a long way the Army still had to go. For all the brave simulation of combat, it was a ragged and sometimes disorderly performance by armies of reluctant civilians. Eisenhower's reputation, however, was considerably enhanced by Kreuger's commendation of his work, and shortly afterward he was promoted to temporary brigadier general. He was favorably mentioned in a newspaper column, and he appeared in a press photograph, along with other officers correctly identified, as "Lt. Col. D. D. Ersenbeing." He observed wryly in his memoirs later that at least they got the initials right.

December 7 was a warm, sunny day at Fort Sam Houston, and Eisenhower was up early. Although it was Sunday, he had paper work to do at the office. A Christmas leave was coming up, and he and Mamie were going to West Point to be with John, then in his plebe year at the Academy. He came home at noon dead tired—he had been working fourteen hours a day for a long time—and he told Mamie after lunch that he wanted to get a little rest. Throughout his life, even in times of greatest stress, he has been able to read himself to sleep, as he did now, in a few minutes with a Western and wake up, after an hour or two, refreshed. The telephone rang beside his bed. One of his staff reported that the Japs were attacking Pearl Harbor. Five days later he was summoned to Washington to become assistant chief of the War Plans Division. The train that took him to Washington, on which he had difficulty getting even an upper berth, was the pumpkin coach.

In the midst of the wild confusion of Washington, one man worked with a calm certitude born of long fore-knowledge of this moment. To try to explain General Marshall and the extent of his contribution to the winning of the war is to come up against an enigma. Most of those close to him came to have for him a regard approaching veneration. Yet the innate greatness which they recognized could never be translated into the terms of mass appeal. In a sense he was an anachronism out of a sterner and more stoical age. And yet he did not set himself up above his own age. To describe him as modest falls wide of the mark, since modesty implies that one puts a higher estimate on one's achievements than one is willing to show in public. As an old soldier he knows a duty well done. But there is no evidence of vainglory, either public or private, in an achievement that has never been fully appreciated because he stood in the background while more colorful figures, such as Eisenhower, filled up the foreground. It is no exaggeration to say Marshall planned it that way.

Something of the enigma and the problem it raises are evident in the man's physical countenance. Portrait painters, during the war and afterward, have confessed to their bafflement and lack of success. The inner man is so much more important than the outer man, and it is the inner man that they failed to portray. To those who pass by quickly, the outer man, the face with the slightly receding chin, might not draw a second glance. This complete lack of the outward glitter of a "personality," in the modern, Madison Avenue sense of that word, may help to explain why he has received far less than his due in understanding and gratitude from the nation.

It is told of him that in cruel hazing when he was a freshman at Virginia Military Institute he received an injury that nearly cost him his life. He never revealed the names of those responsible. The reserve and dignity that made him seem so alien to the hearty camaraderie of the Army life are part of his temperament. The fact that he was graduated from V.M.I. rather than West Point may have had something to do with the attitude that set him apart from the Army caste. Yet it is a tribute to the service that his qualities won early recognition. In World War I he rose from captain to colonel and made a brilliant name for himself as chief of operations for the A.E.F. First Army. Named chief of staff in 1939, he set out to prepare the Army for a war which he was convinced would very soon involve the United States. All too well he knew the fearful inadequacies of the force that in peacetime America had been so neglected. It was deficient in almost every category, and had to be built virtually from scratch.

In the months just before Pearl Harbor, Marshall had gone from one post to another across the country, and, speaking frankly to the assembled officers, he had told them that they must prepare themselves for what was to come. On them would fall the greatest responsibility any generation of American military men had ever had to bear. He did this without official authorization from the Commander in Chief, knowing that if word of it leaked out he would come under the wrath of Congress. In that strange time the popular belief was that if only the United States averted its gaze and avoided as nearly as possible anything that looked like preparation for war, then war would not come. Only four months before Pearl Harbor, Congress had come within one vote of abolishing the draft. The reluctant citizen soldiers wanted out.

In that dark December of 1941 Marshall was looking for a commander. He knew that his choice could not be conditioned by rank and precedence. His commander

must have qualities of leadership, conspicuous, even
showy, qualities, to inspire a mass army and the democracy that must furnish and equip that army. Because
America's productivity and manpower would necessarily
bear such a large share of the total war effort, an American would have command over an allied force. All this
Marshall had foreseen.

He assigned Eisenhower to draft plans for the defense
of Hawaii, the Aleutians, New Guinea, and Australia.
At the same time he was to try to work out a way to
supply MacArthur's beleaguered forces in the Philippines.
That this was impossible, given the extent of Japanese
air and naval power, soon became evident. At best, an
occasional submarine might be sneaked into Manila
Harbor with a bare minimum of the most essential supplies. Put in charge of War Plans, Eisenhower was given
the task of preparing the first outline of a cross-channel
invasion of Europe. Throughout this period he came
under Marshall's constant scrutiny.

Any examination of the relationship between Eisenhower and Marshall is handicapped by the fact that
Marshall has never told his own story. Repeated efforts
have been made to persuade him to write his account
of the great events in which he played such a decisive
part. He has replied more often than not that no honest
history of any war has ever been written, and since he
would not write unless he could tell the truth he meant
to keep silent. He held strong convictions about certain
errors of his Commander in Chief which he believed
prolonged the war for at least a year or a year and a half.
When pressed he would add, with the resolution that is
so much a part of his character, that he had no intention
of airing these convictions in any account that would
be read by his contemporaries. More recently he has
been persuaded to assemble his papers and link them,

with the aid of a trained historian, with at least a part of his own narrative.

Nevertheless, his reticence is so great that we are not likely to know more about the reasons for his choice of Eisenhower than is contained in the official history of the war. To those who today seek a fuller explanation his answer is simply to look at the official record as it stands. The disillusion he is said to have felt over Eisenhower's failures of omission and commission in later years would be one more reason for such a man to withhold his story. Within the limits of what he felt to be proper he did his best to dissuade Eisenhower from a political career. When Eisenhower was a towering hero, importuned on every hand to run for president, Marshall's voice was almost the only one raised in solemn argument against a military man's seeking the highest office in the land.

As the first faint outline of a great military force and a grand strategy began to emerge at the start of the war, Marshall was looking over perhaps half a dozen men in his search for a commander. It was by no means a foregone conclusion that Eisenhower should be the one to become the central figure in the allied command. But the material from which the Chief of Staff had to choose was limited. The long decay and neglect of the years between the wars had been costly. Men who had lived so long behind the khaki curtain, quite outside the main stream of American life, were suddenly confronted with the most overwhelming responsibility, not only for bringing a vast new force into being, but for equipping and supplying that force. The most incredible power was thrust into hands that had been idle or turned to indifferent and time-serving tasks. It is scarcely surprising, then, that some among them drew back in consternation and that others were manifestly unprepared for any but routine command.

In examining the reasons behind Marshall's choice one must put high on the list the Eisenhower quantity of self-confidence. It may be no more than a surface reflection of the temperament of a healthy extrovert. But he seems always, except for rare periods of depression, to have given off this glow as naturally as a stove gives off heat. Another factor was his complete agreement with Marshall on the necessity for a Europe-first strategy. That was at the base of all the plans he submitted to his chief for a holding operation in the Pacific maintained with a minimum of the equipment and supplies in such desperate demand everywhere.

The Russians were clamoring for tanks, guns, planes, and food, with the implied threat, which they were to make again and again in the years ahead, that if the supplies were not forthcoming they would make a separate peace with Hitler no matter how costly it might be. Since everyone from Marshall on down had in the beginning woefully miscalculated Russian powers of resistance, this threat was to send repeated tremors throughout the allied world. Whether with or without the Russians, a war of five, six, seven, or perhaps even ten, years' duration was foreseen in this black time. In such an atmosphere of gloomy uncertainty Eisenhower's confidence must have carried special weight with his chief.

When Winston Churchill came to Washington for his first conference with Roosevelt at the end of December, Marshall saw to it that Eisenhower met him and sat in on at least two or three of the high-strategy talks in which the Prime Minister took part. Churchill is reported to have been attracted to Eisenhower even at this early stage. Not long afterward, at the prompting of the President, Marshall was to take a most unusual step. He sent Churchill a digest of the personal files of three American

generals, covering every phase of their careers from West
Point on. The justification for this extraordinary move
was that since it was anticipated that an American general would in the future command British and French
as well as American troops it was well to have the sanction of the London government. One of the three was
Eisenhower.

Word came back from Churchill that Eisenhower was
his choice. How much weight should be given to this
factor in the selection it is impossible to say. While
Churchill may not have had a veto, his approval must
have counted heavily when added to the other points
in Eisenhower's favor. Harmony in an allied command
would, after all, be of supreme importance. Churchill is
reported to have felt that Eisenhower would be more
co-operative and even more susceptible perhaps to
Churchill's powers of persuasion than the other two
generals.

In late May, Eisenhower went to London with Lieutenant General Henry H. ("Hap") Arnold, Chief of the
Army Air Force, and other high-ranking officers for a
conference on future strategy. The Americans went with
instructions to press for a cross-channel invasion of Europe as soon as possible in 1942. But for Eisenhower this
was also a further test. Reports came back of how well
he got along with the British, of how impressed they
had been by his personality and by the spirit of friendly
co-operation that he seemed to radiate.

Not long after his return, Marshall asked him to write
a directive for the commander of the European Theater
of Operations. He put several days of intensive work in
on it, and finally, on June 8, 1942, he laid the directive
on Marshall's desk. Throughout, the stress was on allied
co-operation and the necessity for suppressing all national
jealousies and rivalries. There have been various versions

of the conversation that followed. Marshall asked his subordinate if he was satisfied with the directive he had written. Eisenhower replied that he was, and in his memoirs he relates that his chief then remarked that this was fortunate since he would in all probability be the one to execute it. Three days later the assignment was definite, and the successive enlargements of the command which brought him to his pinnacle of power and glory flowed logically and, it seems in retrospect, at least, inevitably from that point in time.

While Marshall apparently gave little prior hint of his choice, it can scarcely have come as a great surprise to Eisenhower. Something like a father-and-son relationship was beginning to grow up between the two men. Marshall was putting much of his hope and trust in this officer whom he had scarcely heard of six months before. One by one he had weighed the others and found them wanting. Eisenhower had had very little experience in command of troops. He had never been in combat. He had only recently acquired the two stars of a major general. Yet Marshall advanced him finally over 366 officers who were senior to him. It was a gamble, but it can hardly have escaped the Chief of Staff that for most Americans, unprepared for the responsibility that had suddenly fallen upon us, the war itself was a huge gamble.

Again and again this lack of preparation was to impress itself upon those in high position who suddenly found themselves in situations in which their slightest word carried the weight of America's swiftly developing power. Nor was this feeling confined to the soldiers. Harry L. Hopkins, President Roosevelt's right-hand man, had confessed to thinking, as he walked down a corridor in the Kremlin for his first meeting with Stalin, that there he was, the son of a harness maker from Grinnell, Iowa, about to sit down with the absolute ruler of all the Russians to discuss as an equal the conduct of the most far-flung war in history.

As Eisenhower took over in London a command that was expanding with almost magic swiftness, a similar sense of awe at the transformation that had occurred in his life overcame the boy from Abilene not once but many times. The diary of his aide and old friend, Captain Harry C. Butcher, is remarkably revealing in this respect. In an entry on July 12, 1942, he records that in giving reporters a list of the General's appointments of the previous week he had entirely forgotten to include a duty call on the King of England. That was a measure of what was happening to Eisenhower, and the tone of Butcher's diary is often that of two Yanks, Ike and Butch, suddenly set down in King Arthur's court and told to run the show. As a Yank at King George's court, Eisenhower displayed all the friendly persuasiveness that had been one of the reasons for his selection as commander.

He spent forty-five minutes with the King on that occasion, the first of many that were to follow, talking in his easy, natural way. The King told him about a sightseeing visit to Windsor Castle made by two high-ranking American officers on a Sunday afternoon six weeks earlier. In consenting to the visit, the King and Queen had promised to keep out of sight so as not to embarrass the Americans. But on that afternoon, taking the sun in a secluded garden, they heard voices. They quickly decided to hide and crawled under a low opening in a wall and concealed themselves behind a hedge. Laughing with the King over the episode, Eisenhower confessed that he and General Mark Clark had been the cause of the royal retreat.

Eisenhower was a catalyst. It was in this capacity that Churchill repeatedly called him to Downing Street for those wearisome sessions that went on far into the night. The Prime Minister considered himself a great strategist, and while his own military men took a dim view of his intrusion into their department, they had even less regard for the strategic concepts that came from the American side to be put forward by General Eisenhower. What developed was a long delaying game in which Eisenhower was more and more to feel that he was a pawn moved back and forth on the board between the desires and demands of Downing Street and the White House. It was a difficult, trying role he played out in private, putting him under ever-increasing strain and tension. But all this time, in public his image was growing in an astonishing way, the image of an America moving with a mighty will toward victory.

Four

Eisenhower
Becomes
Ike

In the months immediately before Eisenhower went to London as commander of the European Theater of Operations in June 1942, the United States was just beginning to bring its force to bear in the war. Often in those months, the British, who had stood alone for two and a half years, felt that all was lost.

Russia seemed certain to be forced to surrender. The triumphant Germans and Japanese threatened to join in the Middle East, thereby denying the British a vital source of oil and spelling the loss of the last bastions east of Suez. Malta, the only remaining allied stronghold in the Mediterranean, was about to fall under repeated pounding by German and Italian bombers. Desperately needed guns, tanks, and planes were being sent to Russia on the Murmansk run in the fear that if an effort were not made to supply the Soviet armies they would forthwith yield to Hitler. In a single convoy in June, twenty-three out of thirty-four ships were sunk on the way to Murmansk, and 130,000 out of 200,000 tons of cargo lost. In May and June more than a million and a half tons of shipping were sunk by German submarines, making the total for the half-year more than four million tons. In the first quarter more than 600,000 tanker tons were sunk in the western Atlantic. This was the arithmetic of despair. It seemed impossible to survive such losses.

Eisenhower represented the promise of America's strength and productivity. While that strength and productivity were not yet in being, the new commander of the ETO was the pledge that they would soon be made manifest. With his ebullient confidence he gave new hope to men who had been too sorely tried.

For their part, the British were anxious to indulge him whenever they could. They had been almost pathetically eager to placate the Americans since Pearl Harbor, after they knew they would not have to stand or fall alone. This was vividly shown in the spring when Marshall and Harry Hopkins took to London a plan drafted by Eisenhower, as chief of the War Plans Division, for a direct cross-channel invasion of France in 1942. What they thought of that plan, with its lack of reality, its extraordinary naïveté from the viewpoint of veterans who had been hanging on by an eyelash for so long, the British command carefully concealed at the time. Churchill agreed to it conditionally on an if-and-when basis.

Eisenhower, arriving as the herald of an advancing host, had a welcome ready-made for him. The warmth of the welcome was reinforced by his insistence from the beginning that everyone in his command must start thinking in terms of allied, rather than national, interests. In his first weeks in London he was infuriated by reports of American officers who went out of their way to belittle the English. Whenever he could discover such offenders they were disciplined and in some instances sent back to the United States. Throughout the war the stress was on the common purpose of the allies, with Eisenhower setting the tone at the top for friendly, wholehearted co-operation.

He was so successful that the rivalries and jealousies hidden from view at the time are only now beginning to come to light. It was too much to expect that the image of Eisenhower as the hero of the drama, the chief architect of ultimate victory, should go unchallenged. But at the time that image was an absolute necessity.

Warfare in the middle of the twentieth century is for the scientists and the technicians. It calls for the most complex and exacting organization of every resource. The weapons employed require extraordinary skills. When fighting men are used it is in a faceless mass. There is little opportunity for individual gallantry, courage in the face of great odds, a heroic and well-advertised will to win. It was this that Eisenhower supplied. His ability as a leader, an inspirer, was indisputable, and it was all the more surprising in view of how little experience he had had as a commander of large numbers of men.

With their long hierarchical tradition, the British governing class are masters of the art of ingratiating themselves with the stranger. In various subtle ways they can confer on him a sense of his importance and worth as reflected in the ancient mirror of their own high self-esteem. The utmost that they could do for the new commander who had come like a promise of salvation from across the sea was done. The record shows that again and again Eisenhower drew back from special attentions which were offered to him, trying, more often than not in vain, to make sure that his way of life did not differ too radically from that of the common soldier. This was a preoccupation throughout the war which at times led him to make absurd and somewhat childish gestures.

But whatever his own inmost feeling with respect to the process, the enhancement of the man and his command went on apace. The British press made the most of every scrap of personal information about Ike that came to hand. And this was, of course, as nothing in comparison with the deluge of publicity in the American press. The American command in London was building up at a fantastic rate. The number of calls handled by the American Armed Forces switchboard at 20 Grosvenor Square went from 2,000 to 6,000 a day within six weeks' time. As the command grew, so proportionately did the public-relations apparatus. The vastness of this apparatus staggers the imagination. It was geared to produce news, photographs, broadcasts, magazine articles, on every least aspect of the American war effort overseas. Because the tendency of American public relations is to relate an enterprise to an individual or individuals, General Eisenhower was the beneficiary of a great deal of the build-up.

It was soon evident, however, that the General himself had an intuitive knack for handling the press. He seems never to have held a press conference or dealt with reporters before he went to London. Yet from the first he showed himself a master in this department. He was at his best in the background conference. Two things that he did rarely failed to win favor and friendship: first, he appealed to the correspondents for their help and co-operation, and, second, he took them into his confidence, telling them about upcoming top-secret operations with such frankness as to startle the public-relations officers on his immediate staff. He felt that the American correspondents, as members of the allied team, should be shown complete trust. It was part of their job, too, to help win the war. This attitude was useful in wartime. But it has tended to color Eisenhower's approach to the press in civilian life, and it may help to explain why at White House press conferences he sometimes reacts with irritation and even anger to questions that are particularly provocative. That sort of thing, he seems to be implying, should not come from one of your own team.

Harry Butcher, highly experienced in public relations from coping with the tides of opinion as head of the Washington operation of the Columbia Broadcasting System, pays several tributes in his diary to Eisenhower's skill in handling the press. He noted on September 20, 1942: "When we talk of public relations, I have a feeling that I will gain a reputation as an expert in this field. I'll be getting the credit for Ike's good sense, for he is the keenest in dealing with the press I've ever seen, and I have met a lot of them, many of whom are phonies."

As the image of the leader, the hero, loomed ever larger on the wartime horizon, the General was, for the most part, engaged in harassing negotiations seeking to reconcile the conflicting viewpoints of London and Washington. As he frequently put it, he was chairman of the board, a diplomat, a mediator, a co-ordinator, going through a grinding daily schedule of appointments with British and American military men, high civilians of both governments, Red Cross officials, the press.

The wrangle over which assault, if any, should have priority in 1942 and '43 went on endlessly. General Marshall was eager for an attack across the channel to engage as many German divisions as possible and thereby relieve the pressure on the Soviet armies. Backed by the other service chiefs, he was strongly opposed to what he believed were merely diversionary actions in the Mediterranean. Admiral Ernest King, Chief of Naval Operations, who was constantly pressing for more ships and resources for the Pacific war, was all for a showdown, with the threat implied that if the British were unwilling to go through with a cross-channel invasion at the earliest possible moment then the major strategy of the war should be reversed and the defeat of Japan put first.

But Field Marshal Alan Brooke (later Viscount Alanbrooke), Chief of the Imperial General Staff, was just as stubbornly opposed to an invasion for which he believed the allies were pitifully unprepared, unprepared because they lacked combat-ready divisions, landing craft, and sufficient air support. Alanbrooke was convinced that the invasion proposed by the Americans could end only in disaster, and a disaster that might have a fatal effect on the course of the whole war. On his side were all the British chiefs, and it was a long time before Churchill viewed the American plan with anything but reluctance. His interest was focused on the Mediterranean and the possibility of an attack through the "soft underbelly" of the Nazis' European domain. In the middle of this conflict, trying to bring the two camps together, Eisenhower's position was not an enviable one. He referred wryly to the transatlantic essay contest that was going on as the teletype machines between Washington and London clattered out one memorandum after another.

The raid on Dieppe, undertaken to determine whether a channel port could be seized and held for twenty-four hours, had a sobering effect. Suffering appalling casualties, the Canadian troops assigned to carry out this experiment were driven off almost at once. It would seem, however, that the skill of the British chiefs of staff in presenting their case and documenting it with facts was what really carried the day. This is Alanbrooke's contention, and he supports it with contemporary records that have the ring of authenticity. In any event, by the end of July the decision had been taken to postpone the cross-channel operation and proceed with an invasion of North Africa under the code name Torch. For Eisenhower, who was chosen to command it, this brought an enormous sense of relief. Now he could push ahead with something tangible and immediate.

For all the difficulties of his position as intermediary,

he had established for himself a private life which he was to maintain and jealously guard throughout the war. This corresponded to his peacetime need to have familiar friends and associates around him, to be able to relax with them from time to time in a simple, family kind of atmosphere. Most of the personal memoirs that have been written, with the exception of Eisenhower's own austere, soldier's story, give a picture of easy informality behind the screen of security and military protocol.

Part of Butcher's function was to help the General relax. After a brief stay at Claridge's, they shared a flat in the Dorchester, the clifflike apartment hotel just off Hyde Park. But Butcher soon sensed that this was too confining for Eisenhower's restless temperament. Because of his previous conditioning and background, physical exercise in the out-of-doors is almost as much of a necessity for him as breathing. Butcher found Telegraph Cottage, an unpretentious house on a ten-acre wooded tract with a lawn and rose garden between Coombe Hill and Little Coombe golf courses. When he had an hour or so of leisure, the General could play a few holes of golf without ever going near the clubhouse, or he could practice putting and chip shots on the lawn.

Sergeant McKeogh, his orderly, was another "family" member who devoted himself to the General's well-being. Ike was a hero who could do no wrong to Mickey McKeogh. Convinced that Mickey brought him luck, the General wanted his orderly always within the sound of his voice whenever he was away from the office. Together they were more like an indulgent uncle—an uncle who could also lose his temper—and a nephew anxious to please than a general and a sergeant. The British were always being startled and a little shocked by this informality. Certainly the relationship between Ike and Mickey could hardly have been more different from, say, the formal relationship between a British field marshal and his batman.

It was the same way with all those around Eisenhower; with Butch and with "Tex" Lee, his other aide; with Kay Summersby, his driver and later one of his secretaries, who in her memoirs manages to make the whole thing sound like a prolonged picnic held in various quaint corners of Europe and Africa; and with Sergeant John Moaney, the Negro mess boy who was later to be Eisenhower's valet in the White House. The friendly informality of Eisenhower's military family, duly reported back home, may well have contributed to his popularity. We have always looked with suspicion on military rank-consciousness, and a commanding general who could let down and be just a human being was certain to be appealing. What is more, he was given a Scotty named Telek, and Telek soon became part of this family that stuck together through thick and thin for the three years of the war.

So great was the strain as the preparation for Torch put new and more harassing demands on Eisenhower that no one could quarrel with his need for a little relaxation. While he presents the outward appearance of bluff, hearty geniality, the record shows that he suffers a great deal from inner tension. The surface appearance is part of the resolute optimism that he invariably tries to present to the world.

With final agreement on Torch he was given three separate staffs: one for the European Theater as then constituted, one in anticipation of North Africa, and a third to prepare for the ultimate assault on Europe from the west. The plans for the North African invasion, with all that they involved in mounting an attack along several hundred miles of coast, were a pressing assignment. But what really disturbed him were the political complications with the French. He had little or no preparation for coping with the savage intrigues and rivalries that set one Frenchman against another. It was a poisonous atmosphere, and Eisenhower, with his lack of knowledge and his abhorrence of all things political, could hardly have been expected to find his way about in the maze of French pride, jealousy, and thwarted ambition. The wonder in retrospect is that so much of the responsibility for the problem seemed to devolve on the puzzled and unhappy General.

As he found himself in the middle of the most delicate and difficult negotiations to try to insure that there would be a minimum of resistance from the French forces in North Africa, Eisenhower came to feel that there were almost as many factions as there were Frenchmen. The State Department's Robert Murphy, stationed in North Africa and represented as the foremost expert, came on a brief mission to London and dined with Eisenhower and other top Americans at Telegraph Cottage under the most extraordinary secrecy restrictions. Murphy's visit prepared the way for the adventure a little later of General Mark Clark, who landed from a submarine near Algiers as part of the effort to gain acceptance of the allied invasion. On that famous expedition Clark went ashore with a fortune in gold and ended by losing his pants and nearly losing his life before he got back into the submarine. For soldiers who wanted to fight a war it was all pretty baffling and confusing.

Two months before the invasion was to be launched, General Walter Bedell Smith went to London at Eisenhower's request, to be his chief of staff. With an enormous sense of relief Eisenhower turned over part of the burden to this admired colleague, who soon became a close personal friend. By reason both of temperament and experience Smith could do what Eisenhower was either

unwilling or unable to do. Carrying a crushing weight
of detail through the war, he also had the capacity to
say no and to say it bluntly and abruptly in his rasping,
cavalry sergeant's voice. He was not a West Point graduate, but had served in the Army since 1917, was wounded
in action in France during World War I, and combined
a somewhat broader professional background than Eisenhower's with highly developed intellectual interests. How
large a share of the burden he assumed it is impossible
for an outsider to judge. He himself, in his book *Eisenhower's Six Great Decisions,* gives his boss the most un-
qualified credit as a military leader. But to say that he
was invaluable to Eisenhower is a gross understatement.

Taking off from London for Gibraltar on November 5,
the Commanding General and his staff had a rough flight,
with enemy aircraft reported near as they prepared to
land. Eisenhower had already gone a very long way
toward becoming in the estimation of the American public a central figure of the allied war effort. But it was a
period of acute worry and apprehension for him. In
London a nagging neuritis had developed in his shoulder.
His stomach felt like a clenched fist. This was the evidence
of the complicated individual beneath the simple, ex-
troverted surface the public saw. The symptoms of strain
recurred on the eve of every massive operation, but with
so much at stake, as Torch was about to be set in motion
at his command, his suffering was intense.

There were, however, compensations. As commander
of the whole operation, he was in command of Gibraltar,
and once again the sense of "How could all this be
happening to me?" came over him as it had in London.
Butcher reproduces in his diary a memorandum of the
thoughts that overwhelmed the General as he sat, in his
own expression, in the bowels of the Rock at his own command post giving the orders in this bastion of the British

Empire. Of all the commands he had ever dreamed or
thought of in his Army service this was the last that would
have occurred to him: "I have operational command of
Gibraltar!! . . . I simply must have a grandchild or I'll
never have the fun of telling this when I'm fishing, grey-
bearded, on the banks of a quiet bayou in the deep south."
Someone had told him that it was good luck to see Gibraltar's monkeys, and as the hours were ticking off to zero,
when American troops would first be blooded in battle, he
went with Butcher to visit them. He patted one on the
head to make sure that if there were anything to the
luck theory he would benefit by it.

Torch was a signal success. The allied forces assault-
ing Casablanca, Oran, and Algiers met with only brief
French resistance. But no sooner had the Americans arrived in Algiers than the French presented them with
a political squabble far more embarrassing than the conflicting claims that Eisenhower and his staff had tried
to sort out when they were still in London. Thanks to
fortuitous circumstances, Admiral Jean François Darlan
was caught in Algiers at the time of the invasion. With
some quick work by General Clark he was persuaded to
sign an order calling on French troops to lay down their
arms. But General Henri Giraud, with whom the earlier
negotiations had been carried on, was still in the picture,
and there was at least one other claimant to authority.
To the perplexed and harassed Eisenhower the principal
concern was the possible effect on present and future
military operations. He finally agreed, after consulting
with Murphy but without the official sanction of London
and Washington, to recognize Admiral Darlan as administrative head of French North Africa, with Giraud in
command of French forces.

Almost at once from both England and the United
States a storm of protest broke. Darlan had a dubious

record as a Petainist and a collaborator. In London it was felt that the Darlan deal was a deliberate betrayal of General de Gaulle and the Free French. In America the criticism was more severe than any that Eisenhower was to be subjected to throughout the war. And coming in sharp contrast to the great build-up he took it with acute sensitivity.

President Roosevelt, at a press conference, gave the deal his blessing as a necessity of war. But the reaction was still so unfavorable that General Marshall asked Eisenhower to release the casualty figures in order to show how low they were in comparison with the estimates by those who had planned the invasion, low presumably because Darlan had ordered the resistance to cease, although this is highly doubtful. If I could just get command of a battalion and get into a bullet battle, Eisenhower told his brother Milton, who was visiting Algiers in his job with the Office of War Information, it would all be so simple.

The British were critical at this time and later in the African campaign because they thought the Commanding General was too preoccupied with political problems. Contemporary accounts do not make clear why he should have had to devote so much of his time and energy to straightening out the political tangle. The intimation of his critics was that this preoccupation prevented him from concentrating on swift action to move into Tunisia before the Nazis reinforced it. There were other, readily apparent reasons for the delay: the shortages in shipping and aircraft which Alanbrooke had pointed out in arguing against a cross-channel invasion in 1942, lack of motor equipment, and plain bad weather. In any case, the Germans were able to reinforce Tunisia, and thereby the African campaign was prolonged through the long, cold, miserable winter and into the spring.

This is the sort of point, of course, over which, in the aftermath of any war, the military historians argue interminably. If there was blame to be apportioned for the delay it did not then fall on Eisenhower. At any rate his public was not aware of failures either of omission or commission in his command. In the fury of a war these are not questions, short, that is, of unmistakable disaster, for public discussion, if only because of the necessity for sustaining morale.

Only once in the African campaign was the newly minted reputation of the commander in public jeopardy —when American troops were thrown back at Kasserine Pass in February 1943, and it looked as though a bloody and costly reversal were in the making. The determined confidence Eisenhower had shown was shaken. Sergeant McKeogh has told how the General went up to II Corps headquarters at Tebessa when the Germans were breaking through the Kasserine gap. As he went in one side of the town German tanks were approaching the other side. Back at his villa in Algiers, after a cold and dreary trip, he looked exhausted, and lower, according to his orderly, than Mickey was ever to see him look again. He may have been thinking of Harry Hopkins' words the month before, when Roosevelt and Churchill were meeting at Casablanca. Hopkins, who had accompanied Roosevelt, had taken the occasion to let Ike know that if he took Tunisia he would be ranked with the world's great generals. If he failed . . . While Hopkins was not explicit, plainly the implication was that he would be relieved of his command and the intimations of glory that had begun to gather round his head would go glimmering.

It is scarcely an exaggeration to say that once this danger was past, and the German thrust at Kasserine contained, the whole future course of Eisenhower's career was assured. To Eisenhower himself, in the midst of the never-ending harassments of a far-flung war fought with allies so dissimilar in outlook and background, the future can have had no such certified look. But as Winston Churchill put it, if this was not the beginning of the end, it was the end of the beginning. America's trained manpower and her vast productivity were coming into being to swing the balance against the Axis. They provided the margin for error—and it was soon a very wide one—which had been nonexistent through the desperate months when Hitler and the Japanese seemed almost certain to sweep the world. Only a colossal blunder, which he could scarcely have made, given his abilities, the excellence of his staff, and the careful supervisory eye of both London and Washington, could have knocked him off the high pedestal onto which he had so rapidly been elevated.

He continued to have the watchful, one might almost say paternal, devotion of General Marshall. When Marshall stayed at the villa in Algiers at the end of January 1943, he took Butcher aside and gave him "orders" to take care of his commanding officer—keep him out of the office as much as possible, get him home early, find a masseur for him and have him rubbed down every evening before dinner, make him ride horseback or get some other form of exercise. As Butcher records, this was the attitude of a devoted and anxious father toward a son. But Marshall had a practical objective, too, and that was to keep Eisenhower from going stale under the ceaseless strain. He had a better understanding of his commander than might have been indicated by the military formality of the relationship he outwardly maintained with him.

What seems strange, looking back from the perspective of fifteen years, is that in the fall of that year, with the

African campaign concluded and the Italian campaign well under way, the top-secret cables between London, Washington, and Algiers should have dealt with the choice of a supreme commander for the next great step —the cross-channel invasion. Eisenhower would seem to have been the inevitable heir to this next command. But, in fact, it was Marshall who had already been chosen, in a secret decision made at the Quebec meeting of Roosevelt and Churchill in August. Eisenhower was to take Marshall's place in Washington and was so informed by the President just before the President and the Prime Minister met in Cairo in November prior to the Tehran conference. In his own words, Roosevelt wanted Marshall to emerge as "the Pershing of the Second World War," and it was obviously the post of supreme commander on which present glory and future fame would settle.

Eisenhower told those close to him that he would not make a good chief of staff because he was not enough of a politician. Trying to reassure him, Butcher said that his very "abomination"—the word the diarist used—of politics would make him respected by the politicians, so that he was bound to succeed. His own preference, or so he told his associates at the time, was to stay on as allied commander in the Mediterranean. Presumably this was his choice as an alternative if he were not selected for the great push in Europe. Marshall's personal wishes are not a matter of record; his expressed desire, as a good soldier, was to serve wherever he might be most useful. But certainly he realized that the cross-channel invasion would be the climactic moment of the drama leading to victory.

Under pressure from Admiral King and others to keep Marshall in Washington, the President wavered. Convinced finally that it was best "not to monkey with a winning team," he decided in early December, at the end of the second Cairo conference, that the supreme command was to go, after all, to Eisenhower. On his way back to the United States he stopped over to see Eisenhower and gave him the news.

The star of the drama was cast. Eisenhower was lucky, and the aura of his luck, mirrored in the friendly face now familiar to every newspaper reader, may have been a reason in itself for his selection as supreme commander. While no polls were taken, it is a safe surmise that for one person who could identify Marshall there were a hundred who knew who Eisenhower was. He was over there with our boys, and if anyone mistreated them or pushed them around, as General Patton had been reported as doing, then Ike was there to stand up for them.

It is not at all surprising, therefore, that the question of the presidency should have arisen so early. Appropriately enough, the first notice of it came to Eisenhower's attention through his new friend George Allen, a highly successful specialist in cultivating the rich and the powerful. Allen managed to get to London shortly before the General arrived there, and, as he tells the story in his impudent book *Presidents Who Have Known Me,* he made it appear that the commander of the ETO was already a close friend. Confessing his plight to Eisenhower on the latter's arrival, Allen got the General to back him up with a lunch at the most conspicuous spot in London, Claridge's restaurant. This is typical of the Allen technique of ingratiation. At the same time, Mrs. Allen and Mrs. Eisenhower, both living at Washington's Wardman Park (now Sheraton Park) Hotel, were forming a lasting friendship.

In a letter dated October 6, 1943, Allen enclosed a clipping from the Washington *Post* telling how Tank Corps Post No. 715 of the American Legion in New

York had adopted a resolution boosting Eisenhower for
president because of his "leadership qualities." Butcher
reports that Ike was exasperated and particularly at
Allen's reference to him as a candidate. He scribbled in
reply: "Baloney! Why can't a simple soldier be left alone
to carry out his orders. And I furiously object to the word
'candidate'—I ain't and won't." How many times, in what
a variety of ways—solemnly, angrily, briefly, at length—
was he to repeat that no! The simple soldier who abominated politics was to learn the ways of politicians by a
long, laborious, and often embarrassing route.

The Eisenhower-for-president talk was to continue to
swell in volume from this time forward. After D day hundreds of letters began to come from America saying, in
effect, that having led American boys in war he must
now lead the country in peace. Publicly he brushed this
talk aside as though it were nonsense to be dismissed out
of hand. He cannot, however, have been immune to the
ever more flattering suggestion that he, the national hero,
had become the indispensable man. One of those close
to him in the war years has expressed the private conviction that, as the volume of letters swelled to a flood
following the success of the Normandy landings, Eisenhower succumbed to the presidential virus and never
thereafter recovered. But there is no proof of this except
the negative proof that he at no time used the irrevocable
language of General Sherman.

Hard-pressed as he continued to be with the clean-up
of the African campaign and the launching of the attack
on Italy, he nevertheless found time to see the big-name
correspondents who were continuously coming through.
They were almost all friends of Butcher. Butch took Raymond Clapper in to see Ike, and Ike spent an hour and
a half reviewing the campaign with him. When Clapper

came out he was "on air," according to Butcher's diary, in a state of euphoria in which he had not only nominated Eisenhower for president but elected him. Clapper himself wrote in his syndicated column:

> During a big historic event such as the invasion of Sicily it might be supposed that the Commanding General would be clanking his weight around. After all this is a great moment in history because the Allies at last are carrying the war to Europe.
>
> Furthermore, this is a gigantic operation with 3000 ships involved and it might be expected that the Commanding General would be jumping all over the place issuing orders right and left.
>
> But General Eisenhower returned from the beaches of Sicily looking as if he had just come from a ball game which broke right for the home team. He was more like a big industrial executive who, on the day the plant is breaking production records, will show visitors around the mill as if he had nothing else to do.

Something of the spell the General cast is in this. Talking with him one could not help but be aware of the power that was his. It was very probably an illusion, in view of the intricate chain of command which so fragmented responsibility, but so much for America and for the world seemed to turn on his every word. And yet for all the power and the glory he was a simple, friendly man who seemed to want so little for himself. His office was small, uncluttered, free of the apparatus of prestige of the great man, the only picture on the wall a photograph of Ida Eisenhower seated on the front porch of her home in Abilene, looking, with her white hair and her air of serenity, very much like Whistler's famous portrait of his mother.

In the field he was also unpretentious, going up to startled GIs to ask them where they came from and what they intended to do when the war ended. This was the image projected to the American public by the correspondents who saw him at firsthand.

When he returned to London, the build-up of the man and the force he was to command was rapidly accelerated. Africa and Italy had in a sense been sideshows. This was to be the frontal assault on Hitler's Fortress Europa. Although the pressures were greater in London, he was more accessible there, and the public-relations machine of Supreme Headquarters Allied Expeditionary Force grew along with everything else to incredible proportions.

The man became the legend. It encased him like a golden shell. There is fairly early evidence that he was not altogether happy in this glittering carapace. The duality of his character, the conflict between his innate desires and the whole conditioning of his past life, on the one hand, and the attraction of the public character he had been endowed with, on the other, was evident. Surely he was ambitious and surely he had dreamed in the long years of desuetude of the commands he might one day hold. But this was beyond the dreams of the wildest dreamer. Standing erect and smiling in the hero's role, he was often resentful, longing for the old, comfortable anonymity. It was a duality that was to persist in the years ahead as the discrepancy between private preference and public character became even more marked.

The story of Eisenhower and the final decision on the day and the hour of the Normandy invasion has been told and retold and told again. As with every decision that was taken in the whole course of the war, many, many minds participated in appraising an extraordinarily complex range of factors, from weather to enemy intelligence. But the final responsibility was Eisenhower's, and in the public image he and he alone sweated out those

"Target—Germany"

Edmund Duffy in the Baltimore *Sun*   1944

hours to D day. This has become a part of the national lore, one of those set pieces of history from which a people take heart and courage in times of crisis. It has been recounted so often and with such moving personal detail that already it has begun to take its place with such tableaus as Washington's crossing of the Delaware and Lincoln's reading of the Emancipation Proclamation to his cabinet. History may later grapple with the event, but for the present it belongs to the body of belief by which a nation lives. Often afterward Eisenhower was to say that this was the climax of his life, and he was to add that a man knowing when he had reached such a moment should also know enough to stand on it.

It is a reasonable assumption that the criticism of Eisenhower's conduct of the war has only begun, as one memoirist after another provides new ammunition. In all probability the military historians will still be debating fifty years hence. Much of the criticism has been inspired by those close to General MacArthur, and it centers on the setback of the Battle of the Bulge. They have hinted that General Marshall sent Eisenhower a reprimand so stinging that it seemed it must be followed by his relief from his command. These same sources put the blame for the costly setback at Bastogne directly on Eisenhower. But, as with the other allegations, there is no documentary evidence to support it. The violent German thrust was a last desperate attempt to avert defeat and save Hitler's armies from the giant pincers that were slowly closing from east to west.

The second principal source of criticism, and it is still only in a minor key, is the British. One of Eisenhower's difficult tasks was to arbitrate between the imperious demands of Field Marshal Montgomery and the necessities of his own American field commanders. The feeling was deep on both sides, and Montgomery was a public hero in Great Britain in more or less the same way as Eisenhower was in the United States. General Bradley and other Americans were convinced that Montgomery was vainglorious in public and excessively cautious in the actual direction of his forces. "Quite often during the war," Bradley was to write in his *A Soldier's Story*, "I disputed Monty's views, challenged his decisions, and questioned the wisdom of his moves. For unlike his British associates, I was never so intimidated by the legend of Montgomery that I could unhesitatingly accept his judgment as infallible. Like the rest of us, Monty is mortal; and being mortal, he has made mistakes." Largely hidden from view at the time, this quarrel has left scars which still smart.

From the wartime diaries of Lord Alanbrooke, used by Arthur Bryant as the basis of *The Turn of the Tide*, it is evident that the Chief of the Imperial General Staff had a low estimate of Eisenhower's capacities as a strategist and tactician. This impression is conveyed not so much by what he says as by what he does not say. His references to Eisenhower are chiefly to his charm and to his powers of persuasion. The British never ceased to be perturbed by the casual atmosphere of Eisenhower's headquarters. "A general air of restless confusion, with everyone doing their best under unnatural conditions" is the description by Sir Ian Jacob, Assistant Military Secretary of the War Cabinet, of the Algiers headquarters in December of 1943, as quoted by Bryant. "There is a lack of dignity about the H.Q.," Jacob found, "an air of aimless bustle, a constant cluttering of hangers-on and visitors, and at the same time an amateur flavor that makes one wonder how anything ever gets done."

Whatever the final verdict is, it must take into account the fact that Eisenhower represents a sharp break with the past. He was the military manager, the front-office man, for whom the title of commander was something of an anachronism; the end result of the managerial revolution in the military. But he was also the beneficiary of all past tradition that inevitably endowed the successful commander with heroism and pressed on him a crown of gratitude. As the victor of Europe he was to walk thenceforth with the full chalice of his fame, and, with his reluctance to risk spilling a single drop, his inherent reluctance to commit himself to a course of action that would provoke conflict or hostility was to become even more pronounced.

"Reception Room"
Long in the Minneapolis *Tribune*   May 25, 1952

Five

Return of the Hero

On a hot June day Ike arrived in Washington. A large crowd met him at the airport, and a million people lined the parade route, their welcoming cheers almost drowning out the bands. He stood grinning in an open car with outstretched arms, and when police lines broke before the surging throng he leaned out to shake hands with those who pressed forward. He addressed a joint session of Congress and dined in state that night with President Truman at the White House. In New York he was driven through thirty-seven miles of streets under a rain of paper kept to relatively modest proportions only because of wartime restrictions still in effect. He was honored at a reception and spoke at a dinner, paraded and spoke at Kansas City, Kansas, and again back home in Abilene, and he managed to get to a West Point reunion.

As he tells it in his memoirs, General Eisenhower had no idea that his return to the United States in June of 1945 would cause any outburst. He says that it was his intention to come back just for a day in order to attend his thirtieth reunion at West Point. There was to be no advance notice of his visit or publicity of any kind. He and his colleagues were, he tells us, "so preoccupied in the daily grind of work that we were largely unaware of the enthusiasms sweeping our own countries." He records that he felt "amazement and astonishment" at the hero's welcome given him both at home and throughout Europe.

Such universal acclaim, made manifest in one great overwhelming demonstration after another, has been accorded to few men in history. Woodrow Wilson, in the aftermath of that earlier world war, is the only other American to have received even a remotely comparable tribute outside his own country. June of that victory year was a never-ending triumph, a joyful, million-voiced cry of praise and gratitude offered up to this cheerful, modest American. Parading through London in a landau pulled by white horses, he had delivered the celebrated Guildhall speech and been made the first American member of the Order of Merit. In Paris he had driven down the Champs Elysées saluting from an open car to great crowds, receiving from General de Gaulle at the end of this triumphal procession the Cross of Liberation.

Returning to Europe again, he dissolved SHAEF on July 14, staying on as commander of the United States occupation zone of Germany and U.S. representative on the Allied Control Council, which had been created to govern occupied Germany. At that time, all was harmony and good fellowship. This was the brief period of Eisenhower's famous friendship with Marshal Zhukov, who was the Soviet member of the Council. The two had exchanged decorations at the end of the war—the Legion of Merit and the Soviet Order of Victory, the latter never previously given to a foreigner. Accompanied by Zhukov, Eisenhower went to Moscow in August at Stalin's invitation, and there he was given the full Kremlin treatment.

We now know that even before Roosevelt's death Stalin had begun to present a menacing attitude, but

Eisenhower believed in the genuineness of Zhukov's friendship. He says in his memoirs that Zhukov and his staff demonstrated only an "intense desire to be friendly and cooperative." While they both served on the Council there was a minimum of friction and the annoying incidents that were later to become a calculated campaign of harassment. Until the time that he left Europe, Eisenhower records, his friendship with Zhukov "continued to grow," and the two corresponded in friendly fashion until April 1946, when the Marshal was relieved of his German command and sent into eclipse. It has been surmised that Stalin, hardening increasingly and showing his determination to expand the Communist world, suspected Zhukov of being too friendly with Eisenhower and through him with the West.

On the American side there was little suspicion of this friendship. We wanted to believe that we could "get along" with the Russians, and if these two soldiers could make a go of it perhaps we could hope to live together as we had fought together. Almost anything Eisenhower might have done would have been all right, with the aura of his great prestige shielding him from attack even though the high brass were more and more the object of the average citizen's wrath. Occasionally he was criticized for what was regarded as unsatisfactory handling of displaced persons and for the behavior of our occupation troops. But this was minor, and in the radiant afterglow of the common victory the four-power occupation was uneventful, with no shadow of the perils of the cold war to come.

At the Potsdam conference in July, the General had no official role. This was the occasion on which, according to the Eisenhower memoirs, President Truman remarked to him, "General, there is nothing that you may want that

I won't try to help you get. That definitely and specifically includes the Presidency in 1948." In his televised interview with Edward R. Murrow in 1958 the former President denied that he had made such an offer at Potsdam. But whether he used those words or not, Truman's hero worship was of a piece with that of the great American public, and he was to play an important part in forwarding the General's career.

In November, Eisenhower returned to Washington to succeed Marshall as chief of staff, serving in this capacity until February 1948. Starting with his professed belief that he was unsuited to the post by reason of his abomination of politics, he was to make clear how frustrating and unrewarding he found it. But the chief of staff job is the capstone of a professional Army career, and Eisenhower could hardly have refused it.

The chief of staff tops the pyramid created by the system that was established after the Spanish-American War had revealed the grave deficiencies of the divided command system then in effect. Using European systems as a model, Secretary of War Elihu Root pushed through a reorganization which was enacted into law in 1903. The chief of staff, under the direction of the president and the secretary of war, was given supervision over both troops of the line and staff departments or bureaus. He and the newly created General Staff Corps were made responsible for preparing plans for defense and mobilization, for investigating and reporting on all questions affecting Army efficiency and preparedness, and for assisting the secretary of war and all superior commanders. In 1920 the four-section organization—the four "G's" borrowed from the French by the staff of the American Expeditionary Force—was adopted by the General Staff, with the addition of a War Plans Division. With a few revisions and modifications, and a temporary radical reorganization during World War II, the same system is still in effect.

At the top of the pyramid, Eisenhower made the final decisions. Regular meetings of all the General Staff officers with the chief of staff considered matters of highest Army policy. Questions involving detailed study, as most of them did, were broken down in terms of the various branches and services involved, and each prepared a report on the aspect of the problem within its sphere. These reports filtered back up the line to the deputy chief of staff, and when finally laid before the chief for decision the various parts had been organized and indexed for quick reference and their substance summarized in two or three paragraphs. By the numbers the responsibility is spread from bottom to top until the final yes or no of the chief of staff. The system depends on absolute responsibility at every level and on disciplined subordinates who are required to stay in line come what may.

The job imposed a demanding daily routine. Arriving at his office in the Pentagon shortly after 8 A.M., Eisenhower rarely left before 6:30 or 7:00. The first hour was spent in looking over the most important incoming messages from all over the world and indicating what action was needed. With appointments starting at nine, he saw six to twelve people a day—his own subordinates and, from the outside, members of Congress in particular— plus conferences with the Secretary of the Army, the weekly staff conference, the weekly War Council meeting, and the weekly Joint Chiefs meeting. In between, he worked on correspondence, personally reading in whole or in part and signing answers to a hundred or so letters a day, a carry-over of a wartime practice that has always counted high among his public-relations assets. He was perhaps the most widely traveled chief of staff in history, making frequent inspection trips at home and around the world. Along with these official duties went a stiff schedule of speechmaking. In the first six months he made nearly thirty speeches. To Bedell Smith in February of 1947 he wrote, "One of my worst problems is how to decline a real flood of invitations. . . . Due to my very great desire to promote a few simple ideas in which I so earnestly believe, it is indeed difficult for me to say 'no.' . . ."

The first colossal problem that confronted him was demobilization. The country was hell-bent for peace, and what it cost no one seemed to care. Under a schedule drawn up by General Marshall, the original goal was five million men discharged within the first year. In this there was some faint semblance of order, although it entailed very large losses in matériel abandoned and destroyed. Horrendous tales came back of wrist watches by the thousands in their original cartons thrown into the sea, jeeps and half-tracks pushed off docks by the hundreds, millions of dollars in equipment left to rust and rot where it had been abandoned. But what followed made it look like a cautious and restrained procedure to conserve both resources and military strength in being. Loud, angry outcries came from Congress and the public: the brass were holding back. The pressure was such that Marshall responded by promising in September 1945 that everyone with two years of service could expect to be out during the coming winter and that the separation rate would soon exceed 700,000 a month. As the clamor rose, the rate was upped again, to a million a month. Some direct Communist influence could be detected in agitation in GI camps and depots around the world and in some of the shriller denunciations of the brass. But for the most part it seems to have been the spontaneous demand of a war-weary people determined to get back as quickly as possible to "normal."

Much of modern American history is bound up with our long isolation from the rest of the world. For a century and a half we believed in a natural immunity from the ills that beset other peoples. Foremost among these ills was the cycle of wars that had plagued Europe for generations. If we were drawn into a war it was through some mischance, a wicked intrigue designed to break the happy tenor of our lives. The intriguers under the most immediate suspicion have been the military. Their business is war, and naturally they are forever promoting it, plotting and scheming to gain power over the innocent civilian in order to turn him into cannon fodder.

This attitude came to the surface in the wild rush to demobilize after V-J Day in 1945. The brass wanted to keep our boys in uniform. Of course, we said, since they would thereby retain all their privileges and perquisites. They could go on living it up in big cars and airplanes provided by the taxpayer. While there were other reasons for the reckless haste with which the American military machine was dismantled, this attitude was basic to the rout that took place.

The situation as Eisenhower took over was a difficult one, and he voiced an immediate protest. Testifying before the Senate Committee on Military Affairs in November, he asked, "Are we going so far in weakening ourselves in Europe that we are going to abandon unfulfilled the purposes for which we fought? . . . If our strength in Germany is cut below the point where we can do our job, then we better get the residue out as quickly as possible."

But no one was listening, and the crisis was still to come. By January of 1946 five million men had been discharged, and it became apparent that the Army would be unable to meet even an irreducible minimum of its commitments. The discharge rate was reduced to 300,000 and the plan to have every soldier with two years of service home by March abandoned.

The roar of protest that greeted this move passed all previous bounds. Senators called Eisenhower daily to complain that they were being inundated with baby booties marked "I miss my Daddy." In the Philippines, Hawaii, Paris, London, and Yokohama, GI demonstrations, mass meetings, and near-riots occurred. The tragedy was that most of the men had never really understood why the war had been fought, and now no one explained the importance of trying to maintain order and stability, in the aftermath of the war, with American military strength. Perhaps it would have been impossible in any event, but the effort was never made. The planning for the transition from total war to business as usual was hopelessly inadequate. The GIs were bored, idle, badly disciplined. Belatedly, Eisenhower ordered stern measures taken against the demonstrators, issued a buck-passing order to theater commanders to return to the United States any men "for whom there is no military need," and addressed Congress and the nation on the necessity for retaining sufficient numbers of men, promising, at the same time, an increase in the discharge rate.

The worst of the storm was over at that point, and Congress and the public indicated growing satisfaction with the demobilization rate. In the comparative lull that followed it was possible to view the wreckage of America's once great military force and appraise the damage that had been done. It was almost literally inestimable. With the pressing need to maintain the occupation forces at minimum strength there was not, so Eisenhower testified in March, a single division in the continental United States that was fully trained and equipped. How much of the blame for this should fall on Eisenhower, how much any single individual, even a great national hero, could have done to resist the tidal wave, it is impossible to say. The country was in a mood of frenzied irresponsibility, as though determined after the disciplines of the war to throw off all restraints. In January of 1946 there were 1,750,000 workers on strike, more than in any month in our history up to that time, and more workdays were lost. In such an atmosphere it was perhaps beyond the powers of any man to do more than Eisenhower did.

It was his fate to preside unwillingly over the liquidation of America's military might. In 1947 when the Soviet Union had 208 divisions, a force of 4,500,000 men which could be built to 10,500,000 in thirty days, our Army had declined from its V-E Day peak of 8,300,000, eighty-nine divisions, to a little over a million men and twelve divisions. The National Guard and Army Reserve programs were hamstrung for lack of funds, and Selective Service had been allowed to expire early in the year. America was relying almost exclusively on her monopoly of the atomic bomb, a monopoly that the Russians were not expected to break before 1952. Additional reassurance was found in our control of the sea, great industrial potential, fourteen million veterans, and the comfortable belief that the development of new weapons, missiles in particular, was proceeding satisfactorily under the Joint Research and Development Board.

All the stress from the Pentagon was on the seventy-group Air Force with the atom bomb as its weapon. The total number of men under arms—regarded, it is true, as a minimum—was planned at only a little more than a million and a half. As Eisenhower was completing his tour of duty early in 1948, the actual total of uniformed men and women was only 1,374,000, and the Army had less than three divisions that could be regarded as combat-ready reserves. Occupation troops, as was soon to be made evident by their pitiful performance in Korea, were not regarded as part of the available combat force and were neither trained nor equipped for combat.

In March 1946, Winston Churchill had made his Fulton, Missouri, speech with its warning of the need to stand up to the growing threat of Soviet imperialism. The international situation was rapidly deteriorating, with alarums in many parts of the world. And yet retrenchment and economy were the domestic watchwords; rigid budget ceilings were to be strictly observed. Here again, as in the instance of demobilization, it is hard to say what greater effort Eisenhower might have made to overcome the prevailing mood of both the Republican Congress and the Democratic administration, the mood that was supposedly an accurate reflection of the temper of the country. As Marshall had been before him, Eisenhower, with the support of Truman, became a tireless advocate of universal military training as a democratic substitute for a large standing force, but in the context of the times UMT could hardly have been more unacceptable. And in his major job of selling Congress and the people on the Army's needs and program he obviously cannot be credited with any notable success, comparing unfavorably with Marshall in this respect. His public-relations sense was inadequate to cope with a situation of this magnitude.

Pleading the Army's case inside the military establishment as well as publicly was Eisenhower's responsibility in the controversy over unification that cut across every other consideration throughout his tour of duty. The essence of the controversy was "consolidation," the Army's concept, versus "co-ordination," which was the Navy's position. But behind these innocent-sounding words was a pent-up violence that, as it flared into the open from time to time, seemed to put mutual self-destruction before everything else.

The Army's plan called for a strict chain of command: a single, integrated Department of Defense under a single secretary, a chief of staff and General Staff for the Armed Forces, and three coequal components, air, ground, and sea, each with a commander. The core of the Navy's plan was a continuation of the Joint Chiefs of Staff system inaugurated during the war, to be reinforced by other wartime co-ordinating mechanisms such as the Joint Research and Development Board and the Army-Navy Munitions Board. Co-ordination on basic policy was to be provided by the Joint Chiefs and by an over-all secretary of defense who would not, however, have administrative control over the services. The service departments, including, if the Army insisted, a separate Air Force, were to be autonomous and of cabinet rank. The Navy's views were presented in a report prepared in 1945 by Ferdinand Eberstadt at the direction of the then Secretary of the Navy, James Forrestal. The report envisioned on the highest level co-ordination of military, diplomatic, and economic policy through what were to emerge as the National Security Council, served by the Central Intelligence Agency, and the National Security Resources Board.

From the first, the Navy had an advantage in the effectiveness of its presentation and, in addition, because its plan was far less radical than the sweeping reorganization advocated by the Army. The Army proposed, or so the Navy alleged through the secret propaganda bureau directed by Admirals Radford and Burke, to abolish some of the most cherished military institutions embodying the proudest American traditions. The existence of the Marine Corps in particular was believed to be threatened. The testimony of some Army witnesses and Eisenhower's

views as expressed in his Joint Chiefs papers fed the
suspicion of the Marines and their champions in Congress. The Navy also feared the loss of its aviation to the
Air Force. The Army's command system, the Navy argued, was often inapplicable in naval warfare, and it
would be impossible to apply it to an organization as
vast and complex as an integrated military establishment.
No single authority could administer such an organization. In addition, of course, the Navy simply did not
want its size and power diminished in any respect.

The Army based its arguments on economy—the
billions of dollars wasted in duplicating facilities and
procurement; on efficiency—the elimination of the
wrangling and rivalry of the separate services; and on
the unitary character of modern war—the entire world
might be a single battlefield in another conflict. And
were not the unified command systems of World War II
a demonstrable success, the Army demanded, with the
proof in the experience of General Eisenhower? Testifying himself on that point before the Senate Military
Affairs Committee, Eisenhower argued that the fear that
one service would be subordinated to another in a unified
force had proved to be groundless in the African and
European campaigns. He was sure that "once the step
is taken here, the same result will follow." In the course
of the same presentation he observed, "The pooling of
talent in the field of scientific research and development
is an absolute necessity. Only through a single department can coordinated development of new weapons be
assured."

Eisenhower's public conduct during the controversy as
a whole was exemplary. He expressed himself with obvious conviction in speeches and before congressional
committees, and he was never at any time caught out
in the extracurricular activities being directed by the

admirals. Behind the scenes, however, his role appears to have been limited chiefly to saying "me too" to the advocacy of Robert Patterson, the Secretary of War, while the latter went through the arduous business of seeking some common ground with the Navy.

Forrestal, throwing his whole life into the balance, and paying for it later with his suicide, argued the Navy's position with the kind of detail that proved convincing to Congress and the country and that was largely lacking from the Army's proposals. "Merge now, organize later" was his characterization of the Army's approach, and the Army failed to provide adequate answers to the questions he raised and possible dangers he pointed out. There was a measure of compromise and concession on both sides in the unification legislation that finally emerged, but the Navy's views were predominant. The Army's proposals had originally had the approval of President Truman and considerable backing in Congress, but it was the Eberstadt report that formed the basis of the National Security Act of 1947. The separate service departments were not given cabinet rank, and in subsequent legislation the authority of the secretary of defense over the entire organization was more clearly established, but the Army chief-of-staff, chain-of-command concept was abandoned and the Navy's views on its own roles and missions and the means of carrying them out were in the main adopted.

Opinion, both lay and expert, for the most part accepted the outcome. It appeared that the 1947 law, with all its limitations and inadequacies, was the most that could be achieved at the time. The mere fact that the Navy was so violently opposed to the Army's plan would have, as the Navy anticipated, made it unworkable. And in the opinion of one of America's foremost military analysts, Walter Millis:

. . . experience seems only to have confirmed that in 1947 neither the tactical nor strategic lessons of the Second War, still less the requirements of the future, had been worked out far enough to permit of a unitary solution. Had a monolithic military system been adopted in 1947, it would hardly have worked well in the face of the complex and fluid crises which we were subsequently to confront.

Eisenhower made it clear, however, that he believed that what had been achieved was at best a hesitant first step. The warring tribes had been brought together in an uneasy confederation. It could be assumed that they would join forces against an outside enemy, although to those who remembered the bitter conflict between the Pacific and Atlantic commands during the war even this seemed uncertain. In his farewell report as chief of staff he stated his view that ". . . the constant aim of those concerned with integration of the Armed Forces must be the goal implicit in the Act—a security program in which all fields of responsibility will be covered but from which all unnecessary duplication will be eliminated and in which each arm will be a member of an integrated team. . . ." In that report he made various specific suggestions for effecting true integration.

As he obviously was aware, little progress was made after his departure in achieving the kind of unity he believed in. Through the budget-minded regime of Secretary of Defense Louis Johnson and the great expansion following the start of the Korean War the conflict within the Pentagon continued to smolder and occasionally break out into the open. In September 1952, in an early presidential campaign speech in Baltimore, Eisenhower noted that real unification of the armed forces had yet to be achieved and vividly described the ill effects of permitting each service to spend money developing the same weapons. Looking at both the past and the future he declared:

When I became Chief of Staff, upon my return from Europe in November of 1945, I felt that all our war experience had rendered obsolete the defense organization then existing. I was convinced then, as I am today, that effective coordination of the services in war requires central planning in time of peace. This is the essence of unity in the armed forces. That unity must also extend to the procurement and administration of all the costly material and paraphernalia of modern warfare. It was the hope and expectation of all of us who worked to achieve the passage of the National Defense Act of 1947 that this kind of unity was in the making.

This has not proved to be the case. Such unity as we have achieved is too much form and too little substance. We have continued with a loose way of operating that wastes time, money and talent with equal generosity. With three services, in place of the former two, still going their separate ways and with an overall defense staff frequently unable to enforce corrective action, the end result has been not to remove duplication but to replace it with triplication.

All this must be brought to as swift an end as possible. Neither our security nor our solvency can permit such a way of conducting the crucial business of national defense.

He was soon afterward to be given a new opportunity to try to put these beliefs into action, but while chief of staff he went down to defeat on them, as he did on universal military training and the disastrous demobilization. The times were out of joint, and no single individual, he might well have argued then in his own defense, could have set them right. He must have found his worst forebodings, in the period when he was considered for the post in 1943, confirmed, and he certainly took a dim view of the whole job. In Europe there had been one objective—the defeat of the Germans—while in Washington confusion and conflict of purpose blurred every undertaking. And as chief of staff he had so many peers and superiors.

In November of 1945 he had written his boyhood friend Swede Hazlett, who more than anyone else was responsible for his having gone to West Point, that "there is nothing I want so much as an opportunity to retire." The assignment of chief of staff represented "nothing but straight duty." And in April of 1947 he wrote to Bedell Smith: "Frankly, this job is even more irritating and wearing than I had anticipated. . . . I think the thing that makes me angry is the character of so much of the opposition. So many things seem to be placed above the welfare of the country." This was the politics that the simple soldier liked to think he abominated.

In the public estimation it is unlikely that his actual performance in the job either enhanced or diminished his reputation. He stood clear of the angry recriminations that befogged the Washington atmosphere. There he was, Ike, the hero, doing the job as best he could. And most Americans had only the vaguest notion of what that job was, in any event. They saw him as he made fine-sounding speeches and received honorary degrees.

From the press, which has been so extraordinarily kind to Eisenhower throughout his career, came very little criticism. While some sources found fault with his performance before Congress, others praised it. The sharpest note was sounded in an article in the *American Mercury* in 1948 which reported that ". . . some high Defense officials privately assert that he was the worst Chief of Staff in Army history." His friends exonerated him, however, the article added, because he was concentrating on the White House rather than the military. A suggestion of this same interpretation comes from, of all people, Kevin McCann, one of the principal Eisenhower idolaters. McCann observes that ". . . as burdensome as his responsibilities as Chief of Staff became, his biggest problem at the time was a personal one, having nothing to do with military affairs. It was politics."

Six

Republican
or
Democrat?

At the home-coming celebration in his honor in Abilene in 1945 Eisenhower said to reporters: "In the strongest language you can command you may say that I have no political ambitions at all. Make it even stronger than that if you can. I'd like to go further than Sherman in expressing myself on that subject."

General Eisenhower advanced all the cogent arguments against a man who had spent his entire life in the professional military service becoming president of the United States. It was a remarkable debate that he held in public with his fellow countrymen and in private with himself. The presidency, held out like a glittering prize, one more reward for leading the allied armies, both repelled and attracted him.

But it was over the language of Sherman that he conducted his interior debate, ending always by stopping short of the ultimate refusal. Sherman had said that if nominated he would not run, if elected he would not serve. In arguing the case with himself, and sometimes with his friends, he would say that the Sherman statement, particularly the second part, seemed to him to violate his sense of a soldier's obligation. How could any citizen, and, even more important, any soldier, put a limit on his duty to serve his country in any way that he could? This was the question he came back to, as he discussed it with friends and occasionally with reporters he trusted, and it annoyed him to find that some who heard him, including his friends, put this down as a rationalization concealing, whether consciously or unconsciously, his personal ambitions. He spoke often, too, of the hundreds of letters he received each week from soldiers who had served in his command telling him that he owed it to them to win the peace as he had won the war.

At the same time, he had an intuitive understanding of the nature of the demand being made on him. He sensed that what was expected from him was some kind of magic, the miraculous solution of problems that could be solved only through the long, patient effort of citizens willing to sacrifice their time and their energy to the public good under the democratic process. "They think there's some kind of magic in my name," he would say with impatience.

This was true in at least two separate and distinct ways. The politicians were convinced of the immediate magic of his name, and they meant to exploit it if they could persuade him to say yes. He was a brilliantly decorated package which the public would take without looking inside. For the average citizen the name had a more profound and subtle appeal. A man who could command armies, navies, fleets of airplanes in a global war would surely be able to cut through the tangled knot of politics and show America the way to a secure and lasting peace. Having fought with the Russians as allies he would now be able to put them in their place. Was he not a friend and comrade in arms of Marshal Zhukov? As Eisenhower seemed to understand, all this and much more was in the appeals that were directed at him.

After years of defeat and frustration, the Republicans had begun to have a glimpse of the promised land. Harry

Truman and the Democrats were saddled with all the discontents, the manifold harassments, of the transition from war to peace. Mink coats and Deepfreezes were blown up out of all proportion in the concentrated attack on some of the men around Truman.

Confronted with this golden opportunity, the Republican party was deeply divided. Thomas E. Dewey had failed once, but he was nonetheless anxious to try again, and as governor of New York he was ideally situated to take the nomination. But Senator Robert A. Taft of Ohio was equally ambitious and equally determined. Dewey represented the internationalists of the eastern seaboard, while Taft spoke for the Midwest and its distrust of foreign adventures and foreign involvements. Neither side in this conflict intended, if they could possibly prevent it, to allow a hero-general to walk away with the prize for which they had schemed and hoped and waited so long.

An incident occurred in December of 1947 that, while trivial in itself, illustrated very well the fierceness of the rivalries and the snares lying all about to trap an unwary and unknowing hero. While Eisenhower had an intuitive grasp of the forces in which to an ever-increasing degree he found himself caught up, his knowledge of practical politics and of the fierce currents of ambition and rivalry converging on 1948 was, to say the least, rudimentary.

Late in 1947, toward the end of his tour of duty as chief of staff, General and Mrs. Eisenhower were invited to a dinner at the 1925 F Street Club to celebrate the election to Congress of Representative Franklin H. Lichtenwalter, Speaker of the House of Representatives in the Pennsylvania State Legislature. Lichtenwalter, long since lapsed into obscurity, had defeated a C.I.O. candidate running on the Democratic ticket, and to Repub-

licans this seemed a happy portent of things to come—
a return to power of the Old Guard in Pennsylvania as
represented by Joseph R. Grundy and G. Mason Owlett,
whose man Lichtenwalter was. To this gala came most
of the hopefuls for '48 including Taft, Senator Arthur H.
Vandenberg of Michigan, and a whole stableful of dark
horses.

After dinner, when the men were alone with coffee
and brandy, the conversation turned to politics and specifically to the problem of wages, prices, and trade unions.
With his characteristic warm expansiveness Eisenhower
said that in his opinion in the dispute between labor and
management both sides were thinking simply of themselves and not of the country. The threat of inflation was
therefore very serious. Because management was a more
cohesive group, perhaps it could take the lead in fore-
going higher profits to set an example and call a halt to
the inflationary spiral. This, too, was characteristic of
Eisenhower: the conviction that a little earnest good will
applied in the right place would resolve a conflict no
matter how deep-seated the causes or intense the differences.

The cynics present put this down as the talk of a
candidate. It did not, however, seem important until a
few nights later when a radio commentator close to many
right-wing Republicans, Fulton Lewis, Jr., broadcast a
version of the General's remarks that made him sound like
a wide-eyed idealist if not, in the right-wing view, a dangerous radical. According to the commentator:

General Eisenhower, who has been mentioned as a possible
presidential candidate, pronounced his views on how to cure
the domestic inflation threat, and his proposal was that the
government call in the big industrial leaders of the nation
and put the pressure on them to agree to reduce all prices
for a period of two or three years, so as to eliminate all profits

whatsoever. . . . When it was suggested that maybe the idea would not appeal to them, the General is reported to have suggested that the solution, then, would be for Congress to enact a 100 percent tax on corporation profits, and use the proceeds for a program of subsidies, to bring the prices down by force of government.

This attempt to throw a roadblock in the way of the Eisenhower candidacy was obviously inspired by one or more of those present. By discrediting him with the solid, right wing of the party any ambition he might harbor would be given a setback. A public row followed over what he had or had not said. The General took no part in this quarrel, refusing to reply to any of the numerous queries that were put to him. He was deeply offended by what seemed to him a deliberate betrayal of the rules of hospitality. But in the aftermath of the incident he was touched by the reaction of one of the guests. Senator Vandenberg went over to the Pentagon to tell Eisenhower how outraged he was at what had happened and to say that he intended to make an affidavit stating what he had heard. What is more, he proposed to make this public. But Eisenhower, as he told the story later, dissuaded him, arguing that, in any event, no one would believe that he had not been making a stump speech in the interest of his own candidacy.

This strengthened his ties with Vandenberg while at the same time it seems to have aroused the General to some realization of how formidable was the opposition to him in the Republican party. This opposition, as was evident later, was of an almost conspiratorial nature. Powerful figures on the extreme right believed Eisenhower was a dangerous man. If it was necessary to have a general in the White House, there was MacArthur, the beau ideal of many who found Eisenhower untrustworthy.

In the light of what has happened since, it is difficult

to convey the glow of idealism that was an important part of the Eisenhower appeal, not only for liberal Republicans fearful of the neoisolationists and troglodytes in their own party, but for liberals in the Democratic party, too. In large part this was carried over from the war and the pronouncements of the supreme commander in the conflict with a ruthless and terrible despotism. He had spoken in the war for free men everywhere. The fact that he had spoken through the skillful, thousand-voiced apparatus of a public-relations system intended to inspire the mass of the allied people was irrelevant. He was the beneficiary, and this, for the moment, was all that mattered.

Nevertheless, and this is the extraordinary paradox, the American people were not only ready but eager to select a professional soldier as their president. There were, to be sure, some doubts on this score. The more thoughtful recalled General Grant's disastrous years in the White House. Possible dangers were occasionally pointed out: a soldier-president's lifelong involvement with the military establishment could prevent him from dealing with it with sufficient detachment; he might overemphasize the military or, as General Marshall and others feared, he might self-consciously de-emphasize it to a dangerous degree. But for the great majority neither these reasoned doubts nor their own traditional distrust counted against General Eisenhower.

What took place has occurred in history before, although never, perhaps, on such a scale. The Duke of Wellington after the Battle of Waterloo embodied for the British people all that was good and noble in the defeat of all that was menacing and evil. Substitute Napoleon for Hitler, and the parallel, while far from exact, is nevertheless striking. It was said of Wellington, as the British proceeded to elevate him to be head of their government, that all he had to do was to look the part that his adoring public had determined he was to play. Very much the same thing could be said of Eisenhower at this stage of his career.

It was not enough, however, for the little group close to him who believed that he could and must become president. To what extent they deliberately stage-managed the next phase of the General's career is uncertain, since the stage-managing naturally took place behind the scenes. His tour of duty as chief of staff had ended, and public opinion had turned strongly against "the brass," the military men who seemed bent on keeping America in uniform. This was the reaction of a people for whom, out of long tradition, war and the preparation for war were alien and inherently wrong, a people determined to enjoy the fruits of peace and put behind them the terrible shock that had come with Pearl Harbor on that "day that will live in infamy."

The General, therefore, had to find a civilian occupation, one that would show him as a civilian leader. So those close to him are said to have reasoned. He needed a job—but not for financial reasons. He was at this time in his fifty-eighth year, having spent thirty-three years in the professional Army. As a five-star general, a rank he would retain for life unless he resigned, he received about $20,000 a year, part of it in allowances free of income tax. This was far more than he could ever have imagined when, in the old days, he had thought about retirement to a life of fishing, hunting, golf, and nostalgic reunions with his comrades of the past.

He had also written his book, *Crusade in Europe,* and on the proceeds he had been granted a tax concession believed to be unique. The Bureau of Internal Revenue held that, since he was not a professional writer, he had, in selling his story, in effect sold an asset accumulated throughout a lifetime. He was therefore permitted to pay capital-gains tax on the $625,000 he received, keeping a net of $476,250, which would have been approximately the sum he would have paid to the government in income taxes under normal procedure. Former President Truman has said that he personally directed the Bureau to make this ruling. All the other generals who had written their memoirs had paid straight income tax, and in the Revenue Act of 1950 a provision which came to be known as the "Eisenhower amendment" made this the law for all literary or other creative work.

So it was not economic interest that led Eisenhower in May of 1948 to forego his retirement and accept the presidency of Columbia University. Several of Columbia's trustees had become convinced that Eisenhower was destined to be president of the United States. Among them were Douglas Black, president of Doubleday & Company, the firm that published Eisenhower's *Crusade in Europe,* and Thomas J. Watson, of International Business Machines. Watson played a leading role in getting Eisenhower to Columbia, but denied any political intent.

The fact that Eisenhower had almost no qualifications to be president of a great university, unless it would be his ability to call on wealthy men for contributions, appears to have occurred to no one. The advantage for a potential candidate for president of the United States seemed evident enough. He would hold a distinguished position from which he could legitimately make speeches and pronouncements on the issues of the day. But as a university president he would be out of the direct line of fire of partisan politics. Thus his closest backers reasoned.

They failed, however, to reckon with the deeper, underlying forces of public opinion. In the first place, Eisenhower, as hero and general, never won acceptance as a

"Best of Luck, Ike"
Poinier in the Detroit *Free Press*   1948

college president. He was himself uneasy in the role, and especially so when it was clear that he was expected to raise funds through his friendships and his vast prestige. And the administrative staff and the faculty were not happy with a five-star general whose military aide, Colonel Robert L. Schulz, seemed to have more to say about his appointments than anyone else. Senior faculty members and even heads of departments complained that it was almost impossible to see their president. With his facility for reflecting the optimistic and hopeful outlook, Eisenhower has in retrospect taken a happier view of his experience at Columbia, and he is justly proud of having established the Arden House assemblies on national and world problems at the old Harriman estate on the Hudson. But the two years at Columbia were not satisfying years. The man who read little more than military history and Westerns was not at ease in the abode of learning.

Shortly before leaving Washington he had issued a statement in which every word and every punctuation mark had been weighed and weighed again. This was the letter to Leonard V. Finder, then publisher of the Manchester *Union-Leader* at Manchester, New Hampshire, and one of Eisenhower's most impassioned promoters. Finder had written to Eisenhower to say that a slate of delegates pledged to the General would be entered in the New Hampshire presidential primary to be held on March 9. Victory in the New Hampshire primary is eagerly sought as an advertisement of popularity. Finder enclosed a front-page editorial urging election of the Eisenhower delegates.

Eisenhower spent three days drafting a reply, mostly in the privacy of his quarters at Fort Myer, with the help of his old friend Major General Floyd Parks, then head of Army public relations. This was a crucial decision he was trying to make. State Eisenhower-for-President headquarters were opening, and contributions were being accepted. If it was not stopped now the boom would really begin to grow. But still, in his debate with himself, Eisenhower raised the question of the call of duty to which the soldier must respond.

The letter to Finder is an impressive argument against a military man occupying the White House. It was made stronger by a memorandum put out by Parks when he released the letter. The memorandum said the letter was being made public "because General Eisenhower hopes through this means to inform every interested person or group that he is not in politics and that he would refuse the nomination even if offered." The letter itself stopped short of saying this, although in the sentences that had been so carefully written and rewritten it did go a long way. Significant in the light of events that have followed was the General's expression of his "conviction that unless an individual feels some inner compulsion and special qualifications to enter the political arena—which I do not—a refusal to do so involves no violation of the highest standards of devotion to duty." Here was a public expression of the interior debate. But the argument for the negative was put most convincingly:

Politics is a profession; a serious, complicated and, in its true sense, a noble one. In the American scene I see no dearth of men fitted by training, talent and integrity for national leadership. On the other hand, nothing in the international or domestic situation especially qualifies for the most important office in the world a man whose adult years have been spent in the country's military forces. At least this is true in my case.

If he had cherished the illusion that this was to end the matter, he was to be disabused soon after he went to live in the president's official residence on Morningside Heights. The move to Columbia seems to have been taken as evidence that he could be persuaded. It was known that he had turned down offers from business paying far more than the university salary. If he would take a position of a semipublic nature for which he had no real qualifications while at the same time rejecting large pecuniary reward, did it not signify that he had a further interest in public life?

In any event, he had hardly established himself in his spacious office in Columbia University's Low Memorial Library before a procession of politicians, most of them Democrats, lined up outside his door. At least eight senators and a half-dozen governors made the pilgrimage. They all said more or less the same thing: the times demanded a man of Eisenhower's great stature and prestige, who could rise above ordinary political considerations, and he would therefore have to put aside his personal desires and accept a draft. While they may have received little encouragement, they were for the most part not convinced of the hopelessness of their cause.

No man, however detached and disinterested, could have been unaffected by this prolonged and flattering importunity. With those close to him, Eisenhower joked about it. He told of one visitor franker than the others who came right out and said that he wanted the General at the head of the Democratic ticket because he knew that otherwise he would lose his own race. There was no nonsense in this appeal about the call of duty and the stern demands of the hour. Eisenhower's comment was, "Thank God for one honest man."

On June 6, 1948, the Roper public-opinion poll showed that Eisenhower was the top choice of voters in both parties over all other candidates. As the party conventions drew near, the clamor of the draft-Eisenhower movement rose to a crescendo. The plight of the Democrats was regarded as desperate. Truman's commission on civil rights had recommended a far-reaching legislative program which the President, with characteristic forthrightness, had endorsed. The South was in revolt, and the liberal leaders in the North were, for quite different reasons, disillusioned with the man in the White House. His rating in the polls had dropped disastrously from the peak of his popularity in the aftermath of Roosevelt's death.

As time ran out, a comical coalition of Southerners and New Dealers undertook to draft the General. They shared only a common desire to get a winning candidate at the head of their ticket. Strong support for the draft came from Americans for Democratic Action, the liberal-labor group in which many of the surviving New Dealers had taken refuge. Many ADAers felt that Truman was an expedient politician rather than a true liberal. They measured him against the yardstick of their hero, FDR. As for the President, a party man from start to finish, he had nothing but scorn for what he felt was a collection of ineffectual do-gooders. Labor leaders, including Philip Murray of the C.I.O., gave the draft-Eisenhower movement at least their tacit support.

James Roosevelt, the eldest son of the late President, was one of the most impassioned beseechers, working in private in the General's cause and missing no opportunity to appeal publicly for his nomination. Senator Claude Pepper of Florida, a Southern Democrat with a liberal rating, was equally vociferous. But also on this strange bandwagon were such oddly assorted characters as Governor William Tuck of Virginia and Mayor Frank (I-Am-the-Law) Hague, the boss of Jersey City.

They seem to have had no idea of what views on domestic policy, if any, the General held. Doubts on this score were brushed aside as irrelevant. Once Eisenhower was in the White House he would be surrounded by advisers who would see to it that he made the right decisions. The General was, in fact, both amused and annoyed by some of his supporters. He was, he told a reporter, a strong believer in States' rights, and if he had to name any single individual with whose outlook he agreed it would probably be Senator Harry F. Byrd of Virginia. The idea of using the police power of the federal government to enforce, say, an antilynch law was abhorrent to him, since he was convinced that to turn federal authority to such an end would be disastrous.

On foreign policy the General's opinions were well known as a result of the speeches he had made. He believed in a responsible role for America in world affairs. This meant American aid for Europe. It meant an adequate military establishment with a temporary draft and universal military training. American strength, he had said on many occasions, was essential to stability and peace. For most liberals this was apparently enough. They assumed that he must think like them on domestic as well as foreign policy.

As is traditional, the Republican convention came first. Eisenhower's professed concern was that the Republicans would be deadlocked and that out of the deadlock would come an isolationist-nationalist ticket. Then he would no longer be able to take a detached and impartial view of the political scene. The future not merely of his own country but of Western Europe and the whole concept of a free society would be at stake, or so the General believed as he prepared to sit out the convention before the television screen in the house on Morningside Heights.

He watched through the first day and night, and late in the night he saw the pitifully contrived "demonstration" for General MacArthur put on before an almost empty auditorium. In the hot, churning uncertainty of the second day, the stop-Dewey drive was accelerated. The faster the Dewey machine rolled, with all its well-oiled efficiency, the more desperate were the efforts of those who wanted to bring it to a standstill. The difficulty was that the rival candidates could not agree on anyone to whom their combined strength might be diverted. The strategists made frantic efforts to get in touch with Eisenhower, first by telephone and then by an emissary hastily dispatched from Philadelphia to ask him to permit his name to be placed before the convention. But he refused to talk with the representatives of any Republican faction. He had told earlier emissaries that he knew the Republican party did not want him.

Eisenhower had hoped to see Senator Vandenberg nominated for president with Harold Stassen for vice-president. But when at last the delegates chose Dewey for the first place and Governor Earl Warren of California for second place, he felt that he could relax and go play golf, which is just what he did. He had carefully considered what he would do if the isolationists had won. It was his intention, he said at the time, to issue a statement which might have been phrased as follows: "I will join with anyone who stands for the principles of international cooperation I believe in and who will oppose those who seem determined to take our country back to isolation and unpreparedness." That kind of statement issued between the two conventions would have given such an impetus to the Democratic draft that President Truman might not have been able to stop it.

Even without such a statement, the momentum of the draft movement seemed likely to sweep the Democratic convention. On June 30 President Truman met with some of his closest political advisers in the White House to discuss the danger of an Eisenhower stampede. They recognized that even if the General removed himself at the eleventh hour the net effect might be a repudiation of Truman. With the sanction of the President, it was agreed to try to get Eisenhower to declare his intentions in advance of the convention, and the ubiquitous George Allen was asked to be the intermediary. For Allen, who was to be one of the old friends present at the Eisenhowers' thirty-second wedding anniversary party at this time, it was a delicate undertaking, if only because of his close relationship with both the principals. At least once Allen telephoned Washington from New York to say that he saw no sign of any declaration from the General.

But there were other forces equally determined that Eisenhower should not be the candidate of the Democratic party. Republicans appraising Dewey's chances in November felt that while he had only a limited popular appeal he would unquestionably be able to win against Truman, with the Democrats torn by internal dissension. It would be quite another matter if he should have to come up against a hero with a cheerful grin, whose nickname, Ike, was a kind of talisman. Rumors circulated among politicians that Eisenhower had been put on notice that if he yielded to the siren call of the Democrats he would be destroyed, that his private life would be exposed in such a way as to humiliate and degrade him.

This threat, only thinly veiled, was conveyed by certain right-wing columnists. They said, in effect, that if Eisenhower ran as a Democrat they would make him wish he hadn't. On the eve of the Democratic convention, a reporter visiting the General in his first-floor study in the house at 60 Morningside Drive found him in an unhappy mood. His usually cheerful countenance was somber in the light of the desk lamp as he tossed across at his visitor two clippings that contained the implied threat. Why, he demanded, did they say these things about him?

It was the question of one who had come late and untutored to the savage infighting of American politics. So long and consistent had been the adulation that this small shadow seemed to the man on the other side of the desk to take on menacing proportions. His view of himself was the official view of the Eisenhower personality, the view seen through channels. A personal revelation, even as friendly a revelation as the Butcher book contained, was an intrusion.

Eisenhower seemed to have convinced himself to stay out of politics. He could present so effectively the case against a professional soldier in the presidency at that time. The tension with Russia was not likely to diminish. A military president might be inclined to lean over backward to avoid the appearance of imposing militarization. He would constantly be under the suspicion of furthering the interests of the military. And thus he might fail to do all that he could to maintain a state of preparedness. These were the arguments by which he appeared to persuade himself to exert whatever influence he had outside the White House.

It took first one statement and then a second to stop finally the Democratic draft-Eisenhower movement. Over the July 4 weekend, the General was persuaded that he must speak out or, by keeping silent, lend his consent. Through Columbia's public-relations office a statement was issued saying that he "could not accept nomination for any public office or participate in any partisan political contest." Once again, "could not" had won out over "would not." But after thirty-six hours, when "could not" still seemed to leave the door open a crack, the General's reply to a letter from Senator Pepper was made public saying he "would not" accept nomination to any public

"From Soldier to Civilian"
Tom Little in the Nashville *Tennessean*   May, 1952

office. At last the clamor was stilled. The name of Eisenhower was not spoken during the convention proceedings,
and Truman was renominated without a contest.

As for the General, during the 1948 campaign he spoke
not a word to indicate whether he was a Republican or a
Democrat. When the campaign was over and the Republicans were astoundingly defeated, despite all the
polls, by the cocky little man from Independence, Missouri, the same old vista of the White House opened up
for Eisenhower. It trembled like a mirage in the middle
distance. If he looked the other way there was usually
someone at his elbow to invite him to admire that shining
prospect. And as he had said so often in the long debate,
the ultimate call of duty could not be ignored.

What he had avoided through all the clamor was any
commitment. Was he a Democrat or a Republican? No
one could say with any assurance. He had brought out of
the past some vague prejudices and convictions but they
had little to do with party or political principle. It was too
late to make a partisan of him after his long conditioning
in the Army with its stress on playing the game safe and
offending no one. And politics, or politics American-style,
at any rate, is partisanship, the fierce commitment if not
to principle then to party.

Seven

In and Out
of
Uniform

On October 20, 1950, President Truman wrote General
Eisenhower a two-line note saying that he wished the
next time the General was in Washington he would drop
in because he had something he wanted to take up with
him. In a handwritten postscript he added that it was better not to make a special trip since this would start the
"speculators" talking. When Eisenhower called at the
White House a little later, the President asked him to go
to Paris to be supreme commander of the North Atlantic
Treaty Organization forces in Europe.

At the time, Eisenhower was indignant. He had just
begun to establish himself as president of Columbia, and
this would mean a new uprooting. He would go back into
uniform and be identified once more as a soldier. He felt
that after his service in the war and his tour of duty as
chief of staff the President had no right to make this request. His ardent backers were disturbed, too. They saw
the move as a deliberate effort to interrupt the assimila-
tion into civilian life which the public had begun to accept. But Truman was, of course, as commander in chief,
entirely within his rights in calling on a five-star general,
who, under the law creating the rank, never retires, for
further duty.

In point of fact, it was perhaps the greatest service
Truman could have performed if the General had been

nurturing a deliberate and calculated ambition to be president. In the civilian setting of the university, Eisenhower had been out of character. Every time he opened his mouth on domestic issues he revealed his conservative, not to say reactionary, outlook, and in so doing he puzzled and confused the liberals who wanted to cling to the belief that Eisenhower was one of them. What did he mean when he talked in Aesopian language about going to jail if you wanted real security? As supreme commander of NATO in Paris he would once again be divorced from the domestic scene.

Without straining too hard, one can find a remarkable parallel, when he flew to Europe early in 1951, with his departure in 1942 to be commander of the American forces in Europe. It is the Toynbeean withdrawal and return of the hero and savior, a rhythm of the first importance in Eisenhower's career. The close-up view had not been conducive to confidence or trust. It dimmed the luster of one who had been seen against the vast pageantry of the war as invulnerable, a wonder-worker. Now, viewed again from afar as the friendly proconsul exercising America's authority and power with warm and human discretion, his star would glow on the distant horizon.

The circumstances, too, were remarkably similar. The fall of 1950 was dark with foreboding. The United Nations forces hung by a thread to a small perimeter on the Korean peninsula. The Communist attack from North Korea had revealed once more America's unreadiness. And Korea was believed to presage Communist assaults elsewhere. The conviction was held in the highest places in Washington that Stalin would almost certainly launch some form of attack in Europe. It would most probably come, as the Korean attack had, by indirection through a satellite, but whether it could be confined was an open question.

At the same time, however, decisions had been taken in the West which, against the backdrop of gloom and pessimism, meant the beginning of a new current of hope. The North Atlantic Pact had been signed in Washington on April 4, 1949, committing the United States, Canada, the United Kingdom, France, Italy, Belgium, Denmark, Norway, Iceland, the Netherlands, Luxembourg, and Portugal to the "collective defense and the preservation of peace, security and freedom in the North Atlantic Community." This marked a major turning point in America's postwar policy. And with the spur of Korea and the threat of further Soviet aggression, the flesh was being put on the skeleton structure brought into being by the signing of the NATO pact. Eisenhower's arrival in Paris coincided with the beginning of the determined American effort to help rearm Europe.

As a successor to Marshall Plan economic assistance, Congress in 1951 passed a Mutual Security bill providing $4,700,000,000 for military aid to the NATO powers and $1,020,000,000 in economic aid. Out of the military assistance, vast sums were to be poured into an infra-European structure, linking the Atlantic ports of France with the advanced NATO forces in Germany, into airfields and other installations. And it was widely said that this was only the start. As in 1942, when America's productive power was just beginning to offset the despair of the Nazis' early triumphs, so now Eisenhower was the beneficiary of this new focus of American might. He stood at the front of another host, dedicated this time to fortifying Europe against the encroachments of Communism. Eisenhower in Europe was not the executor of the aid programs, but he was the visible image of authority for Americans and Europeans, the strong confident figure who swept down out of the sky at Oslo or Athens or Lisbon to speak words of hope and reassurance.

It was as the inspiring leader that he had returned, urging the western allies to unity, with a federated Europe as the goal. But, as in the war, he was in direct personal command of multinational ground, air, and naval units along the western front from the Arctic to the Mediterranean. His headquarters at SHAPE (Supreme Headquarters, Allied Powers in Europe), near the village of Rocquencourt, about ten miles from Paris, had the same relaxed atmosphere as did all his headquarters during the war. As one observer noted, it was like a big international club with everyone on a friendly, first-name basis.

Eisenhower has always liked familiar faces and old and tried hands around him. His deputy commander now was Viscount Montgomery. One of his military assistants was Colonel James Gault, a Scots Guards officer who had been a personal aide to Eisenhower from 1942 to 1945. The indispensable man was General Alfred M. Gruenther, chief of staff to the Supreme Commander. Gruenther, who graduated fourth in his class at West Point in 1918, is considered to have the most brilliant and incisive mind of anyone in the service. He was deputy chief of staff of the Third Army, commanded by Lieutenant General Walter Krueger, when Eisenhower was Krueger's chief of staff during the maneuvers in 1941. Their friendship, begun then, continued when Gruenther followed Eisenhower to London and Algiers and was again his deputy chief of staff. A demon for work, considering a day of fourteen to sixteen hours as normal, Gruenther has a surface affability that does not entirely conceal the intensity of his drive. He took over virtually all of the detail work, leaving Eisenhower free for high-level conferences and for the pilgrimages he was forever making to NATO capitals.

In the quickening current of hope that he helped to set in motion, the Supreme Commander singled out those

Europeans who believed that a new continent could be born in unity if not in federation. Or it might be more accurate to say that they singled him out. Foremost among them was Jean Monnet, the small, compact Frenchman who has worked with such quiet zeal to bring a federated Europe into being. Although they are totally different in almost every other respect, Monnet has Eisenhower's incorrigible optimism. He in some ways resembles Paul Hoffman, since without any real political roots he has exerted a strong influence on events in the past decade. This is the type of idealist whom Eisenhower, in his postwar metamorphosis, attracted. Back in America, Hoffman had become one of the most active agents in promoting the Eisenhower candidacy.

As he had done during the war, Eisenhower spoke of the "crusade" that he was conducting. The climate was one of boundless good will. He was enlisting Europeans to be evangels of the new order. One was Paul-Henri Spaak, so long foreign minister of Belgium and today secretary general of NATO. Another was René Pleven, who as head of one of France's splinter parties turned up in various roles, including that of premier, in the endless game of musical chairs which successive French governments have played.

The skeptical observer might have asked what the reality was behind this façade of hope. In his small but excellent book on Eisenhower, John Gunther notes that in 1951 there already was discouragement over the lag in bringing forces of the larger NATO powers under the new command. The total strength of SHAPE at that time was put at thirty divisions, but this was a deceptive figure, since they were virtually all understrength, some merely the rudiments of what might become divisions, and inadequately equipped as well. But Eisenhower wanted to believe that the goals would be attained and the force

filled out. Returning to Washington unexpectedly in November of 1951, he said, "Many things have not come forward as fast as we'd want them to. However, the advances
of the past year have been encouraging. There have been
some fine advancements and some discouragements." After all, SHAPE had been in being for less than a year.

While he had an excellent military staff, made up for
the most part of the old familiars, he also had what could
be called a political–public-relations staff. These men
were dedicated to Eisenhower and served him well. Colonel Paul T. Carroll had a great deal to do with preparing
the General's speeches, and they were often speeches of
a high order. The only rival in the speech department has
been Emmett Hughes, out of *Fortune*. He took over when
Carroll, who went with the General to the White House
and worked with selfless devotion on a murderous schedule, had a heart attack and died in September of 1954.
The chief of public information was Major General
Charles T. Lanham, an old pro in Army public relations.
Part of Lanham's duty was to shepherd the VIPs of press
and radio from Paris to SHAPE headquarters.

When they had been delivered to Eisenhower, the Supreme Commander proved that he had lost none of his
intuitive skill in winning the right friends and influencing
important people. He had maintained in this respect an
admirable record since 1945. His forte was still the background conference, the off-the-record lunch or dinner.
Rarely when he was chief of staff, more frequently when
he came to Washington from Columbia or from Paris, he
would meet with fifteen or twenty Washington correspondents and columnists. As the lunch or the dinner went
on, the General would field the questions with the relaxed
ease that seemed to be a reflex of his self-confidence. He
would often begin by saying, "Now I'd like to get you
fellas to help me. I've got a problem that . . ."

The stories and columns that were written out of these sessions were almost always friendly. The reporters were sitting down with the great hero of the greatest war in history, and he was making them his confidant. When he occasionally said things that seemed quite extraordinary, preposterous even, the group did not let him down. He was not perfect, but, after all, he was Eisenhower. And since the information he put out was "for background" and therefore not directly attributable to him, he had no responsibility that could be challenged. He was obeying the first rule of the Regular Army man—don't stick your neck out—and yet he received a considerable harvest of favorable publicity. The advantages of the background conference over the panel quiz such as "Meet the Press," which Eisenhower consistently refused to subject himself to, were obvious.

At SHAPE the same technique was equally effective with the regular correspondents in Paris or with "names" passing through, with junketing journalists, or, for that matter, with the ubiquitous congressmen on one of the never-ending tours of inspection. Before a small, respectful group in the briefing room, Eisenhower would give an impressive lecture of from forty-five minutes to an hour on America's dependence on the rest of the world for raw materials. Gruenther stood by to second and supplement his chief. An aide displayed maps cleverly drawn to show the long water-borne journey which such vital metals as chromium, uranium, and manganese had to make to supply America's mills.

"Now you take uranium . . ." As he spoke, with fluency and yet with such evident sincerity and conviction, his listeners felt that here was truly a dedicated crusader. A handful of Communists could seize control in Belgium and America's supplies of uranium from the Congo would be cut off. What would we do then for enough of the raw

material for the atomic bombs that were the principal deterrent to war? America had to learn this lesson: that to
an ever greater degree we were dependent on other nations. NATO was in our own self-interest, and if we did
not know it and act accordingly we would find ourselves
in trouble.

It often happened that at the end of forty-five or fifty
minutes an aide would come in, wait until he had caught
the General's eye, then call respectful attention to the
watch on his wrist. The General would pull up short, the
familiar good-natured grin on his face. "Well, they've
come to tell me I've got to go now. . . . You know I get so
wound up with this that I don't know when to stop." And
to Gruenther, "Al, will you take over from here and give
them everything we have? . . . Somebody asked me before we started about our strength in Norway and Denmark, well tell 'em everything." With a handshake all
around, if the group was not too large, he was gone. This
was not only impressive but very disarming. A citizen
soldier had fortunately been persuaded to lead the free
world toward strength.

One of the most helpful members of the political–public-relations staff was William Burnham, a civilian volun-
teer who was ostensibly an "economic analyst" for NATO.
An investment banker, a partner in the Wall Street firm
of R. S. Smithers and Company, Burnham held an almost
mystical conviction that Eisenhower must become president. He went back to America briefly on a mission to
liquidate the existing Eisenhower-for-President groups
and to get an organization going on a higher and more
realistic level. There was something touching and, in a
sense, selfless about Burnham's devotion to his hero. Although he contracted leukemia and was dying in the latter stages of the 1952 campaign, he continued until his
death, shortly after the inauguration. to perform any small

service that he could for Eisenhower. Another friend frequently at NATO headquarters was Clifford Roberts, a broker, partner in Reynolds and Company in New York, a good golfer and an excellent bridge player. Roberts was connected with many important figures in business quietly working for Eisenhower's nomination.

The political activity was all top secret. Reporters taken to see the General singly or in pairs were warned against any questions about politics or the presidency. The General would freeze, and in all probability the interview, for background only, would be terminated. Yet it is impossible to believe that he could have been ignorant of the work of Burnham and others in Paris and in New York. He still lived with the challenge, and scarcely a day went by that it was not put up to him in one form or another. The politicians came not, perhaps, in such numbers as they had at Columbia, but with just as much persistence. One senator, the late Brien McMahon of Connecticut, argued for two hours, fouling up the General's appointment schedule, until his aides thought they would have to come in and bodily remove him.

He was told over and over again that he could have the Democratic nomination for the asking, the Republican nomination by merely lifting his finger. Small wonder, then, if he should have come to believe that he could be the candidate of both parties in an unprecedented example of national unity. Since it was entirely alien to his background, he had no way of comprehending the intensity of party rivalry on the local, state, and national levels, rivalry precluding any such unity.

In October of 1950, shortly before he left Columbia, the General had been forced to respond to a clarion call that came from no amateur. Twice a candidate himself, governor of New York, and a shrewd political operator in tight control of the party machinery in his state, Thomas

E. Dewey proposed Eisenhower for the Republican nomination in 1952. This was quite a different matter from the earnest petitions of the idealists and the one-worlders. In retrospect it can be seen as the start of the serious campaign to put the General in the White House. Dewey and his ally, Herbert Brownell, Jr., were to be prime movers in the campaign for the nomination. The General issued still another refusal through his office at Columbia, adding a curious and somewhat ambiguous postscript: "I put my hand to a job and do my best. I have no desire to go anywhere else if I can help to do what I want here at Columbia. This is the place for me. I don't know why people are always nagging me to run for President. I think I've gotten too old."

After taking the NATO job his attitude toward the presidency became increasingly ambivalent. His half-hearted "no" conveyed implications of "yes." In a letter to a friend in early 1951 he vehemently rejected any interpretation of his "acceptance of military duty as a 'joining of the Administration,'" citing "the extreme degree in which I differ with some of our governmental foreign and domestic policies of the past years." In November he suddenly flew to Washington for "military talks" with Truman. Just before his return, after sixty hours in the capital, he held a press conference at which the "no" was so faint as to be the equivalent of "yes." When he was asked whether Senator James Duff had been authorized to work in his behalf, he replied, "If I have friends that have been my friends so long they believe they know how I would act and react under given conditions, that's their own business and I have never attempted to interfere with any man exercising his own privileges as an American citizen." Both the President and the General emphatically denied a published report that Truman had offered to back him for the Democratic nomination.

The waiting game was ended; the stage was set. It was not without some trepidation, nevertheless, that the first herald walked on to hail the hero in his forthcoming role. At a crowded press conference in Washington on January 6, 1952, Senator Henry Cabot Lodge, Jr., announced that Eisenhower's name would be entered in the March 11 New Hampshire Republican primary. "He will not withdraw," Lodge declared. "He is in the race to the finish." But did he know, did he have assurances from the General? All he could say in reply was that he did not need to have assurances. He insisted that he was confident, and yet his very insistence had an edge of uncertainty about it.

For nearly twenty-four hours the signals from SHAPE were faint and flickering. Then the General issued a formal statement of his position. Confirming Lodge's account of his "political convictions" and "Republican voting record," but stressing the importance of his NATO post, Eisenhower went on to say:

Under no circumstances will I ask for relief from this assignment in order to seek nomination to political office and I shall not participate in the preconvention activities of others who may have such an intention with respect to me.

Of course there is no question of the right of American citizens to organize in pursuit of their common convictions. I realize that Senator Lodge and his associates are exercising this right in an attempt to place before me next July a duty that would transcend my present responsibility. In the absence, however, of a clear-cut call to political duty I shall continue to devote my full attention and energies to the performance of the vital task to which I am assigned.

The hesitant "no" had become a hesitant, conditional, but unmistakable "yes," and two months later, in the face of rapidly mounting political pressure, he was to ask after all to be relieved of his NATO command so he could return to the United States.

"How Do You Like That!"
Burck in the Chicago *Sun-Times*

May, 1952

Behind the khaki curtain, and screened by security, the Eisenhowers' life at SHAPE was pleasant enough. General Gruenther, one of the greatest players in the world, was always on hand for bridge. The Supreme Commander managed to get in enough golf. They fulfilled essential social obligations, but these were not too onerous. After spending a week at SHAPE conferring with Eisenhower to learn his views on foreign policy in May of 1952, John Foster Dulles grumbled privately on his return that the General did not do his homework. He had no time to read anything during the day because his schedule was too crowded. And at night he ignored the memorandums he was given and spent time on his favorite Westerns.

The General was leading exactly the kind of life he had led for thirty-seven years. He was, as he had so often pointed out, a professional military man. If they wanted him to run for president—to be president—it would be on his terms. He had done what he had been asked to do at SHAPE, to bring a command into being, to inspire the West, to lend to the whole enterprise his own confident presence and his enormous prestige. And with his singular luck he was leaving at the climactic moment. Not for many a year, perhaps never, would the prospect for the NATO alliance seem so bright as it did when he left it.

And now he was the candidate. A characteristic of the professional military man is an ability to put one task down and take up another, to sever one set of relationships and pick up another. He learns to do this through years of conditioning; a tour of duty at one post and then moving on, a new assignment totally different from the old. The military mind is of necessity neat and compartmentalized. When Eisenhower stepped from the plane

"All Ready for D-Day?"
Herblock in the Washington *Post*, 1952

May 18, 1952

that brought him to Washington in June he was the candidate.

But in the process of his initiation into politics the soldier was to have some unhappy lessons. When he went to call on President Truman, to report on the conclusion of his tour of duty at NATO and to request retirement without pay, he gave vent to his feelings about the miasmal slanders about himself and his family emanating from the inevitable whispering campaign. What, he wanted to know, was he to do about the things they were saying? As Truman has reported the visit, the President asked what the rumors were. "If that's all it is, Ike, then you can just figure you're lucky," Truman told him.

This was a curious encounter between the two, the professional military man and the professional politician. No matter what he may have come to feel later, Truman had had not a little to do with helping to bring Eisenhower to that moment in the upstairs study in the White House. He had shared the popular view of Ike as hero and victor, and with the President this was reinforced by the respect for generals of one who had risen from the ranks of the Missouri National Guard and had served faithfully in World War I and afterward. Eisenhower, the professional military man, would never, however, understand Truman, the professional politician, mistaking the animus of a political campaign for personal animus, and their relationship was to end in implacable hostility. Yet after Eisenhower was nominated and, at his request, was allowed to resign all the privileges of his rank, President Truman instructed General Bradley to make out a new order restoring his five-star general's pay and perquisites, the order to be dated the day after the election in November in the event that he should be defeated. Eisenhower never knew of the existence of this order.

But whatever the cost of the transition, those on the outside were not supposed to know. That was part of the conditioning of the military man, too. The front that you present to the public, and in particular to your own troops, must always be your best front. You may let down within the caste, among your own kind, but you should never give yourself away to the outsider. Once the decision is taken, the past is irrelevant and the future expendable. How many times had all this happened before? The parade, the review, the farewells, and then, as though it had never been, the new post, the new friends, the new tasks. Taking off his uniform, resigning his five-star rank, with all its perquisites, were merely the outward signs of a transition already achieved. Eisenhower the soldier had become Eisenhower the presidential candidate. If anyone stopped to ask what his equipment might be for the new role, it was certainly not the candidate himself. A man on the move, responsive to the play of forces around him, he had let himself be persuaded and he was eager to get on with it. He was prepared to learn as rapidly as possible the tactics of this new kind of combat.

Eight

The Great Crusade

In his famous speech at the Guildhall in London on June 12, 1945, when he was given the rare honor of being made a citizen of London, Eisenhower spoke eloquently of his sense of kinship between his own home town of Abilene and the gray, ancient capital he had helped to save from destruction. The valley of the Thames, he had said at the Guildhall, draws closer to the farms of Kansas and the plains of Texas in a common determination to fight for freedom of worship, equality before the law, and liberty to speak and act. With this real feeling about the meaning of his roots, he now, as a candidate, returned to Abilene to open his campaign.

As he came down the ramp from the private plane in Kansas City on the way to Abilene, a group of politicians waited, each eager to be the first to shake his hand. The winner was big, hearty Governor Dan Thornton of Colorado, a cattle rancher with high political ambitions nurtured on his success in the cattle business. He grabbed Eisenhower's hand and thumped him on the back, booming out a resounding "Hi'ya, Ike!" The former five-star general recoiled momentarily, shuddered almost visibly, recovered his aplomb, and returned a greeting almost as vigorous. His mentors may have doubted his capacity to adjust to this new and strange world, but from that moment forward they should have been re-assured.

In a sense his second home-coming was a stunt to advance his candidacy, since he had already had one official home-coming at the end of the war. The cars of the private train that had brought the newspaper correspondents, the candidate, and his party from Kansas City stood on the Santa Fe siding while the ritual was enacted for the benefit of the vast publicity apparatus assembled in the little sun-baked Kansas town. But for all the trappings, the spectacle was a moving one. This was the legendary return of the boy who had made good, the fulfillment of the American saga in its purest form. And in his civilian clothes the General lent himself to the role with his characteristic adaptability.

The principal events on the program on that festive day were the dedication of his home, preserved exactly as it was when the family lived there, and the laying of the cornerstone for the Eisenhower Museum nearby. The leading citizens of Abilene had joined together to keep the Eisenhower house on South East Fourth Street as a shrine, and after Ida Eisenhower's death in 1946 her sons had given the property to this cause. The occasion had, despite the equipment of big-time publicity, a friendly, un-assuming quality. A platform had been set up in a field beside the house, and gathered around were most of the townspeople, with many farmers who had come in for the day. Eisenhower spoke with a simple, natural warmth of his gratitude, of the opportunities for everyone in America, of his mother and father and their devotion to God, of his own aspirations and hopes. Here was a man of decent impulses expressing the emotion that welled up in him at this extraordinary manifestation of the American dream.

He has rarely revealed more about his own basic attitudes than when he said: ". . . in spite of the difficulties of the problems we have, I ask you this one question: If each of us in his own mind would dwell more upon those simple virtues—integrity, courage, self-confidence, an unshakeable belief in his bible—would not some of these problems tend to simplify themselves? Would not we, after having done our very best with them, be content to leave the rest with the Almighty and not to charge all our fellow men with the fault of bringing us where we were and are? I think it is possible that a contemplation, a study, a belief in those simple virtues would help us mightily."

In the afternoon General and Mrs. Eisenhower and their party sat on the marquee of the Sunflower Hotel to watch a parade of floats, high-school bands, and marching groups of various kinds. Ike's life was represented on one float after another, from his triumphs in high school to the great moments of the war and the return of the hero. It was homely, sentimental, and yet, again with the quality of the legend come true, moving. In this pageant our fondest belief was vindicated. The boy from the wrong side of the tracks could grow up to be a great figure on his way to the presidency. And no one could doubt that he was on the way to the White House, for all his own modesty and reluctance. He was on the way to the White House because we, the American people, wanted him there.

That night he made a nationwide television address from a stand erected in the town stadium, and the contrast could not have been greater. It was a disaster. The arrangements for the telecast had been improvised without sufficient professional direction, and an unexpected rainstorm just before the scheduled address had made still further improvisation necessary. As apparently no one around the candidate at that time was aware, outdoor television appearances are difficult under the best of circumstances. On the screen the General looked like an old man who read from his manuscript in a halting and uncertain fashion. Viewers around the country were startled. Was this the hero of D day, this old soldier so unlike the image out of the time of victory?

Even more disturbing was the fact that his speech was dull and empty. He had spoken platitudes at the dedication in the morning, but they were homemade platitudes that expressed the man himself. These were the warmed-over clichés of a whole company of speech writers who had managed to comb out of the text any semblance of vitality or conviction. It touched with caution on all the familiar political subjects and succeeded in saying next to nothing. Reporters groped for a lead on which a headline could be built. It was scarcely news that the candidate was opposed to the "evils" of "disunity, inflation, excessive taxation, bureaucracy" or that he believed in "peace with honor, reasonable security with national solvency" and "in the future of the United States of America." The emptiness of his speech, together with his rather lame appearance, brought the great day to an end in anticlimax.

He must himself have understood this. Afterward, he went from one to another of the big houses on the North Side where a series of home-coming receptions were in progress. Encountering a reporter from Washington, he looked startled for a moment. "Why," he asked, "have you come out here?" Told that the reporter had found the speech at the dedication moving, his face lighted with the kind of spontaneous glow that is so much a part of his natural charm. That, he said with genuine feeling, was the kind of speech he liked to make because you didn't have to get into any political stuff. On the verge of the plunge, in the nostalgic atmosphere of Abilene, so little

changed in its essentials in forty years, he was still reluctant to accept the role of candidate in a political contest.
What he had learned in Abilene in the first twenty years
of his life was what in all earnestness he had wanted to
say at the house where he had grown up. This was what
he had taken away and what he had come home with:
that America was a land of democratic opportunity, that
freedom was the greatest benefit of all, that the differences between rich and not so rich were unimportant. If
he had any single fixed goal it was to restore an era of
good will from the simpler America of his memory.

Why and at what point in his postwar career he had
consented to become a candidate for political office is a
mystery. He seems gradually to have reconciled himself
to the inevitability of his nomination. He may himself
have been scarcely aware that step by step he had come
to a place at which he could no longer withdraw without
compromising those who had taken from these successive
steps an implied promise. At Abilene, asked by a reporter
why he was going into politics, he replied, "I hope I
never get pontifical or stuffed shirty with you fellows.
I'm doing this because I feel that I should."

With the end of his sentimental journey into the past,
he found himself in the midst of a hard-boiled struggle
to obtain the nomination of the party he had finally
chosen. He did what he had said he would not do. He
campaigned actively for the nomination, speaking in
Colorado, Nebraska, and Iowa, and arriving at the Black-
stone Hotel in Chicago on the eve of the convention to
lend himself to the maneuvering of his managers. The
outcome was by no means a certainty. With the delegates
complaining that they did not know him or what he stood
for, they were run through his suite in droves, and, as a
good soldier, he shook hands, posed for photographs, uttered the right sentiments, flattered the ladies, and in

private worried about the outcome. Such a rosy picture had been painted while he was still in Paris of the demand for his candidacy, and now there seemed to be a possibility that the convention might take Taft instead. It would be a bitterly humiliating experience.

The chant of "We like Ike" was more nearly a hymn of praise and entreaty to a demigod than a political war cry. In part, at least, it could be put down to the turmoil of the war and the war's aftermath, to the upheaval that had shaken America to its foundations, the earthquake that was never going to stop. Eisenhower represented strength, triumph, unswerving confidence. Millions were happy to take him on faith, on his face, on his smile, on the image of American manhood, on the happy virtue of his family life.

But others, who were more thoughtful, had prepared themselves to believe that he was the way out of what had very much the look of political bankruptcy. The Democratic party had been in power for twenty years. Truman's re-election had come as a stunning surprise to the Republicans, and they were determined not to forgive him for it. Whatever may have been the first reaction to the President's resolve to stand up to the Communists in Korea, the Korean War had become an open sore. It could not be won and it could not be brought to an end. Along with the sense of nagging futility went a casualty list that had grown to a truly appalling total. Divided between North and South, liberal and conservative, the Democrats were on the defensive on the Communist issue, suffering from the hysteria of the time that was partly self-engendered, partly aroused for political ends.

After twenty years of one-party rule it was vital, if we were to have a two-party system, that the Republicans at least offer an acceptable alternative. And for many thoughtful voters Senator Taft was no alternative. His

views on domestic policy had undergone a great alteration during his years in the Senate, embracing federal aid
to education, stronger civil rights laws, and other doc-
trines that put him, when compared with most of his
fellow Republicans, well to the left of center. But on foreign policy he retained all the prejudices that made him,
if not an out-and-out America Firster, then the next thing
to it. He believed that Europe was a worn-out, decadent
continent, and he had voted against most of the measures
to resuscitate America's European allies with military and
economic aid. His was the nationalist wing of the party.
The Old Guard was willing to swallow his domestic here-
sies because he hewed to the concept of Fortress America.
Part of his curious orientation, which made General Mac-
Arthur his close ally, was the conviction that the Democrats had "lost" China and proposed to abandon Chiang
Kai-shek and Formosa. A compound of recrimination over
past losses and extravagant promises to restore the *status
quo ante* was the Taft foreign policy.

While he was not an ally of Joe McCarthy, as were
others in his wing of the party, he did nothing to discour-
age the wilder excesses of the junior Senator from Wisconsin. William S. White of the New York *Times* reported
that Taft had told McCarthy to keep on attacking, since
if he missed one target he was sure to hit another. Taft
himself talked about Communists in government and spies
in the Department of State. Again and again he denounced the Truman foreign policy as appeasement or
worse. The massive tragedy of China in all its complexity
he put down to "Communist influence" in the Far Eastern
division of the State Department.

With his stand on China and his repeated denunciation
of the war in Korea as "Truman's war," Taft drew closer
to General MacArthur. This was the familiar axis of World
War II—the Pacific versus the Atlantic. As a result of

"Oh, Romeo, Romeo, Which Art Thou?"

Marcus in the New York *Times*   June 15, 1952

President Truman's action in dismissing him from his command, General MacArthur's hostility had been inflamed. His bitterness knew no bounds, and he and his friends thirsted for revenge. The allies of General MacArthur in the extreme right wing of the Republican party were determined to destroy General Marshall, as though to punish him, if only for having frustrated the man whom they believed to be the true hero of the war. In calling him a "dupe of traitors," Senators McCarthy, Jenner, and others stopped just short of accusing Marshall of treason. Far from repudiating this attack, Taft seemed to encourage it when, in the spate of words that came from him in speeches and statements as the convention drew near, he declared that Marshall had been sent to China to insist that Chiang Kai-shek take Communists into his government, and that, in revenge when this was refused, aid was cut off from the Nationalists at a critical time. Although it was milder in tone, the Taft attack lent some color of respectability to the savage charges brought against the man who had been chief of staff through the whole war and who had raised Eisenhower to his position of eminence.

It is possible that the real target of this vicious attack was Eisenhower rather than Marshall. Because of his great prestige, his supreme position in the national pantheon, the attackers hardly dared to aim at him directly. By discrediting Marshall they may have hoped to undermine Eisenhower's position in the country. But the Supreme Commander of NATO in Europe, maintaining a discreet silence on politics and on most political issues, was invulnerable.

Faced with the bitter divisiveness that seemed to threaten to split the country apart, it is scarcely surprising that millions of Americans—reasonable Republicans, those who thought of themselves as independent of party, and many Democrats—wanted to believe that Eisenhower could unify the nation in peace as he had in war. He held out the hope of a reform in policy both at home and abroad that would not be a shattering break with the past, such as the extreme right demanded. Evidence of the work of spies and dupes, first in Canada and then in the United States, had been alarming. Yet most citizens drew back from the accusation that those in high places, such as General Marshall, had been directly influenced by the Communist conspiracy. Many were disquieted by Taft's apparent determination to wreak vengeance on the past at a time when the energies of the nation should be concentrated on present dangers. These reservations added up to doubt in the minds of practical politicians, who wanted above all else to win, whatever the name of the candidate.

Standing aloof as the uproar took on hysterical overtones, his image as the crusader for freedom reinforced by his return to Europe, Eisenhower had been the beneficiary of the doubts about Taft. He was above politics. That was part of his attraction for a people who tend to regard the political process as, at best, a dubious luxury, an expensive kind of game in which we are forever indulging the players. In so many respects he was uncommitted, a clean slate on which each citizen could write his own hopes and aspirations. And a great many citizens were doing just that, a number working with zeal and passion to make Ike president and thereby unify the country. Such diverse men as Paul Hoffman, Senator Wayne Morse, Governor Sherman Adams, and Thomas J. Watson, each in his own way helped to enlarge the popular support that would persuade the regular Republicans assembled in convention to put aside their real preference, Taft, and take Eisenhower instead.

If Eisenhower had been pressed, as he returned to take off his uniform and become an active candidate, to give a single motive, it would in all probability have been national unity. As a result of his experience in the war, he had great confidence in the power of words, and particularly his words, to bring men together. Yet, at the outset, he was presented with evidence that he was far less the unanimous choice of the Republicans than his eager friends had led him to believe. The Taft forces were claiming pledged first-ballot votes only sixteen short of the 604 necessary to nominate. It was reported at the time that this came as a shock to him, since he had been given the impression that once he gave his assent the nomination would be his.

Fortunately, he was in the hands of extremely able, not to say ruthless, managers. Governor Dewey's organization was functioning with its customary efficiency. Herbert Brownell had met the Taft forces on their own ground at the Republican state convention in Texas, and if he had not bested them he had come up with a brilliant public-relations gimmick that was to exercise a subtle influence on wavering delegations. This was the cry of "steal," which was made to resound down all the avenues of press and radio. The Taft crowd had stolen the Texas delegation and they meant in the same way to steal the nomination. It was a fine outlet for moral indignation, and all that the Taft crowd could do was to say angrily that it wasn't so. True or not, trumpeted through the convention corridors the charge had not a little to do with moving the uncommitted middle in the direction of Eisenhower.

But before the balloting began, the convention heard General MacArthur as the keynote speaker. While the overtones may have escaped most of the delegates, those who knew something of the intensity of the internecine warfare between the command of the Pacific and the command of the Atlantic after 1941 were aware that here was another act in an ancient drama. Looking remarkably

young for his seventy-two years, but at the same time giving the impression that this was achieved at great cost in
disciplined effort, MacArthur read a solemn speech that
was full of Olympian thunderbolts hurled at the wicked
past. The big crowd gave him a respectful ovation. Many
of his most ardent admirers were waiting for the spark to
start a flame. But it did not happen. There was no real
response. A Texas billionaire had set up a MacArthur
headquarters and had engaged some rather frayed-looking
demonstrators, who paraded halfheartedly about the auditorium. At the end of this "demonstration" one of the Wisconsin delegates complained to the police that his watch
had been taken. He was told that when demonstrators like
that were hired off the street at five dollars a head he had
been lucky to lose only his watch.

The Taft forces had put no little hope in MacArthur's
appearance. The hero of the Pacific was to have been an
offset to the hero of the Atlantic. Taking the convention
by storm, he would stand firm for his friend Senator Taft,
only reluctantly and as a concession to the demand of the
party accepting second place on the ticket. Some of the
General's admirers were even emboldened to believe that
in the storm of enthusiasm he would generate the ticket
might come out the other way round: MacArthur for president and Taft for vice-president. According to the fre-
netic rumors circulating off stage, the Senator was willing
to make this sacrifice. But when MacArthur walked out of
the convention hall and flew back to New York he left not
a trace behind.

The hero of the Atlantic was about to triumph again.
The difference between the response to the two generals
can be explained wholly perhaps in terms of personality.
MacArthur was accorded respectful admiration for his
feats, but the American public never warmed up to him.
They turned to Eisenhower as the archetype of the boy

next door raised to unbelievable eminence and quite un-
touched by it. It is an irony of history that MacArthur,
who had been prepared for so long for the lightning to
strike, should have left that last rendezvous with destiny
unheralded and unsung to return to his lonely retreat in
the towers of the Waldorf-Astoria. One may only surmise
what his thoughts were on the themes of ingratitude and
inconstancy as he flew east.

On July 11 the intricate parts of Eisenhower's triumph
were poised to fall into place. His skillful managers had
done their work well and were certain now of the outcome
of the bitter contest with Taft. It was just a question of
the timing of the climactic moment. As the balloting got
under way that morning in the sweaty, noisy convention
hall, the lead tipped back and forth. With Michigan's
vote, the General finally pulled out ahead, but it soon was
apparent that he was going to be a few votes short of a
majority in this crucial first round. The balance of power
lay with the favorite-son candidates, and California's delegation was standing fast, still hoping that a deadlock
might make Warren the compromise choice.

"Minnesota! Minnesota!" came the cry from the balcony
as the roll call was ending. In the glare of the television
lights Minnesota's banner waved wildly: Minnesota
wanted to change its vote, Minnesota was going to give
Stassen's votes to Eisenhower. Struggling to make himself
heard over the mounting clamor, Senator Edward Thye
announced the switch. Ike was in. While the organ blared
out "The Minnesota Rouser" and "There's Gonna Be a
Great Day," state after state jumped on the vote-switching
bandwagon and the crowd cheered itself hoarse. That
night, again, the crowd roared out its enthusiasm for the
candidate when he appeared to make his acceptance
speech and summon his party to a "great crusade" for
"total victory."

This thunderous acclaim was to have its echoes over and over again throughout the campaign that followed. The image of the confident, smiling hero was to evoke the deepest emotionalism, a kind of release from past cares and present complexities. An early measure of the depth and breadth of this response was provided by the press, as editorial pages in every part of the country hailed the Republican nomination. For the vast majority it was a "new day," if not a "great day," not only for the Republican party, but for the government and people of the United States; with Eisenhower lay the salvation of the two-party system, if not of democracy itself. As the Washington *Post* austerely observed, "It is no exaggeration to say that his nomination reflects the dominant mood of the country."

The course of a political campaign is reported as though it were a sports event. A successful play, and the fortunes of one team spurt ahead. Then as the game continues another sudden shift alters the balance. At the outset, Eisenhower did badly, and his stock sold off on the professional bourse. His televised speech before the American Legion was nearly as lamentable a performance from the technical viewpoint as the address from the ball park in Abilene. He gave halting answers to questions about Communists and the reputation of General Marshall, which his admirers had expected him to answer with alacrity. The famous editorial "Ike is running like a dry creek" appeared on the front pages of Scripps-Howard papers across the country.

Yet to some it seemed scarcely possible that Eisenhower could lose the election no matter what he did or failed to do. The odds were so overwhelmingly in his favor. He had virtually all the press on his side, with the news magazines turning themselves inside out for him. The media of mass communication were, within the restraints of the com-

munications law, the Republicans' to command. The party
could draw on unlimited funds, and in most states the
organization was stronger than it had been for a long
time. The Democrats had a candidate whom almost no
one had ever heard of. Adlai Stevenson appeared as comparatively an unknown. He had been a good governor of
a state that had known much bad government. He was a
short, stocky, almost bandy-legged man whose appearance
was hardly calculated to win the mass television audience.
The Democrats were divided and disgruntled. Most of
this had been true before—only four years before,
and yet the Republicans had lost. What was new this
time was a candidate who was a nationally known hero, a
brand name—Ike—a trade name. Exploited by the most
highly paid talent in the advertising world, the name and
the personality were both highly salable.

In the early strategy conferences Eisenhower had been
diffident. He said that as an amateur he had a great deal
to learn. And, moreover, he hoped to begin slowly and
build up to an all-out attack. His diffidence in this learning
period may have been one reason for the "dry creek" phase
of the campaign. It was not long before he was demonstrating that he knew how to appeal for popular support
as though he had been running for office all his life. Implied in everything he said were certain elemental promises: peace, an end to the Korean War, prosperity, an end
to waste in government.

On his whistle-stop tours of the Middle West, some of
his remarks about the Korean War had isolationist overtones that made an obvious hit with the crowds gathered
to listen around the back platform of his train. He described himself in Michigan as a "Vandenberg Republican," but the next day in Illinois an audience of 15,000 at
Champaign cheered him on as he told them that, if there
must be a war in the Far East, "let it be Asians against

Asians. . . ." South Koreans should be manning the front lines in their country, he said, while Americans "must avoid the kind of bungling that led us into Korea. . . . The young farm boys must stay on their farms; the students must stay in school."

Most Republican speakers went even further than the presidential candidate in denouncing "Truman's war." A large part of the Republican propaganda effort was aimed at exploiting the public's sense of the futility and waste of the Korean War, and the voter was encouraged in a variety of ways to believe that wars always happened under the Democrats, while the Republicans brought peace and with it prosperity. With proper preparations and precautions, America "might easily have avoided" not only the Korean War but one or both World Wars, Eisenhower suggested in a Middle Western talk. And only "war or threat of war" was responsible for "whatever economic gains" had been made since 1932. Senator Karl Mundt of South Dakota came up with the gimmick K_1C_2 as the formula for the critical issues—the Korean War, Communism, and corruption in government. Increasingly, these themes were woven into the speeches Eisenhower read.

As he had done all his life, he was fighting to win, and the means were not nearly so important as the end. Conditioned throughout his career to the chain-of-command responsibility, he delegated to his commanders authority in their respective fields. And on the whole he was ably served by his staff. He was willing to be told what he must do by those with presumably expert knowledge. His G2 had, through years of experience and study, learned the terrain over which the battle was being fought. Naturally, then, the candidate, for whom this was new terrain and a new kind of warfare, relied on the judgment of his staff.

The great crusade moved into Indianapolis, where the General endured one of the most trying experiences of the

entire campaign. Senator William Jenner of that state had
been as virulent as Senator McCarthy in his attacks on
General Marshall as a "front man for traitors." Without
McCarthy's color and resourcefulness, Jenner was nevertheless a rabid isolationist and supernationalist, opposing
everything that Eisenhower through the years had professed to believe. His staff had, however, told him that
Jenner's re-election was essential for control of the
Senate. And it was equally important, to keep harmony
in the party, to make sure that Indiana would end up in
the Republican column in November.

So on the platform Eisenhower submitted to Jenner's
embrace not once but two or three times. He spoke the
proper words of endorsement. His discomfiture was quite
evident as the Senator, with cynical unconcern for the
ideological and other differences separating them, perched
himself figuratively, if not almost literally, on Eisenhower's shoulders. Afterward, the candidate's aides let it be
known that, when it was over, in the privacy of his train,
the General expressed himself in violent soldier's language
about what he would have done if that blankety-blank had
put his hands on him just once again.

But the deed was done, signed, sealed, and publicly
ratified, and his fulminations in private were of small
consequence. From there it was only a short step to the
ultimate compromise with the extreme nationalist wing
of the party, and Eisenhower took that step a little later.
A speech had been prepared for delivery at a rally in Milwaukee. Before the party invaded Wisconsin, scouts
joined the train at Peoria, Illinois. From Governor Walter J. Kohler and Thomas E. Coleman, leader of the party
in Wisconsin, the candidate got a briefing on how the
forces were deployed. The speech prepared for delivery
in Milwaukee contained praise of General Marshall.
Kohler has said since that it was he who advised Eisen-

"Off on a Strange Crusade"

Fitzpatrick in the St. Louis *Post-Dispatch*

September 14, 1952

hower to cut out this passage. The General, so the argument went, was quite justified in praising his old friend
and patron. But he should not do this in Wisconsin from
the same platform on which he was to appear with Senator McCarthy, who was running on the same ticket with
him for re-election. It would be an offense not only to
McCarthy, who had led the attack against Marshall, but
to McCarthy's following, which was represented to Eisenhower as wide and enthusiastic. What Eisenhower replied,
whether he argued and was overborne, we do not know.
The praise for Marshall was not in the speech delivered
in Milwaukee, and on the platform that night the candidate embraced McCarthy as he had Jenner.

To many, including some who had been among the
General's most ardent admirers, he seemed to have lowered the standard of integrity and conviction which they
had followed with such hope and enthusiasm. Added to
the pact entered into with Taft as the campaign began,
resolving their differences of policy, the position of
strength on which the General stood appeared to have
been compromised away. There was even some concern
lest these doubts should be translated into a substantial
loss of support. Stevenson was drawing large and responsive audiences for his literate and informed discussion of
the issues before the country. Several who had publicly
supported the General, conspicuous among them Senator
Morse, now publicly deserted him.

The fears that Eisenhower might lose substantial support as a result of the compromises of the campaign were
seen in retrospect to be wholly groundless. Such fears
were no more than the typical reports of he's up-he's down
that come out of every campaign. What was compromised
away, it seems clear from hindsight, was the hope of re-
shaping the Republican party in a new image. If he had
drawn a line, even a wavering line, between himself and

the extreme nationalists in his party, he would have preserved a position from which he could later, with the
weight of his victory, have enlarged and developed the
acceptance of his conviction of the inevitability of American responsibility for world leadership. That the victory
would have been just as great no one can now doubt. In
Wisconsin, McCarthy was to run behind every Republican
on the ticket, far behind the presidential candidate, with
the then Secretary of State of Wisconsin, Fred Zimmer-
man, who had openly opposed the Senator, leading all
the other candidates.

In the sound and fury of a national campaign such considerations were not even remotely apparent. Eisenhower
was learning fast. He projected his sunny, confident self
to the big crowds that turned out almost everywhere,
evoking a prolonged chorus of approval, and this in turn
fed his own confidence and his lust for battle. His wife,
Mamie, was a splendid asset. Together waving from the
rear platform of their train they were the all-American
couple. This was what Ike had come home to, this was his
reward. As the realists observed, photographs of Mamie
and Ike with their grandchildren at their Gettysburg farm
were worth a dozen speeches.

Carefully and deliberately, the contrast with the brilliant, quick-witted Stevenson was built up. Stevenson had
no wife. His marriage had ended in divorce. His witty
thrusts drew laughter and applause. "It would be very,
very fine if one could command new and amusing language," Eisenhower said solemnly, "witticisms to bring
you a chuckle. Frankly, I have no intention of trying to
do so. The subjects of which we are speaking these days,
my friends, are not those that seem to me to be amusing. . . . Is it amusing that we have stumbled into a war
in Korea; that we have already lost in casualties 117,000
of our Americans killed and wounded; is it amusing that

the war seems to be no nearer a real solution than ever; that we have no real plan for stopping it? Is it funny when evidence was discovered that there are Communists in government and we get the cold comfort of the reply, 'red herring'?" Whether this was the General's own handiwork or that of his staff, it was an effective appeal to a people in a mood of distrust and resentment, encouraged to believe in the corruption and decay of a party in power for twenty years.

Eisenhower's timing of his response to the furor over the private fund provided by a group of wealthy Californians for his running mate, Richard M. Nixon, could hardly have been improved upon. He waited after the first disclosure, letting it be known that he wanted to appraise all the evidence. At the outset, this drew off some of the sting of the attack. Eisenhower was a fair-minded man, and if he found Nixon guilty of wrongdoing then, no matter what it might cost, he would ask him to withdraw from the ticket. Nixon himself seems to have had some such thoughts as he waited with growing impatience and concern for word from the General.

How much serious consideration Eisenhower gave to the ethics of the secret fund there is no way of knowing. From the tactical viewpoint the revelation precipitated a crisis in the campaign. Even such ardent pro-Eisenhower newspapers as the New York *Herald Tribune* called for Nixon's withdrawal. If General Eisenhower had heard of his running mate at all prior to the discussion at the Chicago convention of his eligibility for second place on the ticket, it had been only in the vaguest way. For most Americans, Nixon had been conjured up out of the current political atmosphere; a brisk, brash St. George who had come from California to slay the Communist dragon. There should be no slightest blemish on this eager St. George.

The reconciliation scene at Wheeling, West Virginia, was played to the hilt. The prodigal son was no erring prodigal at all. "That's my boy," Eisenhower said, going out to Nixon's plane, as it arrived, to embrace his vice-presidential candidate. This is the kind of drama the public loves, and when it was played out, against the backdrop of Nixon's television performance with Checkers and the respectable Republican cloth coat, the vice-presidential candidate was a figure in his own right and not just someone who happened to be running with Eisenhower. It is possible that, far from hurting the ticket, the episode may have helped to increase the Republicans' popular majority.

Every aspect of the Eisenhower campaign was calculated to make the American people believe that prosperity and peace could be achieved by electing Republicans to office. Of course we would have to stay strong, and this meant spending money for arms superior to those of any enemy, a superiority that we would always maintain. By cutting out waste in government, eliminating the socialistic frills of the Democrats, and giving free rein to private enterprise this could be done without imposing an undue burden on the taxpayer. Since this was what the average American, sorely tried by a cycle of war, threats of war, and more war, wanted to believe, the crowds roared out their approval, and each new poll showed the Eisenhower-Nixon ticket gaining. If Stevenson had had any real hope of conducting a serious review of the issues facing the country, he was soon disillusioned.

The climax came late in October with Eisenhower's pledge that if elected he would go to Korea himself to see what could be done to bring an end to the war. A Republican administration, he told an audience in Detroit, would "forego the diversions of politics" and "concentrate on the job of ending the Korean war . . . until that job is honor-

"Decorating His Former Hero"
Ned White in the Akron (O.) *Beacon Journal*   October, 1952

ably done. That job requires a personal trip to Korea. I shall make that trip. Only in that way could I learn how best to serve the American people in the cause of peace." This was what most of us had wanted to hear. He was a great soldier, and we could trust what he told us after he had had a firsthand look at the long-stalemated front in Korea. Since he had said repeatedly that it was a futile war into which we had stumbled, and every Republican orator had promised peace at every crossroads, there could be little or no doubt about his conclusion. He would find a way to bring peace.

All but nine states were swept into the Republican column with the landslide for Eisenhower. The jubilation at his headquarters at the Commodore Hotel in New York was led by Fred Waring, who directed the singing of "The Battle Hymn of the Republic" and "Where Oh Where but in America Can You Sing True Freedom's Song?" Raising his hands high above his head in triumph, Eisenhower appeared shortly after 2 A.M. before a wildly cheering crowd in the Commodore ballroom. Of all the climactic moments in the life of the boy from Abilene this was the greatest. He had carried four states in the South which no Republican had taken since the sweep of Herbert Hoover in 1928. Areas long ceded to the Democrats in the big cities went for Eisenhower. This was a stunning national victory, and, while the Republicans had carried the Senate and the House by narrow margins, no one could doubt that it was in large part a tribute to the man, the man as symbol and summation of the hopes and fears of a troubled people. "I recognize clearly the weight of the responsibility you have placed upon me," the man said that night, "and I assure you that I shall never in my service in Washington give short weight to those responsibilities." It was a time "of dedication rather than triumph."

Stripped of all the glitter out of the past, it was seen to

be an extraordinary experiment both for the man and the nation. No president had ever had so little experience of politics and so little firsthand experience of American life. General Grant had, after all, spent seven years as a farmer and store clerk in Missouri and Illinois. Except for the year and a half at Columbia, Eisenhower's entire adult life had been lived in the separate and isolated world of the professional Army.

Shortly after his election, he made good his pledge to go to Korea. This was again the image of the soldier, the general dedicated to bringing peace to the world. Try as he might, he would find it difficult to put aside that identity and establish another. By taking off his uniform and putting on the well-tailored, conservative suits he was to wear, he would not alter the habits of a lifetime.

"One of Them Must Be Wrong"
Fitzpatrick in the St. Louis *Post-Dispatch*
October 29, 1952

Nine

Domestic Affairs

While he was still in the Commodore Hotel in New York recruiting his administration, the President-elect had himself been recruited. An ambitious young clergyman, the Reverend Edward Elson of the National Presbyterian church in Washington, came to sign him up. Eisenhower had never had a church affiliation. He had rarely attended formal church services. But now he wanted to be a good president, to set a good example for all the people. He was the first president to write his own prayer, spoken at the beginning of his inaugural address. He said, in part:

Almighty God, as we stand here at this moment my future associates in the executive branch of government join me in beseeching that Thou will make full and complete our dedication to the service of the people in this throng and their fellow citizens everywhere.

Give us, we pray, the power to discern clearly right from wrong . . . and be governed thereby. . . .

In the great crowd on the Capitol Plaza who heard the President on that cold January day there was an awareness that not since 1920 had the forces of Republican righteousness triumphed in this fashion. And while the Republicans who had come from all over the country to celebrate the great day would have dismissed as absurd the idea that they were there to re-establish the normalcy of Warren G. Harding, they did intend to bring about a break with what had gone before as sharp as that which had come after the last Republican accession. There was a disturb-

"Do Something for Me in November, Son"
Burck in the Chicago *Sun-Times*   July, 1952

ing parallel. The mood of 1953 was something like the popular mood of 1920.

If the Republican orators had not in so many words promised to repeal the unhappy past, that was the hopeful inference which many listeners had taken away with them. It was the wistful belief of the new President himself, who had revealed from time to time, in the clichés of the simple soldier, his distrust of what he believed to be "socialistic tendencies" allied to the menace of big government. This was the attitude of one who knew next to nothing about the technological revolution in American industry and very little more about the vast social and economic upheaval of the Depression and the great expansion of industry that had come with the war and the postwar boom. Spending virtually his entire career within the Army caste, he had for four separate intervals, periods critical in the national life, lived outside the country. What he brought to his enormous task was a simple faith in an earlier America, an America that had all but vanished in a series of cataclysmic events that he had known only from the limited perspective of the soldier.

The men whom he summoned to Washington and put in positions of great power for the most part shared this faith. They were close to the President in age, and, while they came out of the great corporations in which they had made large fortunes, their intellectual bent was very much like his. They shared an orthodoxy based on simple precepts which had filtered down out of the eighteenth and nineteenth centuries. This is the familiar stuff of chamber of commerce speeches: the best government is the least government, anything that interferes with the freedom of business to make profits is inherently evil, a balanced budget is the most vital requirement of sound government, deficit financing and high spending will bankrupt the nation.

But the men who lived by this elemental creed were about to take over the controls of a complex industrial society at a moment when that society, and what it stood for in freedom, dignity, and nobility of spirit, faced the gravest challenge, from Communist totalitarianism, in its entire history. Although they had had a considerable part in the technological transformation of industrial America, the Eisenhower Republicans who came to Washington seem to have had no comprehension of the profound changes, the revolution, that had been wrought.

On the one hand, the new technology had transformed this country's whole way of life, while on the other, the vast concentration of power in a few corporations had utterly altered the economy. A giant corporation operating in twenty-five or thirty of the separate states cuts across all the boundaries of authority on which the eighteenth-century concept of a balance of powers was based. Similarly, national labor unions with centralized control exert a general influence on the economy that can be restrained only by the federal government.

The revolutionary changes of the past three or four decades have redefined the area of free choice within the economy. And one of the responsibilities of the central government, in a role inevitably different from that of the last century, is to serve as a support and a safeguard for the freedoms that remain. An important function of the federal government is to equalize and stabilize the powerful forces that long since broke through the separate political compartments marked out in the eighteenth century. The problem is to conserve what is still valid out of that great charter the Constitution in the face of an utterly changed America. However desirable it might be to return to the age of Thomas Jefferson, or even that of William McKinley, as some of the newcomers on their day of triumph seemed to want to do, this was hardly a feasible objective. The Washington of January 1953 was quite a different capital of quite a different country from the Washington of 1800 or 1900. To try to restore an earlier ideal in the face of radically new circumstances was to risk an enormous dislocation.

All this would have been true if the Communist challenge had not existed. But with the necessity for spending billions of dollars each year to provide a deterrent to war, the problem of keeping a balance between government and a free economy was greatly complicated. Furthermore, the initiative, the leadership, in the struggle with Communism could come only in the first instance from government. A strong and positive voice speaking with the authority of the presidency was essential if the old familiar mood of comfortable complacency was not to claim us again. Even with such a voice, and particularly in light of the rosy promises that had been made in the campaign, it might not have been possible to resist the back-to-normal drive that had wrecked the military establishment in 1946 and that in 1949, on the eve of the Korean attack, had seen American defenses dangerously reduced.

The President had named George M. Humphrey as his secretary of the treasury and Charles E. Wilson as his secretary of defense. Like the President, both were going on sixty-three. They were both good examples of the society in which they had risen from middle-class beginnings to wealth and power. Their honest, deeply held convictions came not out of any organization lexicon, conned with an eye to advancement in the organization, but out of their own background and experience.

Before his election Eisenhower had never met Humphrey. As he was looking about for members of his cabinet in his temporary quarters in the Commodore Hotel in New York, the President-elect had at his elbow his old friend General Lucius Clay. Clay, a shrewd, astute Geor-

"New Do-It-Yourself Devotee"
Justus in the Minneapolis *Star*
September 27, 1954

"General of the Army"
Fischetti. Reprinted by permission of N.E.A.
Service, Inc.   January, 1953

gian, in a key position in the Pentagon during World War II, had demonstrated his skill in helping to organize America's productivity. After his retirement in 1949 he quickly moved into the top echelon of big business as chairman of the board of the Continental Can Company. As commander of the U.S. occupation zone of Germany in the transition period from 1947 to 1949, Clay had known Humphrey when the latter came to Germany as chief of an Economic Cooperation Administration mission surveying German industrial plants. He persuaded Eisenhower that Humphrey was the man for the Treasury post.

It was perhaps the most fateful decision the President was to make, for Humphrey's influence was largely to determine the course of the Eisenhower administration, and it is scarcely an exaggeration to say that he, more than any individual, except the President himself, set the tone of the Eisenhower era. From their first meeting in the Commodore, Humphrey and the President-elect were obviously made for one another. As he walked in to meet his new boss, the balding Humphrey was greeted by Eisenhower with, "George, I see you comb your hair just the way I do." I knew right then, Humphrey says, that we would get along together.

Eisenhower likes men around him who are confident and cheerful, and who give evidence of knowing the job at hand without bothering him with detail. In that first interview, Humphrey laid down one condition for his acceptance of the office: "I want you, if anyone asks you about money, to tell them to go and see George." They understood each other remarkably well in that first talk, and the understanding was to grow into a warm friendship.

The Secretary of the Treasury was not one of your sour conservatives wanting to keep things tightly in hand for the few. On the contrary, he has a genial, generous approach to life based on the belief that every American under our system can enjoy, in kind if not in degree, the same rewards that he has won. Like Eisenhower, he had come from a small town, Cheboygan, Michigan, although his family were of the prosperous upper middle class. After a few years of law practice, he joined the moribund M. A. Hanna Company in Cleveland, gradually took over its direction, and with his drive and energy developed it into one of the most important industrial complexes in America. Largely through his skill and perseverance, the Hanna Company initiated the big Labrador iron-ore-development project to supplement the dwindling resources of the Mesabi Range in Minnesota.

Possessed of a persuasiveness and charm reflecting his own superb adjustment to life, this was the man who, in a close personal relationship with the President and in the cabinet, was to dominate the policy of the administration. Because he controlled the monetary and fiscal policies of the government, he was to set the pace for foreign and defense as well as domestic policy. Humphrey's conviction was not so much that America could not afford to do the things that were being done in the foreign and defense fields, once the Korean War was brought to an end, but that they were in considerable part both wasteful and wrong. He was convinced that federal taxation continuing at the high postwar rate would sooner, rather than later, completely alter the American economy and the American form of government. The individual was being robbed of his right to spend the money he earned as he saw fit. The corrosive effect of continuing high taxes on honesty and morality was changing the American character. The freedom of corporations to decide their own future, apart from government spending and taxation, should at least in some degree be restored.

Much of what Humphrey said in his warm, convincing way struck a deep, responsive chord, not only in the immediate circle of government, but in the country at large. We were fed up with high taxation, we wondered how long we would have to go on helping nations that seemed to show no gratitude whatsoever, we were assured that we had weapons of ever-greater destructiveness, capable of devastating the whole globe, and yet billions more went into them.

Robert Donovan, whose book *Eisenhower: The Inside Story* is an invaluably revealing record of the first term, describes how the President encountered Senator Taft's opposition when he disclosed the outlines of the 1954 budget he intended to present to Congress. Lashing out in a fury, the Senator said that if the President meant to continue with the high spending of the past then the Truman administration might as well have stayed in power. Eisenhower managed to keep his own temper. Taft had to be mollified since if he had broken with the new administration the President would have had a full-scale congressional revolt on his hands.

This was the kind of pressure he was under when, in the spring of 1953, he approved a controversial $5,000,000,-000 cut in the funds for the Air Force. Democrats protested that the size of the military establishment, and therefore America's security, was being determined by considerations of economy and the budget, and high officials of the Air Force expressed their concern. This same protest was to be sounded again and again as funds for defense were repeatedly cut back. The reductions were justified under a new policy in which the President had concurred. The military was to be maintained at a steady level of support through a long period of years, thereby avoiding the wild swings between the exaggerated build-up touched off by some sudden alarm and the decline resulting from the quiescence of apparent peace. In hindsight this seems to have been not so much a new policy as a rationalization for the economies that were arbitrarily being put through. But it was true that in the past the start-and-stop approach, as in the upward swing from the Louis Johnson economy budget to the peak spending of the Korean War, had been costly and wasteful, and General Marshall had often inveighed against this irrational way of trying to maintain the nation's defenses in the face of continuing peril.

The Humphrey influence on military spending was unquestionably great. Between him and Wilson in the Pentagon a curious relationship came into being. Humphrey knew what he wanted; Wilson, surrounded by the admirals and the generals, was not sure. Charlie, Humphrey would say in a friendly but nevertheless chiding voice, you've got to get those people over there under control; they're just throwing the money out the window with duplication and waste. The Secretary of Defense knew the Secretary of the Treasury was right. In his Baltimore campaign speech Eisenhower had called it "triplication." Yet the disorganization, the interservice rivalry that he denounced in that speech, were to continue throughout his first five years without any serious move being made to carry out the drastic revision he had called for until 1958.

Wilson had come out of a small town in Ohio to become the head of the greatest corporation in the world. In his rise he had retained many of the friendly, human qualities of his past. At their best, these were qualities of common sense and understanding which were expressed in the salty language of an earlier America and owed nothing to the rituals of organization. At their worst, his qualities were those of a narrow provincialism ready to contract America's responsibilities to the smallest possible limit. His identification of the well-being of the nation with the prosperity of business was so complete that he could say with perfect conviction that he had always thought that "what was good for our country was good for General Motors, and vice versa." That this should startle anyone came as a complete surprise to the man who was asked by Congress to divest himself of a large part of his holdings in General Motors. The innocent insularity of his viewpoint was shown to even greater disadvantage in October of 1954 when he remarked at a press conference, apropos of the efforts of the unemployed to find new jobs, that he'd "always liked bird dogs better than kennel-fed dogs . . . you know, one who'll get out and hunt for food rather than sit on his fanny and yell." The ensuing uproar, in his own party as well as among gleeful Democrats, obviously astonished him. Protesting that he had been deliberately misinterpreted, he first tried to explain that he had just been pointing up his admiration for "spirit and initiative." The story began to circulate in Washington, as James Reston reported in the New York *Times,* that Charlie Wilson had invented the automatic transmission so he'd have one foot free to put in his mouth!

Like Humphrey, Wilson was a likable person. He was what he was, and no nonsense about it. But what now is apparent in retrospect is that he was totally lacking in the creative imagination that would have led him to accept, if not to understand, the need to push into fantastic new realms of exploration and research in the competition with the Soviet Union for advanced weapons. Prodded by Humphrey, Wilson was a practical man looking about his vast domain for candle ends to pare. In May of 1953 he defended cuts in research and development funds for all the services on the grounds that there had been overlapping and "boondoggling" in the name of research. That word, "boondoggle," out of the New Deal, had a strange sound in this new context. It was the stricture of a man of common sense who had no interest in knowing why the grass is green or why potatoes turn brown when they are fried. The reason the revelation of Soviet superiority in missiles and rockets came as such a stunning shock may lie just here. We had been told by men of common sense, themselves eminently successful in the practical world, that they were cutting away the frills and the boon-doggling.

The Truman administration had been far too niggardly with research and development. The figure in the Truman budget which Eisenhower had inherited, was $1,600,000,-000. The new President revised this down to $1,300,000,-000. Then in June 1953 a further cut of twenty-five per cent in research and development funds was ordered, bringing the total down below a billion. In the light of what has since been revealed about the astronomical cost of developing the new weapons, we can look back on these cuts with dismayed astonishment.

Yet the same attitude persisted throughout succeeding years. In February 1957, Wilson expressed his preference for "direct research" over "pure research." This was again the practical man who wanted to know exactly what you were going to get out of the money you proposed to spend. He had been asked about an appraisal by Dr. Edward Teller, the distinguished nuclear physicist, that the Soviet Union was so far ahead of the United States in training men for scientific work that its lead could not be overcome in ten years. Wilson replied, "I don't know how anyone can be sure what the Russians are doing, and so accurately predict what the situation will be ten years from now." In his opinion, pure research should be carried on by agencies other than the Department of Defense. This was, of course, before the *sputniks* dramatized the Soviet achievement in a way that even the smallest child could not mistake.

The Secretary of Commerce in the new administration was Sinclair Weeks, a New England banker and manufacturer, who at sixty brought to Washington a view of government and business and their relationship that was straight from Calvin Coolidge. While the office of secretary of commerce is not one of the more important cabinet posts, Weeks managed early in the first year to make his viewpoint nationally known, not to say notorious. He undertook to remove the director of the National Bureau of Standards, Dr. Allen V. Astin, because the Bureau had refused to approve a battery additive that a manufacturer wanted to put on the market. Weeks demanded to know what right Astin and his experts had to interfere with the workings of the free-enterprise system. An angry outcry followed, and Astin was reinstated. Weeks apparently had no comprehension of the great body of federal regulatory law, enforced in part through the Bureau of Standards, which had come into being with the nationwide expansion of a consumers' industry and the techniques of national advertising.

One of the responsibilities of the Department of Commerce, and the Civil Aeronautics Administration in that department, is to insure safe and adequate airways systems for the nation's air-transport industry, and nothing illustrates more clearly the inevitable interplay between government and business in the age of technology than the role of government in this connection. As air travel doubled and doubled again from year to year, the Truman administration and previous Congresses had been far too slow to recognize the need to enlarge and modernize the airways. At Weeks's initiative the appropriations were still further cut back. A Senate investigation conducted in 1957 by Senator A. S. Monroney of Oklahoma showed that existing airways, and particularly the flight paths into and out of the great metropolitan centers, were outmoded and already dangerously overcrowded. It was all too apparent that, unless the most drastic emergency measures were taken, the new jet civil aircraft which were to come into use toward the end of 1958 or the beginning of 1959 simply could not be flown into existing airports.

Private business was investing hundreds of millions of dollars in the manufacture of these jet aircraft, and their production and use were a matter of great prestige for the United States and the free world. Yet unless the government played its part, the whole enterprise would come to nothing. A highly qualified expert, retired Air Force Lieutenant General Elwood Quesada, was brought into the White House to push through the modernization program as rapidly as possible. Here was a demonstration of the danger that unless government performed its proper limited function, sustaining private industry and private investment in this highly technological field, it might well in the end be compelled to take over altogether. That, of course, is the Communist system, and the Russians have produced jet transports, which they heralded to the world for their full propaganda value.

So many of the men brought to Washington by the Eisenhower administration seemed to believe in no function for government except perhaps the collecting and distributing of mail, and even here it was suggested that private industry might do a far more efficient job at a profit. They came with the conviction that the mess in Washington could be tidied up in a year or so, and then they could return to their businesses. The administration was handicapped by the turnover in these executives. They stayed a year or a year and a half, barely long enough to learn the different ways of government, and then felt compelled to return to positions from which they had taken leaves of absence.

The antipathy between the business executives and the politicians was considerable. Senator Pat McCarran of Nevada rose in the Senate to pay his respects to Donald

Lourie, who had come from the Quaker Oats Company in Chicago to be undersecretary of state in charge of administration for a brief period. The Senator said he was sure that Lourie was discovering that it was a great deal harder to run the State Department than it was to run Cream of Wheat. A day or two later McCarran again got the floor to say that he wanted to make an apology. It was not Cream of Wheat but Aunt Jemima's Pancake Flour that Lourie had been running when he came to the State Department. Men such as Lourie were unhappy in Washington, giving the impression that they had been thrown into a den of lions and that, like Daniel, they would survive only by their inherent righteousness and godliness in standing as aloof as possible from the whole wicked business.

The President himself had had more firsthand experience with government. He had been a servant of government most of his life. He had been educated at the cost of the taxpayer, and all of his medical care and that of his family had been provided by government. Both as chief of staff of the Army and supreme commander of NATO in Europe, he had repeatedly testified before congressional committees. Yet his own attitude toward government was troubled and uncertain. This was nowhere more evident than with respect to the Tennessee Valley Authority.

An important element in the concept of TVA was the need to equalize through the federal government the imbalance between the poor states, which were the hewers of wood and the drawers of water as they furnished the raw material for industry, and the rich states, in which manufacturing and financial power were concentrated. The strength of exhausted soils was to be restored, the flood waters to be held in check, and, through federally operated dams, low-cost power was to be distributed for sale to municipalities, small businesses, co-operatives, and farmers, who would thereby be able to have some of the amenities of more favored regions. The sale of this power would return to the Treasury the basic cost of the project, aside from such features as flood control and improved navigation, which could be charged off to the taxpayer as contributing to the general welfare. In this last respect TVA does not differ from thousands of flood-control and navigation projects scattered across the land with federal largesse. In a campaign speech he made at Memphis, Tennessee, on October 15, 1952, candidate Eisenhower seemed to accept this concept, at least insofar as the Tennessee Valley went. He said:

In this region, you are deeply interested in the Tennessee Valley Authority and in the part it has played in the improvement of the agriculture and commerce in this area. TVA has served rural areas well and has created new industries in this section. It has helped conserve natural resources, control floods, and promote national defense.

Certainly there would be no disposition on my part to impair the effective working out of TVA. It is a great experiment in resource development and flood control for this particular area.

While he did add that this should not be "a rigid pattern" for similar development in other regions, he gave no indication that he found anything dubious about TVA's status. Not long after his inauguration, however, in a speech to a Young Republican convention at Mount Rushmore, South Dakota, in June, he talked about the "revolution in federal government" that his administration had instituted. Recommended expenditures for the next year, he boasted, had been cut by $4,500,000,000 and requests of Congress for new money reduced by more than $8,500,-000,000. The federal payroll, he told the Young Republicans, was already smaller by more than 50,000 individuals and this meant a saving of not less than $180,000,000 a year. The new government was "finding things it can stop doing rather than new things for it to do."

On the same day, at Custer State Park, Eisenhower gave South Dakota Republican leaders the benefit of some extemporaneous remarks. His spontaneous comments have always been more revealing than his formal addresses, perhaps because they have not been subjected to the inhibitions of a professional speech writer. "In the last twenty years," he said, "creeping socialism has been striking in the United States." He warned that "if this group takes over again, we very gravely run the risk, we've had our last chance." This, he said, was not always the fault of "a few long-haired academic men in Washington." Some people "have not been quick to resent socialism if we thought it would benefit us."

When he returned to Washington he was asked at a press conference shortly afterward to cite examples of "creeping socialism." He responded by naming TVA, trying to explain, in tortured and confused language, what it was he meant. "So we get to this curious thing in the socialistic theory," he told reporters, "that we all of us, provide cheap power, such cheap power for one region that it cannot only—apparently it is subsidized by taxes from all of us all over the country—but then it can appeal and take away the industries from the other sections of the country." He went on, of course, to say that he had stated a thousand times that he was not out to destroy TVA, but it was only one experiment, and in other areas he wanted "local people" to play a greater part.

This was, in a sense, an invitation to business to move in. Business-minded men in the Bureau of the Budget, with the approval of the Assistant to the President, Sherman Adams, were quick to press for the private-power deal under which Edgar H. Dixon and Eugene A. Yates,

representing large utility interests, were to build a plant
and provide power for Atomic Energy Commission installations in the TVA area. For the President this was to be
the source of a most unhappy controversy, and, as he
demonstrated on several occasions, his subordinates had
not kept him informed of the real circumstances of the
Dixon-Yates undertaking. A serious "conflict of interest"
was revealed in the case of a consultant in the Bureau of
the Budget who was serving in the same capacity for
Dixon and Yates, and the A.E.C. ultimately declared the
Dixon-Yates contract invalid on the grounds of this conflict of interest. Altogether, it was a most unfortunate attempt, carried out by dubious indirection, to restore the
private utilities to the Tennessee Valley.

But this episode, along with those of infinitely graver
import for the country and the world, was obscured by the
sound and fury of the McCarthy obsession. While nothing
might have been altered, still it is possible to argue that if
it had not been for this prolonged madness, with all the
destruction it wrought and the attention it compelled
from the government and the public, the normal forces of
political exchange, of criticism and debate, might have
worked to correct, or at least to amend, some of the worst
errors of those years. But it was a kind of national seizure,
suggesting on a much larger and more damaging scale the
devils of Loudun and the Salem witch-burnings.

After embracing McCarthy and Jenner in the campaign,
the President may have expected them to be loyal players
on the Eisenhower team. But almost at once it became
evident that he was doomed to disappointment, as the
Senator from Wisconsin became his greatest trial, harassing the administration at every turn with the same savage
disregard for truth and justice that he had shown when his
party was in opposition. The Republicans had used Mc-
Carthy as a convenient stick to beat the Democratic dog.

McCarthy had gone a long way on charges that were shown to have been almost entirely false, and to think that he would now reform and suddenly become a responsible member of the majority was indeed naïve. Intoxicated with the power that he had usurped, as chairman of the Senate's Government Operations Committee and the Permanent Subcommittee on Investigations, McCarthy began to assault the executive branch of the government more recklessly than ever before.

How much this wild foray cost the President, his administration, and the country it is still too early to say. Accustomed to obedience from subordinates in the chain of command and utterly unfamiliar with the deeper currents of American politics, Eisenhower suffered greatly under the McCarthy goad. He has all his life been quick to anger, and the frustrations and irritations of the presidency, McCarthyism foremost among them, again and again aroused him to fury. The effect on his blood pressure and on the general condition of his health hardly needs to be pointed out. His distress was often visible in press conferences. A question on McCarthy and what he intended to do about the Senator's depredations would cause him to flush and look tense.

He had brought to his high office a civics-textbook concept of the co-ordinate powers of the three branches of the federal government. Under this concept, the executive, the legislature, and the judiciary each kept within its constitutional domain, and the government achieved thereby a neat tripartite balance. As he said in several early cabinet meetings, he intended to play by these rules, and he hoped Congress would too. If the new administration failed to act in cleaning out Communism and corruption, then, but not until then, it would be appropriate for congressional committees to investigate. This textbook approach largely left out the need for the Chief Executive to provide vigorous and positive leadership. And, as in the case of Senator McCarthy, Congress may not play by the textbook rules.

In his early responses to questions about the Senator, the President stressed his belief in the right of Congress to investigate, a right with which the executive branch could not interfere. But as McCarthy encroached with increasing directness on the Eisenhower administration itself, ignoring the effort to placate him by an extension of the federal security system that had been introduced under President Truman, these responses were scarcely adequate.

With the strain he was under more and more painfully evident, the President insisted each time that he would not deal in personalities. His angry private version of this stand, Donovan reports, was that he would "not get in the gutter" with McCarthy. In July 1953, he said he had to remind reporters again that he never dealt "in terms of personality." If a democracy, with all of its different viewpoints and approaches, was going to make progress "someone had to take on the onerous job of trying to search out, analyze and bring together the majority of view or what you might call the bulk of public opinion. . . . You could not get ahead merely by indulging in extremist views and listening to them. . . ." Asked in November whether he thought Communists-in-government would be an issue in the next election, he replied that he hoped it would be a matter of history and memory by then. He didn't believe we could live in fear of each other forever, and he really hoped and believed that this administration was "proceeding decently and justly to get this thing straightened out." But he again acknowledged Congress's right to investigate and said he saw no reason for expressing his "personal opinion" on congressional activities unless it seemed "necessary . . . to the welfare of the country."

A valid argument could be made that the President was taking the wise course in avoiding a personal dispute with McCarthy. So confident was the Senator of his prowess at this point that he would have liked to engage the President of the United States in a public battle. Those close to the President argued that this would only serve to increase McCarthy's stature. The dominant belief in the White House was that McCarthy would destroy himself, with public opinion eventually turning against him for his excesses. For the President to contend with him would merely prolong the evil.

While this sounded plausible enough, it conveniently ignored the grave damage daily being done by McCarthyism. This damage was compounded by the fact that the administration apparently felt no responsibility for coming to the rescue of innocent victims of McCarthy in government. When Harold Stassen ventured to criticize McCarthy for his "negotiations" with Greek shipowners on trade with Communist countries, the President repudiated Stassen's remarks. Secretary of State Dulles conferred with McCarthy and, in Donovan's words, "assured the senator that he had acted in the national interest. . . ." Victim after victim was sacrificed by summary dismissal from government. The demoralization in the Foreign Service and the Voice of America could hardly be exaggerated.

The damage done by the McCarthy obsession was perhaps greatest in the field of foreign relations. When the incredible Cohn and Schine were let loose on Europe it seemed that some kind of limit of insanity had been reached. Flying from capital to capital, they intimidated responsible officials, ordered books taken out of USIA libraries, and generally behaved, as the European press duly noted, like two irresponsible juveniles turned loose with political tommy guns. It was not merely that the whole apparatus for conducting foreign relations suffered

"Have a Care, Sir"

Herblock's Here and Now (Simon & Schuster, 1955)   March 4, 1954

grave impairment. This went so far that five senior retired diplomats of impeccable reputation and great distinction felt called upon to make a public protest. But throughout the world our prestige was damaged as our friends laughed in embarrassment, hoping that the seizure was only temporary, while our enemies jeered and made the utmost use in propaganda of the whole McCarthy madness.

While the effect of the damage in this field is still incalculable, in scientific research and development the toll was also very high. The work of the important electronics research center at Fort Monmouth was seriously disrupted when McCarthy and his agents rode through shooting at everything that moved. As the security system became more extensive and more rigorous in response to the McCarthy hysteria, scientists became reluctant to commit themselves to the security strait jacket. Accustomed to freedom of inquiry and the free exchange of information, they preferred more often than not to avoid government research or even research conducted by private agencies under government sponsorship. These were the intellectuals, the long-haired academic men of whom the President had spoken in South Dakota with implied scorn. In the same vein, Postmaster General Summerfield's boast of Republican "progress in rooting out the eggheads" and Eisenhower's 1954 definition of an intellectual as "a man who takes more words than necessary to tell us more than he knows" were hardly calculated to add to the allure of federal employment among scholars and scientists. And when it came to rewards, industry was competing for their services with far more generous salary offers.

Almost no one took note at the time of what this might cost the nation in the contest with the Soviet Union for the lead in scientific and technological development. In retrospect, it seems to have been taken for granted that the United States would inevitably maintain this lead no matter what we did or did not do. Administration orators rarely failed to claim the inevitable superiority in all departments of the free world over totalitarian dictatorship. One of the few who did express concern on this score was Dr. James R. Killian, president of Massachusetts Institute of Technology and later to be President Eisenhower's special co-ordinator of science and research. Testifying before a House committee in 1954, Killian reported that scientists were "discouraged and apprehensive" about "what sometimes seems a preoccupation with security procedures and policies at the expense of scientific progress." He stated his belief "that the whole problem of security procedures and policies at the present time may be one of the things that is most hazardous to our future research and development activity in this country in relation to military problems."

Yet for all the harm that was being done in a variety of fields, and the evidence was repeatedly made plain, the record shows that virtually no one in authority spoke out in protest. The President, in his speech at Dartmouth College in 1953, did put in an extemporaneous reference to the evils of book burning, prompted by his friend John J. McCloy, who sat on the platform with him. At a subsequent press conference, however, he largely nullified the effect of this warning. It must be said in his defense that his party in Congress was deeply divided. Senator McCarthy had an important following, and Senator Bricker, with his amendment to restrict the treaty-making powers of the chief executive, caused the President as much unhappiness and worry as any single element in the first two years. Only by the vote of one Democrat, who came onto the Senate floor at the last moment, was the Bricker amendment, which the President had said would make the conduct of foreign policy impossible, defeated.

At times it seemed that the strategy of the administration was to outdo McCarthy and thereby prove to his wing of the Republican party that the President and his administration were just as anti-Communist as the Senator from Wisconsin. The trial of Robert Oppenheimer and the decision of the Atomic Energy Commission to revoke his security clearance deepened the division among nuclear physicists and sent a new shock wave through the scientific community. If this was to be the reward for extraordinary services such as Oppenheimer had rendered during the war and after, then the scientist would think twice before putting his neck in the government noose. Dr. Vannevar Bush observed at the time that the morale of scientists was "so low that while they will not refuse to serve, they will serve without enthusiasm and without fruitful inspiration."

As his contribution, the Attorney General, Herbert Brownell, Jr., chose an address before a luncheon club in Chicago to reopen the Harry Dexter White case with the charge that Truman had promoted White despite a report from the Federal Bureau of Investigation showing that he was "a Russian spy." This charge, which Brownell sought to substantiate by making public a secret document from the F.B.I. files, had the most disruptive effect on the relationship between Democrats in Congress and the White House. And not to be outdone, Governor Thomas E. Dewey came forward in a speech in Hartford, Connecticut, to talk of "agents of an aggressor nation . . . permitted to make policy" under the Democrats and to accuse the previous administration of a negligence bordering on the treasonable in the conduct of the Korean War.

In the election campaign of 1954, Vice-President Nixon, exploiting the Communist issue in every speech, proclaimed that he had driven Dr. Edward U. Condon, a physicist who had been in and out of government after repeated security clearances, from his position as consultant to the Navy. Dr. Condon, formerly head of the National Bureau of Standards, has been credited by Edward Teller with advancing work on the hydrogen bomb by as much as a year. "We're kicking the Communists and fellow-travelers and security risks out of the government not by the hundreds but by the thousands," Nixon said. This last was the claim of what had come to be known as the "numbers racket," the practice of lumping government dismissals for a wide variety of reasons in the "security risk" category. As played by the Civil Service Commission, this game stirred angry protest and prolonged controversy.

The long obsessive tragedy gradually drew to an end as a result of McCarthy's attack on the Army. This, for Eisenhower, was a direct blow at the institution that had nurtured him and that he had loved through years of comradeship and service, but he nevertheless continued to decline to oppose McCarthy personally. With McCarthy's outrageous abuse of General Ralph Zwicker and the Army's counterattack on the charges concerning Private Schine, the battle was joined, and finally the instrument that had helped to make McCarthy helped to bring him down. As the Army-McCarthy hearings dragged on and on before the television cameras, the American people had a chance to see McCarthy for what he was. They did not like what they saw, and the way was prepared for the vote of censure by the Senate. Full credit, too, must be given to a few men of courage and determination—Senators Hennings, Benton, Flanders, and Watkins—for their part in checking their colleague's reckless course. With the censure vote, and the Democratic victory in 1954 which deprived him of his committee chairmanships, McCarthy's power rapidly ebbed. It was time then to try to pick up the pieces and count the fearful cost.

McCarthy's downfall must have afforded the President

some consolation for the loss of Congress, and there was cause for real Republican rejoicing in the fact that the economy, after a bad sinking spell which began in late 1953 and continued through much of 1954, was once again in high gear. It was all-out prosperity, the full flowering of the American free-enterprise system, a capital investment boom that seemed to have no limits. And if voices of caution were raised to point out that the capacity to produce seemed likely to outstrip the capacity to consume, and prices and dividends were rising proportionately faster than wages, most of us paid no heed. The genial gentleman in the Treasury was looking after things. Shooting quail on the broad acres of his Georgia plantation, with the President as his companion, he was enjoying life, and so were we all. This was why we elected Eisenhower: no American boy was being shot at anywhere, our taxes had been cut, and we were on our way to making eight million automobiles in a single year.

Ten

From Yalta
to
the "Summit"

It was as a leader skilled in dealing with the troubles of the world, exploring the difficult and dangerous path between war and peace, that the American people had elected Eisenhower to the presidency. He was the hero who could insure our security in the age of nuclear annihilation as he had brought the victory in the greatest war in history. Yet no president in history delegated so much of his constitutional authority over the conduct of foreign policy as Eisenhower was to do. And he found in John Foster Dulles a secretary of state ready and willing to assume this authority. The record of the administration in this department becomes, therefore, largely an account of the Dulles policy and its successes and failures.

At a low point in his remarkable tenure of the office at the end of 1957, Dulles went to the White House to discuss his future with the President. Both in the United States and in Western Europe the clamor of criticism had risen to a shrill pitch. "Dulles must go!" This was the cry raised with varying degrees of indignation on both sides of the Atlantic. The Secretary, remarking on the latest barrage of criticism, said that perhaps the moment had come for him to resign. On February 25 he would be seventy years old. That might be an appropriate time for him to step out.

But the President would have none of it. He protested, as he had before, that Dulles was the greatest secretary of state in America's history and that his equipment made him and him alone capable of carrying on to the end of the second term. It was a warm encomium coupled with a stern rejection of the criticism. If Dulles had had any serious desire to leave in view of his age and the strain imposed on one who scarcely more than a year before had undergone a major operation for cancer, he would have been compelled to set aside his own desires. Returning to the State Department to tell his close associates of the President's words, the Secretary glowed with a new confidence.

In January 1958, at his first press conference after his mild stroke, the President appeared indifferent and somewhat withdrawn. He responded with discursive answers that were so casual as to seem almost perfunctory. Only when a question was put to him about the rumors of Dulles's possible resignation did he show animation. The lines in his face grew taut. His eyes were stern, angry even, as he called the report of the resignation "trash," and said:

The last person I would want to see resign is Mr. Dulles. I don't mind saying this: I think he is the wisest, most dedicated man that I know. I believe he has got greater knowledge in his field than in any other man that I know, and in spite of the fact that many criticisms of him that have been voiced in the newspapers, and so on—I cheerfully admit that—the fact is that, I assume, that I know as many of the leading figures of the world as does the average government official and their personal, intimate evaluations of Mr. Dulles as to furnish—as given to me, by no means indicate any desire except that he stays right squarely on the job and that is where he belongs.

In this way he proclaimed his dependence on the man who had spent his life preparing to be secretary of state and who for five years had carried so large a share of the awkward and awesome burden of foreign policy in a revolutionary epoch. In the course of his preparation, Dulles had incidentally made himself the foremost corporation lawyer in America. For client after client, among them the great utility and other domestic corporations as well as numerous foreign governments, he had shown the most facile skill in arguing a case. His diplomatic experience went back to 1907, when he was secretary to the Hague peace conference. During most of the Truman administration he had acted as Republican adviser on foreign policy, negotiating the Japanese peace treaty and serving in various capacities at the United Nations and with American delegations to one conference after another. Even when, in his campaign for election to the Senate in 1949, he greatly angered Truman by making slurring remarks about his opponent, Herbert Lehman, and the voters in the populous wards of New York City, his predecessor, Dean Acheson, had persuaded the President to take him back.

A mixture of sophistication and evangelism, of great knowledge and a weakness for glib slogans, of shrewdness and windy idealism, of harsh realism and the most naïve wishful thinking, Dulles began with a self-centered confidence that he could quickly remedy the mistakes of the past. And the public wanted at the outset to believe that he could wipe the slate clean and make a new start. The first move, proclaimed in the President's State of the Union Message on February 2, was typical of a great deal that was to follow. The new President announced that he was issuing instructions "that the Seventh Fleet no longer be employed to shield Communist China." This seemed to mean that the way would be opened for Chiang Kai-shek's Nationalist forces on the island of Formosa to at-

"It's All Right—I'm Behind You 100%"
Hugh Haynie in the Greensboro *Daily News*   July 13, 1956

tack the Communist mainland, presumably with American air and naval support. Or at any rate the Communist leaders in Peking were to be put on notice that such an attack might be forthcoming. But, as the President quickly added, his order implied "no aggressive intent on our part," and, since the Chinese Communists knew from their own very thorough intelligence apparatus on Formosa that the Nationalists were incapable of launching an attack on the mainland, the gesture of "unleashing" Chiang had little or no significance.

But if, as a psychological device, the Seventh Fleet order had only a limited and debatable effect on the "enemy," its impact elsewhere was resounding. The Democrats were indignant at the suggestion, which was in fact untrue, that under Truman the Seventh Fleet had in any sense been "shielding" Communist China. In allied countries such as Great Britain and among neutrals such as India the "unleashing" of the Nationalists caused great trepidation and uncertainty. If the announcement meant anything, it seemed to mean that the United States intended to help Chiang return to the mainland, and fear of the war in Korea spreading to all of China and perhaps to all of Asia was great both in Western Europe and among the uncommitted nations. This venture into psychological warfare prepared the way for the embarrassing and dangerous showdown later over the offshore islands.

Among Republicans of the right, Yalta had long been a favorite battle cry. In the extensive folklore cherished by those convinced that all of World War II, or at any rate America's participation in it, was a plot concocted by Franklin Roosevelt, this was the sinister climax. After tricking the American people into electing him to a fourth term, the feeble, failing Roosevelt—deranged, if you accepted the view of the true believers—went to Yalta and there sold out everything that ostensibly the nation had fought for. With the cunning and masterful Stalin calling the turn, he betrayed Poland, confirmed the enslavement of the Baltic states, and acceded to the emasculation of the soon-to-be-formed United Nations. These were the articles of faith of large numbers of Republicans, and, to appease them, Dulles, who put together the foreign-policy plank in the platform of 1952, included the statement that "The Government of the United States, under Republican leadership, will repudiate all commitments contained in secret understandings such as Yalta which aid Communist enslavements."

The new administration had hardly settled into office when the cry went up from leading Republicans in Congress to renounce the Yalta agreements. As Dulles knew very well from his long experience in foreign affairs, this was a dangerous game, at which two could play. He demurred. Then the least that you can do, the nationalists in Congress came back, is to make the Yalta papers public. Surely a Republican administration would want to expose to the honest light of day the secret treachery of that conference in the Crimea, even though it might not be possible immediately to repudiate the agreements signed there.

In this atmosphere, with important Republicans eager to get on with the cleansing of the Augean stables, the name of Charles E. Bohlen was sent to the Senate for confirmation as ambassador to Moscow. A career foreign-service officer, Bohlen had a distinguished record as a specialist in Soviet affairs and the history of Communist Russia. He had served in Moscow for several years and spoke Russian fluently. This seemed an ideal appointment to a post that was of supreme importance, particularly following the death of Stalin and the possibility it seemed to open up of a new relationship with the Soviet Union.

But Bohlen had served both as interpreter and adviser

to Roosevelt at the talks at Tehran and Yalta. He had performed a similar office for Truman at the Potsdam conference, and again and again during the war and immediately afterward he had taken part in high-level allied discussions in the Kremlin in Moscow. As though this was not more than enough to damn him, when he came before the Senate Foreign Relations Committee for a hearing on his confirmation he would not agree that Yalta was a sellout and a betrayal. In response to questioning, he expressed the view that, under the circumstances, the agreement on Poland was the best that could have been obtained unless the United States had been willing, as the war ended, to support with force of arms the establishment of the free Poles who had been the duly elected government of that tragic country. With his own forces occupying Poland, Stalin controlled the situation. It would have taken virtually another major war to have removed those forces, and there was no evidence that the will existed in America for such a war. So, the Bohlen argument before the committee went, the alternative was to agree on the best possible compromise between the two Polands and then to try to persuade and coerce Stalin into living up to that agreement.

This was, however, the voice of reason, and those who wanted to erase the past would have none of it. Led by Senators McCarthy and McCarran, the pack was soon in full pursuit. McCarthy said that Bohlen was obviously pro-Communist, and he meant to block his confirmation. It seems extraordinary, looking back, to realize how much prominence McCarthy's slightest pronouncement was given. While apart from a small fanatical fringe only a few Americans of any position or stature had been shown to have succumbed to the Communist lure, a crisis of confidence lay behind the success of McCarthy's demagoguery. The accusations were magnified far beyond any normal scale, even by respectable sources, and we did not know whom to trust.

Quickly the atmosphere in the Bohlen case became that of a Byzantine palace intrigue. The President said at his press conference that when he had been supreme commander of NATO in Paris he had known Bohlen well. The diplomat had then been attached to the American embassy in Paris. Eisenhower had played golf with him and knew and liked the members of his family. Bohlen was the ablest man available for the position. Yet the controversy, if such it could be called, went on. Quite apart from the personal ordeal that Bohlen was undergoing, the usefulness of a valuable public servant was being impaired. This was, moreover, a grave encroachment on the prerogatives of the executive branch. Short of some conspicuous defect, an ambassador has always been considered the personal choice of a president. McCarthy and the extremists on the right were refusing to play by the civics-textbook rules.

Into this situation, which was more and more an acute public embarrassment, stepped Senator Taft, with his shrewd knowledge of the political realities. He agreed to come to the President's rescue. A remarkable understanding, calculated to assuage all but a few diehards, was arrived at in the privacy of the Senate cloakroom. Taft and Senator John J. Sparkman, Adlai Stevenson's 1952 running mate, would read the material contained in the F.B.I. file on Bohlen and report to the Senate whether it contained anything of a seriously derogatory nature. This was in itself something like a vote of no confidence in the President. The F.B.I. is a subordinate service of the executive branch of the government, and if the chief executive cannot be relied on to appraise the material contained in its files, then the essential trust on which the balance of powers in our system must be based breaks down.

The two Senators duly announced to the Senate that, after reading the Bohlen file, they found it contained nothing that would in any way indicate that he had had any connection with Communism or any leaning toward that ideology. Bohlen was confirmed by a vote of seventy-four to thirteen. Of the thirteen votes in opposition, eleven were Republican.

While Senator Taft's maneuver had saved the administration from a crucial defeat, or at any rate from prolonged public discomfiture as the controversy continued, the price he exacted was high. According to Robert Donovan, he told the President that there must be "no more Bohlens." In other words, the appointments sent to the Senate for confirmation were to be free from even the slightest suspicion that might arouse the prejudices of the extreme right of the Republican party. Nothing could illustrate more forcefully the price that Eisenhower paid again and again for even the most limited co-operation from the members of his own party in Congress. Cabinet meetings and staff meetings were taken up day after day with the consideration of how to get around or appease the prejudices of a few men who had come up through the congressional ranks to hold positions of power on key committees. It is not to be wondered at that the President repeatedly expressed his sense of bafflement and frustration. He was learning in the most painful way the harsh realities of the politics that he had so long deliberately eschewed.

In April, speaking before the American Society of Newspaper Editors, the President seemed to stand apart from the divisive disputes of the past which had already involved him so deeply that he no longer seemed a free man. He spoke out in the clear and resolute accents that in the years since 1945 had inspired so much hope. In charting a course for American foreign policy that was both strong and conciliatory, he seemed to be opening the way to negotiation of the outstanding issues of the cold war. Taken along with the changes occurring in Russia following Stalin's death, this was a moment of hope, when the threat of an onrushing nuclear doom seemed to promise to lift.

The President had flown up from Augusta, Georgia, where he had been having a golfing holiday, to make his speech to the editors in Washington. Those sitting close to him could see before he was halfway through with his address that something was wrong. He was very pale, and beads of perspiration stood out on his forehead. The fact that he did not falter and come to a halt before the end was due only to a remarkable effort of will. The announcement was made afterward that he had been suffering from food poisoning when he arrived for the luncheon meeting. There were those who believed subsequently that he had suffered from an attack of the chronic ileitis that in 1956 was to send him to the hospital for a major operation. In any event, it was an unhappy portent of things to come.

As economies cut more deeply into the military establishment, Dulles, the skillful lawyer, made the best possible case for his clients. In the first instance his client was the President of the United States. The Secretary has been scrupulous about consulting with the President on foreign policy, since the President under the Constitution is empowered to conduct the foreign relations of the United States, but this has been, as one of the Secretary's closest associates put it, for approval of decisions already taken and plans already evolved in considerable detail in Dulles's ingenious and tireless mind. Speaking before the Council on Foreign Relations on January 12, 1954, he unveiled the policy of "the deterrent of massive retaliatory power." We would, said the Secretary, maintain "a great capacity to retaliate instantly, by means and at times of our own choosing." While he did not say so, this meant also that the conventional forces available to fight smaller wars were rapidly being cut back. The United States was relying more and more heavily on preserving peace with the threat of all-out nuclear retaliation. Among America's allies and the neutrals, this multiplied the fears that America might use nuclear weapons hastily and indiscriminately.

The increasing rigidity of the Dulles policy line was apparent from this point forward. Sometimes by implication, naïvely, sometimes with remarkable frankness, the Secretary of State revealed his conviction that if only we held fast behind the massive deterrent, which was the Strategic Air Command with its hydrogen bombs, the Communist empire would certainly collapse from its own inner contradictions and distortions. Since the time was therefore bound to come when the Communist leaders would give in, no slightest concession, or even negotiation that might imply concession, was called for. This is an oversimplification of the Dulles position, but it is in essence the viewpoint around which his policy hardened. It parallels in a striking way the basic tenet of Communism that holds that capitalist society must fall by reason of its own inner contradictions. For Dulles, the moralist, because Communist rule is inherently immoral it must inevitably fail. For the Marxists, with their own rigid orthodoxy, because capitalism, in their view, is inherently wasteful, contradictory, and self-destructive it must inevitably fail.

How completely the President subscribed to the Dulles line of "massive retaliation" to deter a shooting war until the Soviet system should collapse, it was difficult to determine, since he was so often preoccupied with trying to reconcile not only the opposing elements in his party but within his administration. He had brought to the presidency a seemingly unbounded faith in his own ability to

" . . . We Don't Like to Worry Him . . ."
Conrad in the Denver *Post*   February 29, 1956

reconcile conflicting viewpoints. You got people around a table, and when all the opposing views were threshed out, you came up with a consensus that was a proper guide for a middle-of-the-road course of action. In this spirit the President presided over meetings of the cabinet and of the National Security Council, seeking to subordinate his own views as if they were really no more important than those of anyone else present. In some of his appointments, it seemed as though the President had gone out of his way to test his ability as a reconciler so that he might prove the validity of his thesis.

During his visit to Korea, Eisenhower had been greatly attracted to Admiral Arthur W. Radford, then in command in the Pacific. Wilson, the new defense secretary, was also impressed by Radford. Widely known for his Asia-first views, the Pacific commander was an articulate champion of air and sea power and in particular of the giant aircraft carriers. He was reported to be close to Senator Taft and those who believed America should tell the neutrals in Asia that it was join our side "or else." Radford made no secret of his conviction that the United States should seek to keep Communist China isolated even if this meant a cold war, or for that matter a hot war, of fifty years' duration. This was the man whom Eisenhower selected as chairman of the Joint Chiefs of Staff, the most important position in the military establishment, with great influence in shaping policy. And it was not long before the reconciliation thesis was put to a severe test.

In December 1953, the President met in Bermuda with Prime Minister Winston Churchill and French Premier Joseph Laniel. At the end of that conference the President flew to the United Nations in New York and made one of the truly constructive proposals of his administration, the atoms-for-peace plan that was to become a reality in a new United Nations agency. But while this was a happy conclusion, the conference in another respect proved to have been a sad deception. The heads of government and their foreign ministers in reviewing the world situation had accepted from Georges Bidault a rosy picture of the war in Indochina that was almost entirely false. The United States was paying up to nearly a billion dollars annually of the cost of that conflict, and Bidault encouraged the hope that with only a little more time and a little more money the war against the Communist Viet-minh would be brought to a successful conclusion. Whether American diplomatic reporting from that area was hopelessly deficient or whether the President and Dulles preferred to accept the optimistic view, they seem to have put full credence in Bidault's wishful dream, which concealed such a fearful reality.

By the late winter and early spring it was impossible to obscure any longer the full horror of that reality. With very little support from a people sick and tired of a corrupt regime headed by the corrupt Emperor Bao Dai, the French were about to be pushed into the sea. And what threatened was a holocaust of blood as the Communists swept toward the delta and the cities of Hanoi and Saigon. Desperate appeals came from Paris. A thousand American planes manned by American crews, plus at least one and a half or two paratroop divisions from America, were essential if a disaster was to be averted. To symbolize their plight the French had dramatized the resistance of their forces in the jungle stronghold called Dien Bien Phu.

But even if American troops had been available to send into the Indochina jungle, the last thing the administration wanted, with the Korean conflict so recently ended, was to become involved in another Asian war. A trial balloon was sent up. Vice-President Nixon told a meeting of American newspaper editors that if worst came to worst he believed American ground troops should be sent in. Reaction in Congress was sharply unfavorable, but the Communists must surely have known that it would never happen. A conference of the powers involved, including Communist China, was called for late April in Geneva, and it appeared that unless France could somehow be extricated by negotiation the eight years of the Indochina tragedy would come to a climax in bloody disaster. Shortly before the conference, Admiral Radford tried in Paris and in London to persuade America's allies that by an atomic strike from aircraft carriers in the Gulf of Tonkin the stronghold of Dien Bien Phu could be saved and ultimate victory snatched from what seemed to be certain defeat. Radford had advocated unilateral intervention by the United States, but the President had ruled that the British and French must go along. Churchill and Anthony Eden were adamant in their opposition.

Still, on returning to Washington, Radford pressed for approval of the atomic strike. The most determined resistance came from General Matthew Ridgway, Chief of Staff of the Army, who believed that supposedly limited intervention would inevitably lead to full-scale military involvement of incalculable cost. After a period of uncertainty, with rumors of war springing up on every hand, the President finally overruled the Chairman of the Joint Chiefs. Instead of achieving any sort of "reconciliation," he had been compelled to devote himself to arbitrating a built-in conflict between two deeply opposed points of view.

Dulles's performance at the Geneva conference was one of the saddest of his career. Having faced at last the inevitability of negotiation to conclude the conflict short of disaster, the Secretary remained for only a week of preliminary talks, although Eden pleaded with him to stay in order to help obtain the best terms that could, under

the circumstances, be salvaged from the general wreckage. During that week Dulles scrupulously avoided even
looking in the direction of Communist China's Premier
Chou En-lai. It was a pathetic role for the representative
of the greatest power in the West, the power chiefly responsible for maintaining order and security in the face
of Communist aggression. After long and painful negotiations, Eden and France's then premier, Pierre Mendès-
France, agreed to a settlement that brought the war to an
end.

The cost of that settlement was very great: half of the
peninsula ceded to the Communists. But the American
people were never made aware of what this loss meant or
of the tragic miscalculations that had led up to it. Along
with so much unpleasant news, it was swept under the
thick-piled rug of American peace and prosperity. The
war in Korea had been brought to an end, and for that
most Americans were devoutly thankful, even though the
terms were those that the Truman administration had felt
the public would never accept. Half the Korean peninsula
remained in Communist hands, and a war-ravaged population, swollen by refugees from the north, was left
crowded in the southern half. While a few hardy souls
spoke out in protest, most people were ready to accept
the peace that the Eisenhower administration had promised. If the President was Dulles's first client, the public
ranked a close second. With his amazing energy Dulles
argued the case for the West, and if at times the threats
of total destruction seemed to outrun the promise of total
victory, the net effect was to reassure, if not to enlighten,
the citizenry.

What was left, once the Korean and Indochina wars had
been ended, was a situation as frozen, as implacably resist-
ant to change, as it had been before. We found ourselves,
as before, reacting to the probing of the Communist colos-

sus. And once again, in the fall of 1954, the President was faced with the necessity of trying to reconcile the irreconcilable. When the Chinese Communists began to bombard Quemoy, one of the small islands off the China mainland that the Nationalists have held on to, it was Admiral Radford, again, who wanted to use American air power, including atomic bombs if necessary, against the mainland in order to deny Quemoy to the Communists. And in a repetition of the drama as before, General Ridgway was his chief opponent, while Dulles was listed in the Radford camp. The President overruled Radford at that time, but the debate over whether or not to intervene on behalf of the offshore islands continued for the next several months as Communist belligerence increased.

These were costly exercises. They were costly in time, in effort, in frayed tempers, and not to the end of constructive action, but solely in order to preserve the *status quo* of an uneasy peace. They were exercises in restraint, principally devoted to deciding what *not* to do, which should never have been necessary at all. That was the irony of the frustration and the constant harassment under which the President was so often impatient and angry. He was making a mighty effort just to stay in one place. This was a man on a cruel treadmill, who often seemed to wonder why he found himself in so unhappy a position.

In the spring of 1955 a hopeful vista suddenly opened up. It had been heralded by the abrupt reversal of the Soviet Union's long-standing opposition to a treaty ending the occupation of Austria. Coming first in an announcement in Moscow, it seemed almost too good to be true. But as the ambassadors of the four powers concerned held exploratory talks in Vienna in the early spring, the reality began to emerge. A new atmosphere seemed to be developing in which anything might be possible. When the North Atlantic foreign ministers sat down together in

Paris in May, Harold Macmillan, then foreign secretary for Britain, informed his colleagues that his government believed a high-level meeting with the Soviet Union was imperative. It was imperative first of all because the Conservative party had decided to go to the country with an election challenge. As prime minister, Anthony Eden could proclaim his intention of achieving a peaceful settlement of the cold war. This was a recognition of the deep desire in England, articulated by the Labor party, for a determined and persistent effort to try to resolve the outstanding differences threatening destruction for East and West alike.

Dulles was not happy when Macmillan informed him that a summit meeting was a necessity if the Conservatives were to stay in power. The Secretary's deep, abiding conviction of the futility of negotiation with the Soviets was not shaken by the achievement on May 15 of a treaty restoring the independence of Austria, with the evacuation of all foreign troops. A summit meeting would, in Dulles's gloomy view, serve chiefly to strengthen Moscow's hold over the Communist empire, and it could not possibly resolve the issue of a divided Germany, which was fundamental to any settlement. But Dulles recognized the political necessity confronting Eden and Macmillan. After all, the Republicans had waged a peace campaign in 1952 that had been eminently successful. In May, therefore, the three powers—France, Great Britain, and the United States—proposed to the Soviet Union a conference of heads of state accompanied by their foreign ministers. The Soviet Union accepted the invitation, and the conference was set to open in Geneva on July 18.

There is some reason to believe that President Eisenhower's attitude toward the proposed summit meeting was different from that of his Secretary of State. By this time the Eisenhower reputation was sadly frayed. The image of the crusader had been blurred by the McCarthy madness and by the nagging, persistent futility of his efforts to bring his party together behind many important, constructive measures. The Democrats had won control over both houses of Congress in 1954. With the dimming of the Eisenhower luster, his critics were becoming bolder, although he still had a powerful hold on the country as hero, a folk figure larger than life-size, and a large proportion of the press continued to treat him with veneration, if not with awe. With his intuitive sense of drama and popular response, and with the precedents of 1942 and 1950, the meaning of a return to Europe in the role of peacemaker can scarcely have escaped him. The symbol of the hero-leader was in need of refurbishing. His mandate, out of the great electoral victory of 1952, had been to bring peace to the United States and the world. And so this new opportunity glowed against the murky horizon of the recent past with both a challenge and a promise.

Dulles was telling his associates with foreboding that he knew just what would come out of the conference. The bright façade of good will, with innumerable vodka toasts and hearty handshakes and smiles all around, would be advertised to the world through the media of mass communication concentrated in Geneva. The photographs and the newsreels would be used by Moscow in the satellites to prove that the West now sanctioned the Soviet grip on every part of the Communist domain. Back of this view was Dulles's preoccupation with the "liberation" of the satellite nations. In public he suggested that the Soviet Union was on the point of economic collapse, implying that this was why the Russians were willing to come to a summit meeting. The President disagreed with this estimate of Soviet strength, and Nikita Khrushchev employed a Russian idiom to warn the West against any thought that the Soviet delegation would be coming to Geneva "on broken legs."

In England the Eden government had won a handsome majority with a gain of nearly thirty seats. Posters emblazoned with the word "peace" beneath the distinguished face of the Conservative leader had set the tone of the campaign. In America, Senator McCarthy had, a few months before, paid the President the backhanded compliment of "apologizing" to the voters for supporting him in 1952, and now he denounced the coming conference. But McCarthy was almost alone. The manifest hope for peace in America was nearly as strong as it was in Britain. Thus was the stage set for the summit meeting.

The drama of the President's arrival in Geneva was perfect. In the late afternoon, with the blue-gray sky brushed with color from a gentle sunset, the presidential plane, the *Columbine,* came out of the west. The great gleaming silver ship circled down onto Cointrin Airport in a perfect arc and rolled slowly to a stop before the group of dignitaries waiting at one of the big hangars. A little way off, bleachers had been set up for the press, along with a platform for newsreel and television cameramen. It was extraordinarily quiet as the ramp was rolled up to the plane. The door opened and the President appeared. A kind of hush of expectation fell as he slowly walked down the steps.

The oppressive weight of all that had gone before argued against a miracle. And yet the name, the face, the ready, confident smile—these were the irresistible symbols evoking that earlier crusade when, with the odds at the outset so heavily against him, he had nevertheless brought salvation. Whatever the wisdom or the unwisdom of his going to Geneva, this must be put down as one of the great moments in Eisenhower's career. Only one other president in office had gone to Europe, and Woodrow Wilson paid a disastrous price for his adventure. One may argue that under the circumstances Eisenhower had no choice and that in any event the times had completely changed since 1919. But still he risked much: failure and repudiation and the grave heightening of tensions in the aftermath of failure. One wondered, watching him move briskly and correctly down the line of Swiss soldiers drawn up in his honor on the apron of the airfield, whether he had weighed these consequences. A man little given to reflection, he must have believed that he would pull it off or, like a good commander, he could, at the worst, disengage his forces without too much harm having been done.

Dulles had been so right about the vast apparatus of publicity concentrated on such a meeting. This is one of the handicaps of a high-level conference: the showy personalities move through an elaborate quadrille of lunches and dinners and talks, their least movement recorded by hundreds of cameras, with only the conference room, which seems to become steadily less important, shielded from the intense glare. The vodka flowed and so did the Martinis, and in the absence of any very tangible information out of the discussions in the council chamber of the old League's Palais des Nations, the inevitable rumors sprang up: Marshal Zhukov had had a long and friendly talk with the President and they had agreed on the peril to all mankind of a nuclear war; the conference would break up on the rock of German unification; Molotov had said that the Soviet Union would never approve a communiqué calling for unity of the two Germanys through the formula of free elections. This is another handicap of the high-level conference: the inadequate way in which information filters out of the private discussions through the briefing system. Because it all happens at two or three removes from those who are trying to report the news, the effect is one of shadow-boxing behind a lighted screen. The performance is cloudy, opaque, conveying little of the urgency and the momentousness of the issues of war and peace in a nuclear age.

On the fourth day of the conference the President threw in his "open skies" proposal calling for an exchange of blueprints of the military establishments of the two powers and the right of aerial inspection over their respective territories. It was a bold, dramatic, radical plan that would have swept down the whole structure of secrecy on both sides of the iron curtain if it could have been agreed to. But in an earlier form it had previously been rejected by the Soviet Union, and because it was so sweeping, some observers felt that it was no more than a propaganda device tossed in to catch the headlines and show up Soviet unwillingness to relax their own barriers.

The Soviet delegation was reported to be indignant at what they considered a maneuver disruptive to serious discussion of ways and means of resolving the long-standing causes of tension. According to one report, coming from the British delegation, in the meeting of the foreign ministers on that same day Molotov had declared the willingness of his delegation to reverse the position taken originally by Marshal Bulganin and agree that German unity and a European security pact were interdependent. The question of the relationship between German unification and European security had been one of the sticking points from the beginning. Then, if one accepted the British account, into what had begun as a meeting of minds on the principal sources of dispute came the device of the "open skies" proposal—a bombshell that threw the conference into confusion and uncertainty.

A great deal of the time that remained was taken up with acrimonious argument over the wording of the final

communiqué. The Soviet delegates insisted that their concept of European security, based on a pact between the
east and west halves of the continent, should come first.
The American delegation, with the backing of the British
and the French, held out for putting German reunification
by free elections first. As so often happens, the final wording, agreed to just in the nick of time as the great men
were due to return home, was a pale compromise from
which both sides might pluck the meaning they desired.
According to Dulles, it had been necessary to blend the
two positions in order to get a final communiqué at all.
There was no mention in it of the "open skies" plan. To
the embarrassment of the other delegations, Bulganin included in his last speech, for propaganda purposes, all the
familiar Communist demands, ranging from the recognition of Communist China by the United Nations to the
abolition of nuclear weapons. There were those who suggested that this was the answer to the "open skies" proposal.

In his own final talk, the President felt compelled to
enter a polite but firm demurrer to the familiar propaganda
points that the Soviet premier had thrown into his address.
But with this one exception, the President spoke at the
end in tones of lofty idealism. The high note of hope was
what the world had expected from the conference—and
above all from him.

"In this final hour of our assembly," he said, "it is my
judgment that the prospects of a lasting peace with justice,
well-being and broader freedom are brighter. The dangers of the overwhelming tragedy of modern war are
less."

Whether this was true or not, and many who were
later to dismiss the whole conference as inconsequential
or worse subscribed at the time to the belief that a beginning, however small, had been made, the President's opti-

mism corresponded to the desire and hope of the great
mass of people everywhere. In the brief interval at Geneva
the President had become again the soldier of peace.
Again the image was bright of a confident leader who was
not afraid to voice his belief that peace could be achieved
if only men put their minds and hearts to the task. Prime
Minister Nehru wrote a remarkable letter to the President
expressing his faith in his efforts to achieve peace and urging him to visit India, where he said he would be received
with great joy and acclaim by the people. This was the
widespread response of a world weary and sick of war and
the never-ending threat of war. For a brief time it seemed
that Eisenhower had reached another and even more
memorable climax to his remarkable career.

Disillusion was not long in coming, since what the heads
of government had done was to put off onto the foreign
ministers' meeting in October all the unsolved problems
out of the past. Any real agreement was hopeless from
the beginning if the formula of free elections in the two
Germanys was to be made a first condition. It was, of
course, a convenient formula if the intention was to prove
that negotiation was in fact impossible. More than two
years later Walter Lippmann was to write:

. . . the ambiguous formula about the unification of Germany which was adopted at Geneva has not worked. I myself cannot believe that Mr. Dulles, who, of course, knows
the record, can ever have imagined that he had really reached
an agreement about Germany with Mr. Molotov. If he did
imagine that, as he now says he did, he was much more
gullible and far less astute than we all know him to be.

The words of good will at the summit that the world so
longed to hear had obscured some frightening realities.
Although Dulles had had word at the conference of Moscow's proposal to sell arms to Egypt, the Soviet heads of
government were not confronted with this first evidence

of the initiation of a major intrigue in the embattled Middle East. When he was taxed with it at the foreign ministers' meeting, Molotov could blandly shrug it off as merely a concern of Czechoslovakia. The opportunity had passed to put up to the two men exercising the greatest power in the Soviet Union the question of whether they proposed to endanger the peace anew with still another military adventure. If the West had raised the question of the Middle East at the summit, the Russians would almost certainly have countered with their geographical and other claims in that area, and this was the last thing the western delegations wanted to discuss. So much was glossed over by a frail formula of agreement that was so soon to be merely another field of battle.

Eleven

A State of Health

After a brief interval in Washington, the Eisenhowers flew to Denver for what was intended to be a long, relaxing vacation. The President was gratified by the worldwide praise which had come to him for his efforts at Geneva. But he was showing signs of strain that concerned those immediately around him. It was important for him to get away and forget about it all as nearly as any man could in the prison of the presidency. This was the advice of Sherman Adams, the old reliable right hand, always there, always ready with an answer in his dry, understated New Hampshire fashion, an answer or an opinion delivered with an unassuming, cracker-barrel gravity that never failed to impress "the boss."

Adams had begun as a woods boss, and gradually he had worked his way up the political ladder; a term or two in the New Hampshire Legislature, election to Congress for one term, and then the governorship. He happened in this office to be in a strategic position to advance the Eisenhower candidacy in early 1952, and he risked his future, going all out against the dominant Taft faction, to insure a victory for Eisenhower in New Hampshire's early primary. That is a conspicuous advertisement which politicians in both parties prize.

From there it was a short step to Ike's campaign train and the beginning of the close relationship between the

President and the taciturn New Englander. His title in the White House, "The Assistant to the President," gives only a faint idea of the scope and authority he has assumed. As Adams has put it privately, he has done whatever the President has not done. Theoretically, the assistant to the president is a kind of political chief of staff. But with a commander whose interest in politics is at most academic, the chief of staff of necessity gives the orders. In this anomalous role, as a deputy president, Adams has drawn down the fire of criticism that otherwise might have been concentrated on the Chief Executive.

The President needed little urging from Adams or anyone else to get away. He had never resigned himself to the irksome confinement of his daily routine and the incessant demands pressed on him from every quarter. Except for the two wars, he had not been accustomed to an exacting, relentless schedule, and always he had had access to the out-of-doors. So now it was with a great sense of relief that he took off for Denver. In the careful phraseology of Press Secretary James Hagerty, it was to be a work-and-play vacation. But in the temporary White House offices at nearby Lowry Air Force Base the President soon found that he could finish off the work in an hour or two in the morning, and then he was free for the rest of the day.

Gradually he settled down to the kind of life he likes, regaining, in the solid, comfortable, undistinguished house of his mother-in-law, Mrs. Doud, something of the anonymity that he had reluctantly surrendered as part of the price of his high office. It was not repose that he sought. Just as quiet introspection and reflection are not part of his nature, so he cannot tolerate inactivity for very long. During every waking moment he threw himself into the games he has always found so absorbing. At the Cherry Hills Country Club he rarely played fewer than twenty-

seven holes of golf, eighteen in the morning, a quick lunch
in the locker room, and then another nine in the afternoon. At night there was bridge or canasta. He liked to
go into the Doud kitchen and cook one of his favorite
beef stews. Here was a man on the move, early in the
morning, late at night, and everyone who saw him com-
mented on how well he looked, his ruddy color, his jaunty
step. On August 24 he flew to Philadelphia to address a
meeting of the American Bar Association. In a suite at
the Bellevue-Stratford Hotel, where he was meeting some
of the leading members of the Bar Association, he was
asked whether he was getting a good rest. "Well, I sure
am," the President is said to have replied. "They'll hardly
let me do any work at all."

The days slipped into weeks as the work-and-play vacation continued into September. It was a perfect time of
the year, clear and dry, with the aspens on the higher
slopes already beginning to turn to gold. But a slight note
of acerbity had begun to mar the chorus of praise which
had reached a new crescendo after the President's performance at Geneva. Querulous editorial writers were
questioning whether the country could run without a
president. How long and how often was he to absent himself from Washington? Some unkind commentators compared him to Calvin Coolidge as the press reported his
trout fishing in the high Rockies. Could a president in
times such as these stand aside with detachment as Coolidge had done? If the summit conference had indeed been
a start on the road to peace, then great and persistent
efforts were essential to continue the difficult exploration
of that road. And could all this be left to Dulles? The
noise of a waspish discontent, small as yet, but nevertheless insistent, had begun to come up from the country.

If Eisenhower heard it, he gave no sign whatsoever. He
was, as on other occasions in the past, almost entirely shut

off from the world. He held no press conferences, and his personal contact with the press was confined to a casual word or two exchanged as he went in and out of the Lowry offices. The image was projected by Hagerty through the little group of White House correspondents who had gone out to Denver. Then Hagerty himself went on vacation, to be replaced by his assistant, Murray Snyder, and the regular correspondents were given temporary relief from an assignment of great tedium.

There was one good story. On September 10 the forty-eight Republican state chairmen flew to Denver to hold a breakfast meeting with the President which turned out to be a long hosanna for Eisenhower and his re-election in 1956. Responding, the President gave them what, in retrospect at least, many felt was a serious warning. Humans, he said, are frail and they are mortal. "Finally you never pin your flag so tightly to one mast that if a ship sinks, you cannot rip it off and nail it to another. It is sometimes good to remember that."

With this brief task completed, the President took off for the Byers Peak ranch of his friend Aksel Nielsen, a Denver investment banker. With Nielsen, George Allen, and his personal physician, General Howard Snyder, he resumed with a boyish zest the kind of life that he loves best. Up at five, he cooked a camp breakfast, and not long afterward he was whipping an icy trout stream. At 9,000 feet the air was thin and heady, and it seemed to give him more energy than ever. His companions would remember later that he had been so eager to start for the camp that he had been standing out on the curb in front of the Doud house ten minutes before the others were ready.

On the morning that they were to go back to the city he was up at dawn to cook hotcakes, pork sausage, fried mush, and beef bacon. As he departed, with not a little regret at the end of the outing, he said that he had never felt better in his life. But Bulganin had written a note, and it was necessary to go down to the office and talk on the long-distance telephone with Dulles. The presidential cavalcade pulled away from the Nielsen ranch almost before the reporters were aroused, and the President and his party drove at high speeds over the Great Divide. After about two hours at Lowry he went out to the country club to play eighteen holes of golf with the club pro. He lunched with Allen and other friends, a hamburger and raw onion wolfed down, and then went out to play another nine holes, walking this time rather than using the golf cart. Twice he was called off the course, once to talk to Dulles in Washington about the reply to the Bulganin note. It was September 23, and there was still no sign of when the long vacation would end.

The news out of Denver the following afternoon shocked the whole world. The President had had a heart attack. It seemed incredible. He had been so well, a vigorous, full-blooded man enjoying the life that satisfied him so completely. Those who went through the next twenty-four hours will never forget the atmosphere of that vigil. Murray Snyder's first announcement, coming when the President had been taken to Fitzsimons General Hospital nearly twelve hours after he was first stricken, called it a mild attack. As the night wore on, the full meaning of this sudden tragedy gradually made itself clear. And with each successive bulletin the gravity of the President's illness became more apparent. Mild was changed to moderate. Mrs. Eisenhower moved to the room next to her husband's to be close to him. Specialists from Walter Reed Hospital in Washington were being flown to Denver. Cots were set up in a corridor adjoining the press room, where reporters would keep the death watch. More and more medical details were provided by the Assistant Press Secretary. The President would continue to be in danger until it was established that the attack had run its course.

This was the beginning of a personal drama that was to absorb the attention of the American public to the exclusion of almost everything else. Three days after the seizure, the period of greatest danger had passed. The expectation was that, barring another attack, the President would live. But naturally all thought of a second term would now be dismissed. A man who had had a heart attack could not endure the intolerable strains of the White House. For one who had all his life been blessed with the most extraordinary good fortune, this was perhaps the greatest piece of luck of all. Or so it seemed to some of those close to the President. The evidence points to his intense dislike for most of the aspects of the job of president. He had looked forward with mistrust and doubt to a second term. Now he had a perfectly valid reason for saying that, not merely in his own interest, but in the interest of the country he must retire at the end of his first term. Only a man in full possession of his powers could begin to measure up to the impossible office of the presidency. He had just taken a new initiative for peace in the world, and the country was at the height of prosperity. Whatever might come afterward, no one could blame him. He would retire to his farm at Gettysburg to assume, if and when called upon, the role of elder statesman.

Whether the President seriously contemplated this vista we do not know, nor are we likely to know unless one of the three or four persons really close to him should choose to reveal any thoughts he may have expressed on this score. What seems evident in retrospect is that, short of taking a firm decision on his own initiative in the first ten days or two weeks following his attack, the President's opportunity to elect the course he would follow was to a large extent foreclosed. The whole apparatus of the White House staff and the top command of the Republican party closed around him with two principal objectives.

The first objective was to convince the country that the business of government was being conducted as usual by "the team" during the interval of the President's convalescence. The cabinet was taking over just as the President wanted it to. From confidential cabinet minutes made available to him, Donovan reveals that what happened at that first meeting in the cabinet room in Washington a week after the President was stricken did not differ markedly from the meetings at which he presided. Secretary Dulles, we are told, reported that the Soviet arms deal with Egypt was causing grave concern, but he gave assurances that the United States was not without plans for dealing with this situation. What those plans were he did not say, and apparently he was not asked. This reflected the same sort of personal responsibility that Dulles had been carrying throughout in the administration. After Dulles's report, the Vice-President took over, outlining to the cabinet the way in which the government would be conducted during the President's recovery. At the end of the meeting a statement was issued saying that it had been determined that there were "no obstacles to the orderly and uninterrupted conduct of the foreign and domestic affairs of the nation during the period of rest ordered by the President's physicians." Adams, the statement said, would leave for Denver at once and be available there in consultation with the President's physicians "whenever it may later become appropriate to present any matters to the President." Thus did the executive apparatus smoothly encompass the presidential sick room, with the Assistant to the President assuming more or less openly such powers as have rarely, if ever, been exercised by an official who had not been elected to national office.

If there was a conflict over power in the first forty-eight hours, and there were reports of such a conflict, the organization, the "palace guard," closed ranks and the surface aspect was one of quiet efficiency. James Hagerty arrived in Denver twelve hours after the President's attack, and from that moment he was in command of the flow of the news, making himself indispensable not only to the President, but to party leaders determined that nothing should stand in the way of a second term.

As legislative correspondent of the New York *Times* in Albany at the age of twenty-nine, Hagerty had attracted the attention of Governor Dewey. In 1942, after eight years on the *Times,* he joined Dewey's staff and quickly proved his skill in dealing with the press. Twice for Dewey and once for Eisenhower he went through the fearful grind of a presidential campaign. In the White House, as press secretary, he showed the same dexterity in a punishing job. His ability was in holding the confidence of the regular White House correspondents while at the same time keeping them within the bounds of the news as he sought to define it. Beyond that circle, as when he ventured to brief the press at Bermuda and at the summit, he was out of his depth. During the President's illness he functioned with shrewd skill.

The second objective of those managing the difficult situation growing out of the illness was to convince the public that the President was not only on the way to recovery but that he could resume the full authority of the office and be re-elected. This objective was achieved over a period of several months with the same deftness, thanks to Hagerty and to Dr. Paul Dudley White, who stepped into the fierce glare of publicity surrounding this crisis in the nation's life as though he had been waiting in the wings for just such a role. On the third day after the heart attack Dr. White was already saying that within two weeks the President could hold conferences and that it was conceivable that with a good recovery he could run for re-election. As the weeks passed, his statements grew increasingly optimistic, until he gave the President ten more years of life including five more years in the presidency. A distinguished heart specialist believing in techniques to enable heart-attack victims to be restored to usefulness, Dr. White was happy to make an object lesson of the President of the United States. But to some observers it seemed that he ignored the fantastic demands made upon a president if he is to serve in the office with full executive energy and with the capacity to initiate high policy.

Hagerty continued to give the most thorough and comprehensive daily reports of Eisenhower's condition. The details poured out as the public was told not merely of the President's respiratory rate and his pulse and heartbeat, but of his meals, his intestinal tone, and every aspect of his digestive processes. In keeping with the intensely personal character of American journalism, this fed and whetted the appetite of reporters. Their regard for Hagerty grew as he went to great lengths to supply the material for the script of the drama out of Denver.

Concern with the President's recovery obscured almost everything else. As the good soldier determined to do his duty, he was reported as cheerful, confident, eager to get back into battle. The utmost was made of the brief visits to his bedside by cabinet officers and others who flew out from Washington to "confer" with the President. The sympathies of the American people were deeply engaged. Nothing seemed to matter, not even the breakdown in November of the foreign ministers' conference, if in fact anyone had been paying any attention to it, until we were sure that he would be entirely well again. While the stock market had taken the greatest drop since the depression of

1929 on the first day of trading following the attack, the recovery had been rapid and the Eisenhower boom was
gathering fresh momentum. From various government departments came statements of new records in production
and income. This seemed to accompany the return of the
hero to health, as though his survival as symbol were in-
extricably linked with the national well-being.

At his farm at Gettysburg and during a period in the
sun at Key West after Christmas, the drama of his recovery
and his future was as engrossing as ever. It was a great
guessing game—would he or wouldn't he? From members
of his administration and from prominent Republicans
statements had been coming with greater frequency and
ever firmer confidence to the effect that of course he
would run and that certainly he would be re-elected. But
at his first press conference after his illness, in Key West,
his remarks seemed to underscore the gravity of what he
had just been through. He spoke of how "critical" it was
"to change governments in this country at a time that is
unexpected." By a ratio of five to one the reporters present expressed their conviction that he would not seek a
second term.

But while he himself may still have been wavering at
this time, all the circumstances, including those carefully
cultivated by the group around him, conspired to leave
him no escape. Not only the members of his administration, but old friends, such as Lucius Clay, in whom he
had complete trust, were telling him that peace in the
world and prosperity in America depended on his continuing in office. The pressure brought to bear on him was
in many ways like that which had induced him to run the
first time. But it was buttressed now by the appealing argument that, since he had already shown how well and
how easily he could manage the affairs of state, there was

no reason in the world why he should not consent to bless the country by serving for another four years.

On February 14, following tests at Walter Reed Hospital, the doctors announced that the President's health continued to be satisfactory. "Medically I think we would agree," said Dr. White, taking over the press conference, "that his present condition and the favorable chances in the future should enable him to be able to carry on his present active life satisfactorily for this period, as I have said, for five to ten years, knowing full well, as we have just emphasized, the hazards and uncertainties of the future."

The following day the President and Mrs. Eisenhower went with Secretary and Mrs. Humphrey to the Humphreys' Georgia plantation, and if there were any last, lingering doubts in the President's mind, Humphrey seems to have resolved them, exercising once again his remarkable influence on the man and the era. The setting itself helped to underscore the genial Humphrey optimism: the quiet luxury of the white-columned central lodge and surrounding guest cottages, the six hundred acres of beautiful, unspoiled country. The President and his Secretary of the Treasury went quail shooting, and as they tramped through the tall grass behind the dogs, the President felt a return of his old vigor and confidence. Humphrey is said to have supplied a gentle running commentary on the theme that as chairman of the board, acting in a supervisory capacity, the President could serve another four years without undue strain. It was not that he owed this duty to his country. He had long ago fulfilled any such obligation. But he had demonstrated so well his ability to delegate authority that it would be a shame to break the continuity of progress he had initiated both at home and abroad. And there would be younger, equally capable men to take over from the older members of the team in the second term.

The announcement, the drama's grand climax, came on February 29, first at a press conference and later in a broadcast. While in his broadcast the President expressed full confidence in his personal well-being and in his capacity to perform as well as he ever had "all the important duties of the presidency," he added some fine print to the effect that his performance in the future would require "a regime of ordered work activity, interspersed with regular amounts of exercise, recreation and rest. . . ."

As happens with most fine print, the public didn't read it. Republicans were jubilant. The effect of the long drama played out in such calculated detail on the national stage was obvious. The criticism that had begun to grow over the President's neglect of his office and his long vacations was forgotten. Ike was a hero again. He had won out over an illness increasingly common in America with an aging population. There he was on the television screen, smiling, radiating the confidence that we had come to trust implicitly.

Kenneth Davis says, in his biography of Adlai Stevenson, that immediately after the heart attack certain of Stevenson's advisers were convinced that, if the President should recover and if he should run again, the sympathy generated by his illness would, leaving out all other considerations, be sufficient to re-elect him. Through the spring and early summer the two leading Democratic candidates, Stevenson and Senator Estes Kefauver, were engaged in a fierce, internecine struggle in the presidential-primary campaigns. In Minnesota, in Florida and California, and in at least a half-dozen other states they went after each other with charge and countercharge. They were supplying the ammunition that the Republicans would use to excellent advantage against either candidate in the fall. Speaking to crossroads gatherings, at picnic suppers and ice-cream socials, they campaigned as though they were running for sheriff. It was a senseless, exhausting procedure that could benefit only the party in power. The immense advantage of the "ins" was demonstrated once again. With the sounding board of the White House, particularly as manipulated by so skilled an operator as Hagerty, the President almost without effort made his most commonplace remarks heard across the country.

Even when, in June, Eisenhower was taken seriously ill for the second time in less than a year, the question of his fitness to serve another term was given scant consideration. The second illness was handled just as the first had been. It seemed that the patient had hardly come out from under the anesthetic when he was reported by Hagerty as conferring with Dulles and members of the White House staff. As before, a massive volume of detail about his illness was funneled to the public through Hagerty. This time, however, the press had less opportunity to question the doctors who had performed the operation and who were supervising the President's convalescence. Every effort was made to dispel any doubt the second illness might have created as to whether the President would, after all, run for a second term. It was considered almost bad form to raise the question. He himself would take care of that little matter at his first press conference when he returned to the White House.

Before the ileitis operation, he had agreed to go to Panama for a meeting of the heads of government of the Organization of American States. The meeting was postponed for a month, and although he had been out of the hospital only three weeks, the White House announced that he would attend. It was to be a demonstration of his fitness. The three-day conference was little more than an occasion for the expression of ceremonial good will. But the pictures of the President smiling and shaking hands with his fellow heads of government were supremely important back home. It was reported that in response to questions he admitted feeling pretty tired, not himself. But he had proved that in spite of the odds he could carry on. That was the lesson of Panama advertised to the nation with careful public-relations techniques. The time for the national convention, with the campaign to follow, was drawing close, and the President was ready, willing, and eager.

But there was one slight rift in the sedulously smoothed façade. Although the President had earlier indicated that Nixon was acceptable to him as his second-term running mate, Harold Stassen said publicly that the Vice-President would be a liability to the ticket and should be replaced. This was quite out of character for an administration that had consistently and with considerable success tried to hold back any news likely to be adverse or divisive. Moreover, it was out of character for Stassen, who, since his failure to capture the nomination in 1948, had proceeded with the caution of an elephant walking on eggs. The belief persisted that someone in the White House, perhaps even the President himself, had given encouragement to this lonely heresy.

Devout Republicans were outraged. Nixon had worked hard at making the vice-presidency something more than an empty, time-serving office. And the President had encouraged him by inviting him to sit in at meetings of the cabinet and the National Security Council. He was certainly better informed on both domestic and foreign policy than any previous vice-president. On his good-will trips to Latin America and Asia he had kept himself in the public eye while playing the role of statesman.

His choice in 1952 had been, insofar as Eisenhower was concerned, an accident. The two are utterly different in almost every way, and their relationship has largely been on a formal and official level. It was this last that seemed to lend some color to the belief that the White House had sanctioned, if not encouraged, the one-man revolt. But it was soon checkmated by the President. At a hastily called press conference after he had gone to San Francisco for the convention he said that Stassen had informed him that he wanted to second Nixon's nomination. Thus the Eisenhower team was restored to perfect public harmony.

The political struggle within the party between the old right-wing Taft faction and the "modern" Republicans of the eastern seaboard had been deliberately obscured, but it was nevertheless of great concern to the President. Donovan discloses that at one point he was so disturbed that he thought seriously of starting a third party, but cooler heads persuaded him that this was impractical. He has lacked both the knowledge and the capacity to do very much about making over his party.

During the first term, liberal Republicans found it difficult to get access to the White House and to make their influence felt. Eisenhower seems to have had no understanding of the uses of patronage and power, which must be taken into account if a president is to fulfill his role as leader of his party. He strongly resisted, in fact, the suggestion that he use such tools to get his way. These realities simply did not fit into his textbook concept of government. Those who suffered as a consequence were men such as Senator John Sherman Cooper of Kentucky, who tried repeatedly to see the President to warn him off the Dixon-Yates deal. The principal obstacle was said to have been the indefatigable Sherman Adams. Similarly, Senator Clifford Case of New Jersey reported that he could count on little or no co-operation from the man in the executive office. Eisenhower often spoke the words of liberal Republicanism, of men such as Paul Hoffman who

"Walking on a Delicate Issue"
Eldon Pletcher in the Sioux City *Journal*

September, 1956

had so much to do with electing him, but too often he
showed no understanding of how to go about translating
his words into deeds or even, for that matter, of the fact
that he had a personal responsibility in this connection.

At the 1956 convention, the President seemed about to
take a stronger grip on his party. He had found in Arthur
Larson someone to articulate the philosophy of the new
Republicanism. Larson's book, *A Republican Looks at His
Party*, is an effort to chart a course between the New Deal
and the reaction of the right wing of the Republican
party. This rather ambiguous prescription, drawn up by
one himself a novice at politics, was what the President
proposed to champion. As one of the authors of the President's acceptance speech at the Cow Palace in San Francisco, Larson sounded the theme of "modern Republicanism," which, in various versions, Eisenhower has tried to
use as a definition and rallying point for his political
views. The convention itself was at best a ceremony of
ratification, since there never had been the slightest doubt,
once the flickering Stassen rebellion had been put down,
of the outcome.

After the convention, the President went to stay at the
Cypress Point club on the Monterey peninsula with a
group of business executives. These were the men who
had been close to Eisenhower throughout his first term,
his only intimates. They were representative of the core
of the business community that has supported his business
administration. Among them were Robert Woodruff,
chairman of the board of Coca-Cola, Charles S. Jones, president of the Richfield Oil Corporation, Barry Leithead,
head of Cluett-Peabody, Frank Willard, a New York investment banker, Leonard Firestone, and John Hay Whit-
ney. During the day they played golf over the beautiful
Cypress Point course, with the Pacific at its edge alter-
nately shrouded in fog and brilliant with sun. At night

they played bridge. The President's stay at Cypress Point occasioned some concern among his advisers, or so it was reported at the time, because the publicity about his association with so many rich men in that lush atmosphere was considered unfavorable.

If there was any such concern, it surely was a little ludicrous, for this was the pattern—the easy geniality of a few business friends in a closed atmosphere—of all the Eisenhower years. And even with the caution of professional politicians, there can have been little or no doubt about the outcome in November. The image of a vigorous, confident Eisenhower had been restored despite two serious breaks. The party had unlimited money to draw upon, thanks to just such men as were around the President at Cypress Point. The press was once again, outside the South, almost unanimously for the Republican candidate, and even in the South important newspapers long Democratic were now for Eisenhower. The Democrats at Chicago had displayed their divisions and advertised their doubts and disunity in the choice of a candidate who had grown weary in the primary struggles and who knew all too well the heavy odds against him. In this strangely unreal interlude Eisenhower may have believed those who told him that his worries in the second term, when he would be chairman of the board, would be far less than those in the first term. With the soldier's will to win and, as he himself put it, to win big, he set out on still another campaign that was to be one long shout of victory.

But if the foreground was a glowing, sunlit landscape, in the shadows at the rear the unfortunate Dulles was overwhelmed with troubles. In June he had abruptly and with public disdain dashed the hopes of Egypt's President Nasser for American help in building the Aswan Dam on the Nile. The cotton senators from the South had been breathing down his neck, threatening to add a rider to the

foreign-aid bill prohibiting any assistance to Egypt which
would increase competition with the cotton of the South
on the world market. The consequences of this public
brush-off were not long in coming. On July 26 Nasser na-
tionalized the Suez Canal. It was a grave blow to the security of Western Europe, since virtually all of the oil on
which Europe depended came through that waterway.
With the canal in his full possession, Nasser would be able
to slow down or choke off entirely the flow of this economic lifeblood.

Nasser's action, which seems to have come as a complete surprise, found Dulles in Peru attending the inauguration of a new president. This most traveled of secretaries of state quickly flew back to Washington. The reports he found on his return to the capital were deeply
alarming. The British and the French were threatening to
go to war to regain possession of an artery of traffic on
which they believed their very existence depended. The
issue was complicated by the long history of British domination in Egypt and the rising tide of Arab nationalism
of which Nasser was determined to be both leader and
symbol.

In response to an urgent message from Robert Murphy,
whom he had dispatched to London to make a preliminary
survey, Dulles went over to take command. He used all his
considerable skill to persuade the British and French to
try an alternative to force. From those first talks there
emerged the outline of a plan that seemed to offer a way
to end once and for all Western Europe's dependence on
the whims of the dictator Nasser, with his hatred of the
West. It was bold, imaginative, and it promised to put the
whole relationship between Europe and the Middle East
on another and more solid footing.

The plan had a first emergency phase and a second
long-term phase. In the first phase tankers would be

routed around Africa, and the additional cost of the long haul to Britain, France, and the other Western European powers would be met by loans or grants from the United States. In the second phase a whole series of steps would be taken. Large tankers specifically designed to carry oil around the Cape of Good Hope, at very little additional cost because of their size, would be constructed. Pipelines would be built across Turkey, partly through private investment and partly by government subsidy, and perhaps also across Israel. These pipelines would carry the oil of the Middle East to ports safely on the other side of the canal. As Dulles outlined the plan on his return, he said confidently that the canal would become a dry ditch. No longer would Europe be at the mercy of the wayward and unstable Nasser. Moreover, the capacity of the canal had long been overtaxed, and large amounts of new capital would be necessary if it was to be enlarged and modernized. Obviously, with Nasser in control, that capital would not be forthcoming.

If it had done nothing else, the proposal appeared to have averted the danger of war. While this was not strictly a brink of Dulles's making, he had succeeded in pulling the scuffling participants back from it. That, at any rate, was the impression given wide currency as Nasser and his canal sank below the headline horizon.

But between the conception and the execution of the plan something went wrong. America's partners in Europe complained that when Dulles returned for a later conference the hopeful commitments he had apparently been ready to make had faded away to nothing. The explanation in Washington was that Secretary Humphrey had exercised his veto. In the first year the plan would have cost $500,000,000, which presumably would have been supplied to Europe by the Export-Import Bank or some other lending agency. Humphrey is said to have viewed this as a threat to a balanced budget. There was grave doubt in England, furthermore, about assuming another loan which would mean long and continuing dollar demands to meet the interest and principal.

Following Nasser's rejection of international control of the canal, the Canal Users' Association was formed, at Dulles's suggestion, with the hope of working out a compromise with Egypt. While it seemed most unlikely that Nasser would yield to either pressure or persuasion from the association when he already had physical control of the waterway, Dulles continued to express the optimism of the trial lawyer who must, before the jury at any rate, keep up the illusion of the perfect case.

It was not that he failed to receive a warning of what was to come. In early September he was told by Douglas Dillon, the American ambassador in Paris, that the French would attack and would probably be joined by the British if some way were not found to gain at least a degree of control over the canal's operation. Dillon even set a date, predicting that a resort to force would come sometime after October 20. The Secretary is said to have replied that he was confident that Eden and Guy Mollet, then premier of France, would never do such a thing in the midst of an American political campaign.

The election was not far off, and whatever Dulles's private anxiety may have been, peace was an essential ingredient of the Republican campaign. There was no place for troubling doubts as the campaign got under way with an old-fashioned rally at the President's farm at Gettysburg. The theme was to be a simple one: peace and prosperity. And that theme was to be personified in Dwight Eisenhower. Put your trust in him, and you were assured four more years of the same prosperity and the same peace.

The Republican campaign resembled in many ways that which Franklin Roosevelt waged when he first ran for re-

election in 1936. In the same way, Eisenhower moved
across the country as the popular pledge that all was well,
the image of a cheerful father, a kindly pastor, a modestly
confident hero. He touched on issues only tangentially.
With a long sustained rhythm, sometimes with cheer-
leaders, sometimes with massed bands, the crowds
chanted "We like Ike." That was what they had come out
for in the soft Indian-summer weather—to cheer, to shout
and laugh, to sing and wave banners for the triumphal return of Ike and Mamie and what they stood for: peace and
prosperity. As Roosevelt had done twenty years before,
Eisenhower deliberately refrained from mentioning the
name of his opponent, referring to the opposition with
scorn and sometimes with half-humorous mockery. There
were, to be sure, references to dangers ahead and trials
still to be met. But they were made to sound as hardly
more than a further challenge to one who had already
achieved so much.

How much all of this was the work of the skilled public-
relations and advertising experts available in such numbers to the Republicans and how much it was due to the
intuitive sense of Eisenhower, now the experienced cam-
paigner, it is impossible to say. At times the praise was
extravagant to the point of absurdity. Senator James Duff
of Pennsylvania, in a close race for re-election, introduced
the President at Pittsburgh with the words that had been
reserved up to then for Washington: "First in war, first
in peace, first in the hearts of his countrymen." It was one
long gala, a kind of political barn dance to the sustained
chant of "We like Ike."

As for the opposition, Stevenson's campaign seemed to
lack the fire that it had had four years before. Divided
counsels sent the Democratic candidate here, there, and
everywhere around the country in a race against time and
against the great resources of money which enabled the

Republicans to blanket the television networks. He tried hard to get public attention on the question of ending nuclear tests, charging that the radioactive fallout, adding to the pollution of the atmosphere, brought peril to mankind.' But people were not listening. And, after all, wasn't Eisenhower a soldier, and couldn't we believe him when he said that it was necessary to go on with the tests? Stevenson attacked on the issue of a part-time president, adding up the number of days Eisenhower had been absent from the White House, often at times when national and international crises were threatening. Republicans came back with the cry that they would rather have Ike half-time than Adlai full-time.

Not until almost the close of the campaign did Stevenson raise the question of the President's health and his capacity to serve out a second term. It was Vice-President Nixon, he said, in his final nationwide address on November 3, who would be the dominant figure in an administration in which "the Chief Executive has never had the inclination and now lacks the energy for full-time work at the world's toughest job." He told an election eve Boston audience that there was every indication that "a Republican victory tomorrow would mean that Richard Nixon would probably be President of this country within the next four years." Most of his advisers had opposed that tactic, believing that it would only arouse more sympathy for Eisenhower. And they felt they had been vindicated when angry cries of foul play came up from the Republican camp.

As the campaign had advanced and his supporters felt the heat of battle, the pressure on the President to extend his speaking engagements had grown greater. He had said that he would play only a limited role, but before long he had agreed to go to the Pacific Northwest with a stop in Minneapolis on the way. Other cities were added to the

Tom Little in the Nashville *Tennessean*   November, 1952

schedule. But he looked well, and he seemed to be enjoying the whole experience. Everywhere he went the familiar chant burst on the air and the banners hailing him waved wildly in front of the rostrum.

Early on the morning of October 29 the President started out on a one-day tour of the South. As the party assembled at the airport, rumors spread that the trip might be called off. Israel had invaded Egypt, and the imminent peril of a small war that might grow into a big war could not be ignored. But almost at the exact time scheduled for departure, the President, looking his usual cheerful self, arrived to take off in the *Columbine*.

The first stop was Miami, and there under a brilliant, hot sun a considerable crowd, in the variegated costumes of that resort, was out to cheer the President. He read the text that had been prepared for him well in advance of the explosion in the Middle East. Stressing the familiar peace and prosperity theme, the President also made a direct bid for the southern States' rights vote. With no mention of the 1954 Supreme Court integration decision, he said he believed the South should solve its problems on a state and local level. In 1952 the President had carried four southern states, and the strategists of the 1956 campaign meant to do at least as well this time. Of the cloud on the eastern horizon, so threatening to the peace of the world, nothing was said.

In Jacksonville the President abandoned the prepared text that had been handed out in advance to reporters accompanying him and spoke, from a platform at the airport, in his own informal and often rambling fashion. Although shortly before he began to speak he had been given an Associated Press bulletin telling of the continuing advance of the Israeli forces and the alarm in the Middle East and in Europe, he made only a brief, passing reference to the new peril. His homely assurance of America's well-being, expressed in the awkward and hesitant locutions that characterize his extemporaneous remarks, seemed singularly out of key now with the evidence that a major crisis confronted America and the world. On the press plane reporters were given in a remarkably short time mimeographed copies of a transcript of what the President had said at the Jacksonville stop. It was one of the ironies of the Republican campaign that the words spoken, words so muted and so minor, were transmitted with so much efficiency and dispatch to a waiting world.

At Richmond, the *Columbine* and the press plane dropped under a low cloud cover in gathering darkness and rain for the last appearance of the day. And there, before another airport crowd, the candidate did speak of the danger that had intruded itself on the American ritual of a presidential contest. He was introduced by the Assistant Secretary of State for Far Eastern Affairs, Walter Robertson, a Virginia gentleman, who had resolutely held the line against any change in American policy in Asia. The President spoke in admiring terms of Senator Harry F. Byrd, the senior senator from Virginia and the inheritor of Virginia's aristocratic tradition, who had done perhaps as much as any single individual to resist the course of integration as ordered by the Supreme Court. In the text there was praise of still another Virginian, General George C. Marshall, and this time, unlike 1952, the reference to the President's friend and patron stayed in the address as delivered.

The fearful onrush of events swiftly broke through the cherished illusion of all's well with the world. Following with inexorable logic from the intrusion of the Soviet Union in the Middle East through the Egyptian arms deal, one crisis now succeeded another as Britain and France joined Israel in the attack at Suez. The public, absorbed in the election campaign as, in a sense, a continuation of the

Eisenhower personal drama, was unprepared for these shattering events. What were our allies doing, going behind our backs and treacherously attacking a sovereign power? This seems, in the first instance at least, to have been the President's own reaction. Yet there is evidence that he would have moved much more quickly than his Secretary of State was willing to, to repair the breach with London and Paris. No matter how one looked at it this was a cruel dilemma. To have sided with Britain and France at the outset would have been to risk alienating the whole Arab-Asian-African world. In the Dulles view, therefore, the United States must come down on the side of the former colonies and in opposition to Britain and France. But could the western alliance survive such a break? With the persistent optimism that had come from Dulles, obscuring the whole nature of the growing crisis in the Middle East, there had been no intimation that a question with such devastating implications might soon confront the country.

Compounding the nightmare was the horror of the revolt in Hungary. When the Soviet tanks and troops entered in force to put down the government of Imre Nagy, the conscience of the western world was profoundly affronted, and yet any form of intervention contained the threat of a nuclear war. Whether intervention by observers of the United Nations, at the very least, might have been possible during an interval of from three to six days before the Russian onslaught is debatable. The head of the American delegation, Henry Cabot Lodge, Jr., has been reproached for failing to take some initiative that might have interposed the moral authority of the U.N. between the defenseless Nagy government and the Soviet tanks. Lodge has denied that any such opportunity existed, and perhaps it would have made no difference. In any event, the presidential campaign was drawing to a close, and any move that appeared to jeopardize the widely advertised peace would hardly have been welcome.

On Election Day, November 6, events came to a wild climax. Allen Dulles, director of the Central Intelligence Agency, has told how he was en route to his voting residence on Long Island to cast his ballot when a courier hastily dispatched from Washington overtook him. The word the courier brought was of Marshal Bulganin's notes of the day before to Britain and France which seemed to imply that the Soviet Union would use rocket weapons against them unless the invasion of Egypt was stopped immediately. Dulles turned around and flew back to Washington to spend what he has said was perhaps the most agitated and frantic twenty-four hours in his entire career. On the basis of thorough and intensive work by the C.I.A., Dulles had every reason to believe that the Soviet Union had launching bases in place capable of sending missiles with nuclear warheads in the direction of the European capitals up to a range of 1,500 miles. His agency had been plotting the trajectories of missiles since late in 1954. So the Bulganin threat was not an empty one. In high government offices in London and Paris, where there was also a relatively realistic appraisal of Soviet capabilities, something like panic prevailed.

By November 7 the belligerents had agreed to a ceasefire in Egypt. The official American view was that the action of the United Nations had brought about this result. But it is idle to pretend that the nuclear threat from Moscow did not have a considerable, perhaps decisive, influence. Here again, as in the instance of Indochina and the offshore Chinese islands, a situation had been brought to the point of disaster. On the very edge of the abyss, peace had again been salvaged, and for the time being, as with the end of the Indochina war, allied losses were obscured by the wave of relief over catastrophe averted. The cost of this kind of brinkmanship would be fully appreciated only at the next brink.

It was the belief of Stevenson's advisers that whatever chance he might have had, and certainly it was slight, was wiped out by the new threat of war. The President was a military man, and if we were in danger again then we needed him for another term. In his last speech of the campaign, Eisenhower talked wisely of the need to repair as quickly as possible the breach with Britain and France. It was a careful utterance, calculated to calm the emotions and prepare the way for putting together the shattered pieces of the alliance.

Election night was for the second time a swift sweep to victory. The returns from the very first showed the extent of the Eisenhower landslide. By ten o'clock that night the President was confident of victory. At quarter to two, shortly after Stevenson conceded, he made his triumphal entry into the ballroom of the Sheraton-Park Hotel in Washington, where a crowd of his supporters, long confident, had been impatiently awaiting him. With something of his old effort to disassociate his person from his office, he expressed his belief that the tremendous vote he had received could not "be merely for an individual." It was "for principles and ideals," he felt. It showed that "modern Republicanism has now proved itself and America has approved of modern Republicanism."

Second thoughts were in order in the sober morning-after when it was seen that for the first time in over a century a president re-elected to office had failed to carry in with him the two houses of Congress. In state after state where the President had called for the election of Republican senators and representatives the voters had chosen Democrats. In Oregon, once considered safely Republican, the former Secretary of the Interior, Douglas McKay, had been rejected in favor of the maverick Wayne Morse, in spite of the fervent personal plea the President had made on behalf of McKay. Similarly, in the state of Washington, Governor Arthur Langlie, contesting the seat held by Senator Warren Magnuson, received the President's personal accolade and yet he was defeated. Only in Kentucky, where two able candidates wearing the modern Republican colors, John Sherman Cooper and Thruston B. Morton, both were elected, could the President be considered to have scored a success. To many observers the result seemed to forecast the end of any serious attempt to reshape the Republican party. Against the Eisenhower majority of more than nine and a half million, a great personal tribute in a nationwide popularity contest, the failure of the Republicans who had tried so hard to ride the hero's coattails was all the more glaring. In this striking discrepancy was the suggestion of a recurrence of the old unhappy sickness that had seen the G.O.P. out of power for the twenty years from 1932 to 1952.

But with the second inauguration the illusion of all's well seemed to have been restored once again. Eisenhower was back in the White House for another four years. His State of the Union message was a middle-of-the-road document that forecast a balanced budget and even a surplus to reduce the national debt by a small amount. Secretary Humphrey started an argument over the size of the budget, but the President said he agreed that it was right to try to cut it wherever it was possible. Dulles had made a remarkable recovery from the operation for cancer of the colon, and with the amazing stamina and will that are two of his principal characteristics he had taken up again, as he entered his seventieth year, the reins of American foreign policy.

What, if anyone had stopped to think about it, was so miraculous was that the imminent perils seemed never to have happened at all. Where was the threatening night when nuclear missiles had seemed poised to become a terrible reality? Where the dreary failure of the British and French at Suez? Where the crack that had split the alliance open? It had all been just another bad dream which we would forget as quickly as possible. Thus was the comfortable calm of the Eisenhower era restored after a fretful hiatus.

Twelve

The Image Fades

Before the first six months of his second term were out, the President was asked in press conference not once but twice whether he regretted having made the decision to seek re-election. With quiet dignity he answered that if one did one's duty then there was no room for regret, and, moreover, regret was a form of self-pity in which he did not choose to indulge. But the question reflected a change in the atmosphere. Under the Twenty-second Amendment to the Constitution the President was not eligible to run for his high office again; the day after he received his huge popular majority he was a lame duck, certain to retire at the end of four years. And the preoccupation with McCarthy, the heart attack and the President's recovery had meant that so much during the first term had been evaded and postponed.

The attitude toward the President was both more critical and more expectant. He had been given a great vote of confidence, and the feeling was growing that he should now get on with trying to solve the problems facing the nation. Foremost among these was the issue of integration in the schools and the related question of the serious deterioration of the American public-school system. It was just here that the weakness of the Eisenhower concept of the presidency became most evident.

The President had been urged repeatedly to take the

244

lead in helping to ease the way toward a peaceful adjustment to the profound social change that had been de-
creed by the Supreme Court under Chief Justice Earl
Warren, whom the President had named to that office.
He had been pressed to take various steps: to call a national conference of the moderates from the South, both
white and Negro; to tour the South speaking for order and
reason and respect for the highest court of the land; to
go on television with an appeal to all the people for patience and understanding. But he did none of these things.
From his cautious remarks in press conference it could
even be inferred that he did not approve of the decision
on integration. The previous September he had been asked
whether he endorsed the finding of the Supreme Court on
the segregation question or whether he merely accepted it
as the Republican platform did. He replied: "I think it
makes no difference whether or not I endorse it. What I
say is the—the Constitution is as the Supreme Court in-
terprets it; and I must conform to that and do my very
best to see that it is carried out in this country." He made
himself sound rather like a police officer who must wait
for a riot call before he can intervene in a family quarrel.
No president in a long time had so narrowly interpreted
his role. What was most revealing was the suggestion that
his own personal opinion did not matter. It was as though
the President were a detached spectator who would do his
duty when called upon but only then.

From the South came an angry muttering punctuated
by an occasional explosion. The Federal Bureau of Investigation put together an ominous report showing the
extent to which guns and ammunition were being pur-
chased in southern communities. The extremists on both
sides had begun to demand the impossible.

The radical change brought about by integration, particularly in the border states, where it was occurring on

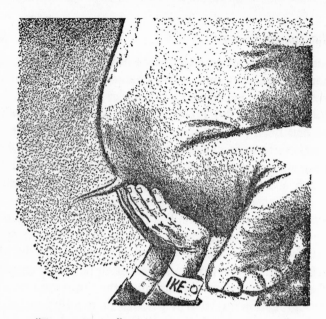

"Upsey Daisy"
Hesse in the St. Louis *Globe-Democrat*   October 25, 1954

"Elephant Boy"
Marcus in the New York *Times*   November 9, 1952

a large scale, took place in school systems already seriously overtaxed. The cost of construction had been rising
steadily, and states and school districts were unable to
keep up with the demand for classrooms. The shortage of
classrooms was estimated at 180,000. In hundreds of communities children were attending school on a half-day
basis, and classes were much too large. The shortage of
teachers was nearly as great as that of classrooms. Teachers had been perhaps more defenseless than any other
group in the face of the postwar inflation. All this meant
a grave decline in the standard of education. The fiction
of "separate but equal" had encouraged the illusion that
the Negro was being given the same kind of education as
the white pupil. We had deliberately shut our eyes over
the years to the profound social differences separating the
two races. Conditions of inequality were created long before school age was reached, and it was idle to pretend
that the schools, even if they had really been equal while
separate, could compensate for these inequalities. These
were the troubling realities that came to the surface in the
aftermath of the Supreme Court decision.

The President said several times that laws could not
change men's hearts, and with this no one could argue.
By no *fiat lux* could the old order be changed from one
day to the next. But only through action by the federal
government, with its superior resources and its overriding
powers, could the transition be made easier. The Eisenhower administration had consistently put the emphasis
on state and local responsibility in the whole school situation, but in two previous years modest programs of federal
aid for school construction had been submitted to Congress—and failed to win approval.

In the aftermath of the President's great victory the
time seemed right to put through a program of federal
assistance. The Secretary of Health, Welfare and Educa-

tion, Marion Folsom, was determined to do everything possible to see to it that Congress adopted a reasonable aid program. The President on several occasions spoke the right words in favor of the proposal put forward by Folsom. But, as in the past, when it came down to the practical business of using the political tools that other presidents had employed, he simply withdrew. Despite the stiffening attitude of the South, it should have been possible to have reached an equitable compromise between the position of the Democrats, who favored a measure that would help all states regardless of need, and the Republican program, which based federal assistance on the degree of need in the individual state. It should have been possible to have persuaded individual Republicans in the House to go along with the administration. But on a parliamentary technicality, which destroyed all hope for any measure for that session of Congress, most leading Republicans voted against what the President had said he wanted. Apart from the very real efforts of Secretary Folsom, the whole matter had been handled with such a lack of conviction and earnestness as to leave a strong suspicion that the President had been doubtful that a federal aid bill was really necessary or desirable.

The budget dispute touched off by Secretary Humphrey had had an unhappy effect on relations between the White House and Congress. The Democrats in control of congressional committees took Humphrey's observation about the government's tax take producing "a depression that will curl your hair" as a challenge to them, and they set out to whack up the Eisenhower budget. What an extraordinary performance Humphrey had put on: a member of the President's cabinet, the Secretary of the Treasury, the man who determined the government's fiscal policy, openly attacking a budget that had been presumably agreed to within the entire administration. At a press conference, the President was to say that he had approved Humphrey's remarks, but this hardly explained what was behind the curious maneuver. In any case, if the President and his Secretary of the Treasury felt that it was so important to cut down spending, then perhaps they were just as pleased that a school aid bill had been checkmated by a parliamentary blockade in the House.

Outwardly nothing seemed to have changed in those first months of the second term. The President went down to the Humphrey plantation in February for his winter vacation. If he was concerned over the state of the nation or the world he showed no sign of it. A strange rumor sprang up in some parts of the country: the rumor that he intended to resign and turn the presidency over to Nixon. When he returned, he characterized this, in answer to a question, as the worst rot he had ever heard. He might have added that, after all, he had proved that he could delegate authority. He was chairman of a board of directors in whose integrity and capability he had implicit faith. In April he went to Augusta for golf. He had said, when he announced that he would run again, that he would intersperse his work with regular intervals of rest and recreation.

To those who looked closely at the economy, the first small signs of a business decline were apparent. Democrats such as Representative Wright Patman of Texas and Senator Robert Kerr of Oklahoma were attacking the "tight money" policy of the administration and the Federal Reserve Board. They charged that the Eisenhower policies were benefiting the bankers at the expense of the average citizen. But this was the customary grist of the political mill. In order to check the price rise which went on month after month some measures of fiscal restraint were necessary, and if this meant a temporary increase in unemployment, it would be a small price to

pay for stability, or so the policy makers in the administration argued. There was no reason, in Humphrey's opinion, why the tenor of the second term should not be very
much like that of the first. Employment, production, and
spending were still at very high levels, and for the moment the headlines reflected a comparative calm in foreign relations. It was time, Humphrey was saying, for the
old men to get out and make way for newcomers lest it
should seem at the close of the second term that it was
not merely an administration that was coming to an end,
but a party as well. He was planning to leave, and he
urged Dulles, too, to make way for a younger man.

But while only the first faint rumblings could be heard,
an earthquake was in the making that would shatter the
familiar surface calm. It began with a somewhat louder
subterranean rumble, which caused consternation in the
White House, although, as with so much that has gone on
in the Eisenhower years, the public had only the slightest
intimation of what was happening. In late February and
early March the top command in the Pentagon became
aware that the Air Force was overspending its budget
by a very large amount. This was due in part to the inflation and in part to the fact that commitments made long
before were beginning to mean greatly increased pay-
ments for the fantastic "hardware" that modern warfare
demands. Secretary Wilson and the Under Secretary,
Donald Quarles, kept hoping that by some means or other
this runaway spending would be brought under control.
But as the weeks passed, the situation grew worse instead
of better. It was like trying to dam up a raging torrent.
Stop it at one place and it broke out in another. The
budget ceiling fixed for the military was $38,000,000,000,
but largely because of the excess spending by the Air
Force, the rate of expenditure was close to $42,000,000,-
000. Obviously this could not be concealed forever from

the Treasury and the White House, and if the flood could
not be checked, a frank confession was necessary.

The anger of the President when he was finally confronted with the truth is said to have known no bounds.
Beneath the public exterior he has always been a volatile
man, and in the first outburst he was determined to fire
Quarles. When he had quieted down somewhat, he was
persuaded that such hasty action would almost certainly
mean a scandal. If Quarles went, then Wilson would also
have to go, and this would be a public confession of disastrous error. After the storm had subsided, the decision
was taken, with Humphrey in command, that expenditures must be ruthlessly cut back and the budget ceiling
restored over the Pentagon. The proudest convictions of
a conservative administration were at stake here. If the
runaway were not halted, the budget would be unbal-
anced, and this might even force an increase in taxes. At
the very least it could mean the necessity of going to
Congress to ask for an increase in the ceiling on the national debt, and Senator Byrd, whom the President has
praised as a master of government comparable to Thomas
Jefferson, would stoutly resist any such change. Nothing
less than the whole public position of the first Republican
regime since Herbert Hoover was in jeopardy.

With the Bureau of the Budget in charge of field operations, the economizers went to remarkable lengths. Programs for aircraft procurement and missile development
were arbitrarily lopped off. Aircraft manufacturers were
told that their bills would not be paid until after the end
of the calendar year, and these bills in some instances,
such as the Boeing Aircraft Company's, added up to hundreds of millions of dollars. But even in the smallest matters, such as the payment of electric-power charges, the
economy squad hacked and chopped and postponed. The
director of the Bureau of the Budget, Percival Brundage,

a close ally of Sherman Adams, had long since enlarged the powers of his office to the extent that he was accused of usurping the right of Congress to determine what moneys shall be appropriated for a particular function and how they shall be spent. Before the economy squad went to work in the Pentagon in this sudden emergency, Brundage had taken it upon himself to say in a variety of instances that money appropriated would be withheld in whole or in part.

The drastic measures taken in the late spring and early summer were soon felt in those industries in which defense contracts are the chief bulwark. Workers on the assembly lines, and, with them, technicians and engineers, were dismissed from aircraft plants on the West Coast. This sudden, sharp blow at the structure of defense spending coincided with the retardation deliberately achieved by the "tight money" policy. Another important factor was the slowing down of the great capital-investment boom. As a consequence, what had been a mild lag soon began to threaten to become a fairly rapid retreat.

In the atmosphere of challenge created by Humphrey's warning on the dangers of excessive spending and a large budget, the House had cut away $2,600,000,000 from the President's national defense request for the next fiscal year. In the Senate, with great effort, Senators Saltonstall and Symington succeeded in restoring $971,000,000 of the House cut. Earlier, the President had issued solemn warnings about the danger of economies at the expense of national security. He said that he himself had seen in the past the peril to the nation's defenses of such unwise economy. But not long after Symington and Saltonstall won their victory, while the Senate and House were in conference on the defense figure, messages from both Wilson and Brundage were sent to the Capitol to say that the administration did not, after all, want the appropriation that the two senators had salvaged. This drew a particularly outraged cry from Symington. The year before, the former air secretary had conducted a lengthy investigation into American air power, and while the conclusions of that inquiry were expressed in somewhat subdued terms, they left little doubt that the size of the budget, determined for reasons of economy and politics, had brought sharp reductions in America's deterrent striking power.

Others joined the chorus of protest. Why should the President, in a short space of time, warn against the dangers of economy in the defense structure and then repudiate those who had made a valiant effort to save what he had told Congress was so essential? The reason, of course, was the hidden overspending, which was not only a threat to the political position of the administration, but illegal as well.

Through the fretful months of summer Congress remained in Washington. The question was raised now and then about the President's vacation. The doctors were said to have decided that Colorado was out for a recovered heart patient because of the altitude. The Wisconsin lakes were reported to be a possibility. The President could hardly go away before the session of Congress ended, and yet those close to him were aware that he was in need of relaxation and change.

On September 4 the President and Mrs. Eisenhower flew to Newport, Rhode Island, to settle in at the Navy installation on Coasters Harbor Island. This, too, was to be a work-and-play vacation, and since the distance was so short, not much more than an hour's flight, the President could be expected to return to Washington from time to time. But he had hardly established himself in the handsome residence put at his disposal and started to play his customary intensive game of golf on the lovely rolling course of the Newport Country Club before a new and even more ominous rumble intruded on the vacation quiet. It came from Little Rock, Arkansas, where the Federal District Court had ordered the high school to be integrated. The governor of the state, Orval Faubus, in order, he claimed, to prevent violence, called out the Arkansas National Guard and stationed the troops around, the high school. They were instructed to prevent the entry into the school of the nine Negro pupils determined to attend.

The President was presented with the most serious challenge in his entire tenure of the presidency. He must either persuade Governor Faubus to cease his defiance of the federal court and permit the Negro children to enter the school or act himself to sustain the authority of the federal government. To ignore the challenge was to endanger the whole structure of federal authority as it relates to the states.

Since the cost of maintaining the Arkansas Guard was, as in all the states, met largely with federal funds, the President might have served immediate notice on Governor Faubus that if he did not employ the troops to uphold the order of the court then it would be necessary to federalize the guard, as the President has the power to do. It was, after all, extraordinary that a force should be supported by the federal treasury which was deliberately defying a decree of a federal court. But the President was very reluctant to take such action. He had expressed so often his abhorrence of the use of federal power to enforce federal laws in the states. In the early summer he had said that he would do everything he could to avoid the use of troops, the mere prospect of which obviously filled him with deep distaste. So he delayed, hoping for reconciliation.

There followed the tragicomedy of Governor Faubus's

visit to Newport. For an obscure governor of a little-known state, up for re-election, this was a ten-strike. The governor exploited it for all it was worth, with the world looking on. Men of good will had hoped that he might be persuaded during his talk with the President to follow the reasonable course. One of these was Representative Brooks Hays of Little Rock, a deeply religious man, who was convinced that right must triumph without the ultimate recourse to force. Hays had been an intermediary in arranging the talk with Eisenhower, and, as so often happens to intermediaries, his fate was not a happy one. For when Faubus had had his day before the television cameras he made it clear that he had in no way altered his position. By treating with him and, in effect, giving him the last word, the President had been made to look very foolish.

With Faubus's shifty, reckless performance, the tensions in Little Rock were further inflamed. A mob spirit of prejudice and hatred began to grow. The Negroes in the community, and particularly those who had been courageous enough to insist on what they believed to be their rights, were one target. Another target was Harry Ashmore, an editor of fortitude and stamina, who had continued to say in the Arkansas *Gazette* that the Governor could not defy the law of the land. More than a hundred reporters had converged on Little Rock, among them several correspondents from abroad, and they, too, were the object of insult and slander and even the threat of physical abuse. Benjamin Fine, education editor of the New York *Times,* was taunted as a Jew by the shouting mob, and some bolder members made as if to seize him and carry him off. The ugly menace of what was happening in Little Rock, reported in the press of the world, could not be exaggerated.

As the prospect of violence grew, the President continued to try to keep his vacation schedule. In the morning he would take the *Barbara Anne,* the Navy yacht named for his granddaughter, across to the mainland and then motor to the country club. As always, the game he played was fast and furious. He was said to have remarked to a friend that the best thing about golf was that when you were playing it you couldn't think about anything else. That was the impression he gave on the course —of a man determined to shut out everything else from his view except that small white ball and the green or the sand trap just ahead. The contrast with the ugliness of Little Rock—the splendid course, with the sweep of ocean in the distance, the houses of the rich or the once-rich standing out against the clear blue Indian summer sky, the President in easy sport clothes intent on his game— could not have been greater. It was a contrast that disturbed certain of his advisers, and especially when news reporters told of his being called off the golf course for telephone consultation about the situation in Little Rock. As in the crises of the past, Hagerty was the medium through which he was presented to the public. Reporters observed the President on the golf course, but he held no press conferences.

The situation that finally presented itself was so grave, so ominous, that any course of action other than the one he took had virtually been ruled out. When the nine Negro pupils appeared again at the high school, and the swelling, stormy mob that opposed them defied the President's command to disperse, there was no response left but the intervention of federal force. The President's statement of September 23 warned that he would "use the full power of the United States, including whatever force may be necessary." In his executive order of the following day, the Secretary of Defense was "authorized and directed to take all appropriate steps to enforce any orders" of the district court "for the removal of obstruction of justice" with respect to integration. The Arkansas Guard was federalized, and troops from the 101st Airborne Division were ordered to Little Rock to join in patrolling the high school. It was an agonizing decision for the President, wrenching his cherished convictions about the separation of powers and the rights of the states.

Many northern newspapers gave him a measure of praise for having acted to end an intolerable situation and to uphold the authority of the federal government and for his patience in the most serious federal-state conflict since the Civil War. But this was grudging tribute from those who felt that, if only he had acted more quickly, the worst consequences of this shameful episode might have been avoided. In the South there was cold fury directed at one who had seemed up until Little Rock to stand with the embattled believers in the states' right to live separate and alone in ways of their own choosing. But partisan praise and blame to one side, the President by his action had damaged the popular image which had been sustained through nearly five years in the White House. He had always before been above the battle, a friend to all alike, the symbol of the whole nation's well-being. It was not so much that the South would harden against him and his party politically. That was relatively minor. His position before the country had been profoundly altered. He might from this point forward become a different, more positive, active leader. But after Little Rock nothing would be the same, and a sense of this was in the clear, crisp air as he went out for the last time to play golf, ending his troubled Newport vacation.

This was the great divide, the first of a series of cataclysmic events that were to bring to an end an era to which the President had given the color of his hopeful, buoyant temperament.

Looking back, the marvel is how totally unprepared we were for what was to happen next. Before October 4, our complacency, our comfortable conviction of inevitable superiority, was a suit of armor that nothing could penetrate. A warning of sorts had come earlier in the summer when reports were printed that American intelligence sources had verified the successful testing of a Soviet intercontinental ballistic missile with a range of up to 5,000 miles. Not long afterward, the Soviets announced that they had perfected an operational ICBM. The fact was that the Central Intelligence Agency had known of these successful tests for many months. The information had been kept back, so it was said, to see when and how Moscow, in its own good time, would make known this great advance. Important as it was, signifying that Russia was at least two to three years ahead of the United States, the news created only a mild stir. One reason, of course, was that administration spokesmen in the Defense Department and elsewhere began to cast doubt on the report. This was in all probability no more than a test prototype of a long-range missile. From these first tests it would be a long way to an operational weapon. These were the comfortable words that came out of Washington, and so deeply ingrained was the assurance of superiority that it was easy to shrug off this latest claim by the boastful Russians.

But when for the first time man pierced the envelope of the earth's atmosphere and put his mark in the sky, then people everywhere were filled with wonder. The first reaction in America was one of intense fascination with the achievement itself. At last man had triumphantly broken through to the stars. A flood of news about the *sputnik,* some of it more fanciful than real, was poured forth. The

Soviet rocket experts, whether by coincidence or design, were in Washington when the announcement came from Moscow, and they were interviewed on every conceivable aspect of the orbiting satellite. The public could not learn enough about this venture into outer space.

As the wonder wore off, however, the realization of what it meant in terms of Soviet science and military advancement brought deeply disturbing second thoughts. The *sputnik* with the equipment it carried to broadcast signals back to earth weighed 184 pounds. That was nearly ten times as much as the twenty pounds of the unhappily named Vanguard, which was to have been the American entry in the satellite race. And what had happened to the Vanguard anyway? Gradually the story came out: the decision to concentrate on a modest project, with the Navy in charge, as part of the International Geophysical Year, the meager funds available, the complete lack of any understanding of what it would mean to be first with such an achievement. As though in a deliberate effort to make matters worse, administration apologists came forward to belittle the whole business. That down-to-earth New Englander Sherman Adams called it nothing more than an interplanetary basketball game. Clarence Randall, a former steel-company executive and one of the innumerable "special assistants" of the White House, dismissed it as a celestial bauble. But with his intuitive sense of the tides of public opinion, Vice-President Nixon spoke of the seriousness of the Russian achievement and what it meant to America. Addressing the International Industrial Development Conference in San Francisco, he warned that "we could make no greater mistake than to brush off this event as a scientific stunt. . . ." It was a "grim and timely reminder" of the "great magnitude" of Soviet scientific and industrial capacity.

In the most immediate and practical terms, it meant

that the Soviet Union had an engine capable of launching a rocket weighing perhaps as much as 150 tons into outer space. The Vanguard rocket with its satellite would weigh not more than eleven tons. Hardly had the impact of this been absorbed when, on November 3, Moscow announced the successful orbiting of *sputnik* number two. This satellite, containing the dog Laika, weighed 1,200 pounds. Now it was not wonder, but something close to consternation that overwhelmed the capital. Members of the Senate Armed Services Committee, including the chairman, Senator Russell of Georgia, returned to Washington for two days of intensive briefing at the Pentagon. At the end of that briefing, Russell, normally a moderate and careful man, said that he was shocked and appalled by what he had heard. What the Soviets had achieved was an advance so great that it was not even in the planning stage in Washington, according to Russell. If anyone had taken the administration's assurances literally and had doubted the Soviet capability to launch an ICBM, all doubt was now dispelled. As the two *sputniks* streaked across the sky, the naked truth could no longer be obscured.

The shock to the American people was described at the time as not less than that of a second Pearl Harbor. But Pearl Harbor had been a physical attack that brought an instant, fighting response. This was so much more subtle, this insidious object that without let or hindrance traversed our skies from one end of the country to the other. Slowly we became aware of what lay behind this great scientific achievement and its practical significance in weaponry. It meant a science and technology at least as advanced as ours and certainly more concentrated on objectives that we had slighted or ignored. We had been told that these people were peasants, barbarians, capable of advancing only when they stole our secrets. And now they had been the first to take this giant stride beyond the reach of earth-bound man.

One consequence of the mood of disillusion and distrust that followed was a diminution of the President's stature. Whatever else he might have been blamed for in the first five years, he was a military man, and we had a secure sense that all was well with our national defenses so long as he was in the White House. This had been a common theme in both the first and second presidential campaigns. But now, with the successful orbiting of the two *sputniks,* this confidence was for the first time shaken. A rash of jokes, some of them colored with bitter irony, sprang up about the President and circulated through the country, as they had with other presidents. There was the story about the slogan supposedly seen on automobile stickers in Texas and elsewhere: "Ben Hogan for President. If We're Going to Have a Golfer, Let's Have a Good One." And there was the one about the President and his party asking permission to play through a foursome ahead of them on the Burning Tree golf course. "What was the hurry?" "New York has just been bombed." Until that point he had been immune to the common touch of humor.

In the lurid light of the two man-made comets, certain harsh realities that had been hitherto screened from notice suddenly were in the forefront of the public consciousness. Soviet Russia was exceeding the United States in the training of scientists and technicians. Soviet primary and secondary education was thoroughly grounded in the sciences and in mathematics. A thirst for learning in Russia sent young people into the bookshops with a passion for texts in physics and chemistry. All this and much more we had been told before, but we had listened to the glib assurances that all was well and that a free society was bound to outdo a slave society.

It was a time of searching, almost fearful self-examina-

tion. We asked ourselves how we could have fallen into
this pit so blindly. To some, the moment seemed comparable to England's hour of trial and tribulation in the
spring of 1940, when Winston Churchill had told the
British people that he could offer them nothing but sacrifice, blood, sweat, and tears.

In this troubled mood, the country awaited the first of
the speeches the White House had announced the President was making to tell us where we stood. When it came,
it was judged as adequate enough as another Eisenhower
middle-of-the-road talk. It was disclosed that Dr. Killian
of M.I.T. was to be named as a special adviser to the
President for science and technology, and the federal government meant to take steps to increase the training of
scientists and engineers. What the speech most strikingly
lacked was any sense of urgency. It failed to lift the spirit.
There were many who believed that a frank confession of
error, coupled with a determination to ask for any sacrifice to make up for the time we had lost, would have received an overwhelming response. While the principal
author was said to have been Arthur Larson, removed
from his position as head of the United States Information Agency and put in the White House as a consultant
on psychological warfare, the speech had a stale, bureaucratic, combed-over tone that did little or nothing to alter
the mood of the country. The second "chins-up" speech
suffered from the same blight of bureaucratic language.
As the President read with scant ardor the awkward sentences, it was hard to believe that this was the inspiring
hero whom millions had cheered.

The government is stepping up its basic research program, the President said, but he immediately added, as
though to quiet the old fears of government domination,
that the bigger share of the job would be in the hands of

industry and private organizations. "We want adequate security. We want no more than adequacy but we will accept nothing less. My friends, it has always been my faith that the eventual triumph of decency and freedom and right in this world is inevitable. . . ." Coming from one who had dealt for so long and so generously in the rhetoric of inspiration, the words had a pinched-off, unnatural sound.

As the determined effort to throttle down the steam of defense spending coinciding with the beginning of the business decline had unhappy consequences, so the coincidence of the drive of the economizers with the advent of the *sputniks* also produced inauspicious results. Newly aware of the threatening lag in both science and development, the public read of research programs curtailed despite the assurances of the administration that this would not happen. The mood of the country deepened to a dark gray. This was the winter of our discontent following on the autumn of our disillusion. In many respects the reaction to the *sputniks* was irrational, since the loss we had suffered was not actual and immediate, nor irretrievable. With an inspiriting leadership, reviving the will, the resolution, we would be on our way again. The gloom and pessimism could be seen as a reaction to the unthinking optimism that had been the mood so short a time before. Less than a year had passed since the "all's well with the world" political campaign and the bland assurances of that campaign which had obscured the drift of events in the Middle East toward a truly frightening major crisis. If the downward swing toward despair seemed wild and unreasonable, it could be accounted for in part, at least, by the fact that we had been living in a state of euphoria which had been induced by the deliberate effort of the administration to make us believe that we were the bravest, richest, strongest, and happiest people in the world.

The disillusion, the discovery of what lay so close below the surface of our charmed contentment, took many forms. An increase in the price of new automobiles made some of us take a new look at the exaggeration of tail fins and chromium on cars that were beginning to be as gaudy as circus wagons. Were we trading tail fins and chromium for national security? And the temper of growing distrust played a part in the decline of the economy for, as we have been told so often, confidence under our system *is* supremely important to a healthy economy. Thus the chain of events created a whole series of unhappy coincidences.

We were newly aware that while the military budgets had seemed large in dollars—inflated dollars—they were each year smaller in relation to the nation's gross national product. The interservice disputes in the Pentagon sounded louder and angrier than ever. As the controversy over whether to proceed with the Air Force's missile, the Thor, or the Army's Jupiter became public, few could doubt that these disputes had impeded the development of advanced weapons. Later evidence made it quite clear, in spite of the official denials, that the Army had been delayed in the development of the Jupiter's potentials, both in weaponry and in the orbiting of a satellite. All this had a disturbing effect as generals and admirals sought to bring their case before the country.

The President's reputation in the field in which he had spent his life was further shaken. He had shown in his campaign speech of five years before that he had known so well what to do about making over the defense department, and yet he had not done it. His popularity dropped nearly twenty points in the polls, but this seemed to reflect not so much a change in his personal relationship with his public as a growing distrust of his administration. Perhaps it was simply that the image was growing too dim to cast its glow much beyond the man himself.

To what extent was the President aware of the mood of the country? Fewer and fewer people, aside from the little circle of intimates in the White House, saw him. Almost his only direct contact with the outer world was the press conference, and after October 30, preoccupied with preparing and delivering the "chins-up" speeches, he held no conference for several weeks. Yet for all his seclusion, he can hardly have been unaware of the shock to opinion of Little Rock and the *sputniks* and what this might mean to the status of his administration. The conference with Prime Minister Macmillan was an attempt to restore confidence at home and abroad. And while the communiqué that came out of that meeting was merely another expression of earnest determination, the decision was taken then, at the urging of Paul-Henri Spaak, Secretary General of the North Atlantic Treaty Organization, to have the heads of government, rather than just the foreign ministers, attend the December meeting of the NATO Council.

On November 25 the President went out to the airport to greet the King of Morocco and accompany him to a public ceremony of welcome on the way to the White House. He stood hatless in the cold, damp air while the King was accorded the customary honors. In a role that was familiar and congenial he looked his normal self. Then, for the third time since he entered the White House, he suffered a serious illness.

At the time of the heart attack and the ileitis operation he had still been in the ascendant. His presence, using that word in its broadest meaning, was essential to his party and important to the country and the world. Now, in the context of doubt and uncertainty over his powers, it was no longer possible to feel that with his recovery we as a people would also be restored to our former strength. Too much had happened for that, and this time Hagerty, in Paris preparing for the NATO meeting, was not on hand to take firm control of the shaping of the news. The first word given out was that the President had suffered a chill which would prevent him from attending the state banquet in honor of the King. In the tense interval that followed, the most sensational rumors circulated. The President was going to resign; he was paralyzed; he was dead. It was not until the next afternoon that it was revealed that he had suffered a mild stroke which had caused some impediment in his speech and would necessitate several weeks of rest and recuperation.

All this was depressingly repetitive. The shock to the country was not so great as it had been on the other occasions, although the stock market dipped sharply downward in the first reaction. In the time of prosperity and well-being, the President had been a happy symbol of confidence and optimism. In the time of discontent and disillusion, the fact of the chief, the leader, having been stricken was just one more blow. Less than a week after his stroke, he attended church with Mrs. Eisenhower. It was a courageous, if perhaps foolhardy, gesture in recognition of the need to restore in the public mind the sense of his presence and all that it might still mean to the country. In their first discussion following the diagnosis, Adams, Nixon, and Dulles had decided that the illness would certainly mean that the President could not attend the NATO meeting in Paris. Word of this as given out by the White House was reported to have greatly angered Eisenhower. He was represented as determined to go unless the doctors should flatly refuse their permission. He would not be an invalid, those close to him said; he would die with his boots on.

It was important that he attend the NATO meeting. In Europe the image of the man and the nation was a wavering and uncertain one. It was widely believed abroad that he was a dying man, with the government run by a junta of his close associates in the White House. Dulles, with his constant no-saying, his constant moralizing, his self-righteousness, could not have been more unpopular in Europe and, for that matter, in Asia. It was important, too, because the President before he left Washington had had no idea of the popular pressure to negotiate, or at least to seem to be willing to negotiate, with the Russians.

For a man of sixty-seven who had had three serious illnesses in two years, it was an ordeal. He went through it with soldierly resolution. He had virtually mastered the lingering traces of the speech impediment, and in addition to the formal meetings that went on for four days, he met privately with one head of state after another. Europe had a better impression of the President as a result, and out of the conference came an agreement, in effect a concession from America, to explore the possibility of negotiation through diplomatic exchanges and perhaps eventually through a meeting of foreign ministers that might lead to another summit conference.

In this last illness was a poignancy, a pathos, far greater than in the highly dramatized medical recital of the heart attack and the ileitis operation. Here was no struggle waged with the help of doctors and medicines. It was one man trying to stand up under a severe blow in an impossible office in a time of unparalleled crisis at an age when most men had retired to quiet and ease. One morning during the NATO conference he had driven out to his old headquarters at SHAPE. On the immediate and practical side this was to advertise the military resolution of the alliance. But it was also a sentimental journey to an old scene of glory.

When the band of the Garde Republicaine had played
the "Marseillaise" and "The Star-Spangled Banner"—and
as a concession to his condition he kept his hat on against
the raw dampness—he made a little speech standing on
the steps of SHAPE headquarters. Confessing that he was
homesick for his old command, he told a story about a
hard-boiled sergeant who had served under General Patton before the war and who had had a great struggle trying to whip some raw recruits into some kind of military
form. The sergeant had at last said to the General that
they were "only fitten to be civilians." The President went
on:

> Now I must confess, that there is certain of that feeling in
> my heart today. After forty years of wearing a uniform it
> would be strange if I felt quite as natural with my civilian
> hat as I did with my military cap. But I want to indulge for
> just a moment this feeling of homesickness, the fun of going
> and seeing some of the people of SHAPE, not because they're
> the same ones, because there's only a few left here of five
> years or so ago, but they are the same ones carrying the same
> mission, doing the same job that all of us here started in 1951,
> I believe it was. . . .

With the growing concern over his failing powers, it
followed that his every public word and movement would
be watched and analyzed to try to determine his real
condition. Some newspapers that had been most ardent in
his support at the outset were impelled to call on him to
resign for his own good and for the good of the country.
But it was clear, once he had recovered from the first
phase of the stroke, that he had no intention of resigning
short of a second attack that would incapacitate him.
What is more, Congress had failed to provide a law that
would clarify and define the terms of the resignation of
a president. Still another factor to be considered, if he

had wanted to resign, was the newly added rigidity in the American system which would confront his successor. The Twenty-second Amendment to the Constitution provides that a vice-president who serves more than two years of the unexpired term of a president who has died or resigned shall be eligible for only one elected term. This meant that if Richard Nixon became president before January 20, 1959, he would automatically face the handicap of being a lame-duck president in the event of his election in 1960.

In January Eisenhower went to Capitol Hill to read his State of the Union message to Congress. So much had been expected of it, far more than was reasonable. It was to repair his prestige and dispel the gloom and pessimism. No single speech could do that, and certainly not a State of the Union message traditionally devoted to generous assurances covering every possible field of human endeavor. The comment was sharply divided: he looked well and he spoke vigorously; he was failing and sick, and he spoke with hesitation and difficulty. While members of Congress were on the whole kind in what they had to say about the content of the speech, their remarks had the air of charity for one in need of patience and tolerance. Uncertainty tempered the attitude of both friends and critics. Always more or less removed from the ordinary give-and-take of politics as a soldier-hero, the President now stood on precarious ground, his great hold on the popular imagination shaken, but still with a claim for sympathy and understanding in his ordeal.

On January 15, at his first press conference since October 30, the same watchfulness prevailed. Reporters, crowded into the balcony as well as on the main floor of the conference room in the old State, War and Navy building, were anxious to assess the man whom they had seen only on two or three ceremonial occasions since his latest illness. The most common verdict was that he had greater difficulty expressing himself, that he was more discursive, and that his answers were noticeably less responsive to the questions.

But it could be argued that this was merely a matter of degree. Time and again in the early years, reporters had left the press conferences baffled by what seemed to be either his ignorance or his disinterest. He simply did not engage himself in the flow of world events which more often than not were matters of headline knowledge. This was now accentuated. A striking illustration was his reply to a question about whether he thought Robert Oppenheimer should be invited back into government in order to try to bring about a better relationship between government and the scientific community. The President said he knew nothing about it; he thought the Oppenheimer case was settled. He added that if any new information were available then he would have no objection to the matter being reopened "because personally I don't know the individual."

As often in the past, the President was speaking as though his personal opinion or personal knowledge about a momentous issue was irrelevant to the discussion of that issue. Again, at the same conference, in discussing the reorganization of the Defense Department, he referred to the fact that he would be commander in chief for only three years more, adding that his "personal convictions, no matter how strong," could not be the final answer. This detachment, his insistence on standing apart from controversies involving the nation and the world, may have been more pronounced, but it was in fact a matter of degree. This had been his attitude on the integration of the schools prior to Little Rock. It was the attitude of one who seemed to regard the presidency almost as a ceremonial office, a lofty platform from which to view the scene, and concur when concurrence seemed to be called for. The explanation would seem to go back to that persistent belief, originating long before his nomination to the presidency with the friends who were working on him to say yes, that he would be president of all the people, standing above the battle, unifying the country.

There seemed to be nothing to do but carry on in the same way as before. The budget for the fiscal year 1959 was almost entirely the work of an old-fashioned budget-balancer, Percival Brundage, aided and abetted by Sherman Adams. With a total of $74,400,000,000, it actually called for expenditure of a smaller percentage of the estimated value of the gross national product than the budget of the previous year. In short, for national security as well as for spending for other than defense purposes, it was a smaller slice of what was available. The total appropriation requested for federal aid to education was only slightly more than half of the total that had been sought for the fiscal 1958 budget, since the new request contained nothing for school construction.

As has happened before under our system of divided powers, the party in control of Congress challenged the party in control of the executive. The Democrats, with the exception of some of the Southerners, championed in one field after another the view that the federal government must act to advance the public good and the growth of the economy. They were quick to point out that for at least a year and a half the economy had ceased to grow. The division was sharp over how to cure the recession that deepened in the late winter, with five million unemployed. It was sharp, too, over what to do about agriculture, since, after more than ten years of tinkering with one program

"Mr. President, the Carriage Awaits"

Low in the Manchester *Guardian*. Reprinted by permission of David Low, "Copyright © Low All Countries"   November, 1954

and another, agricultural surpluses were still very large
and farm income was continuing to decline. But when the
powers of government are divided between the opposing
parties, a kind of double veto operates to prevent action
by either branch. A hostile Congress can frustrate the
plans put forward by the executive. The executive, in turn,
can, by impounding appropriations and by simply failing
to act, as the Eisenhower administration has so well demonstrated, thwart the will of Congress.

With such a stalemate in effect, the atmosphere in
Washington was incredible. Thanks to the work of Washington *Post* reporter Chalmers Roberts, the content of the
Gaither report, withheld by the administration, became
known. In this prolonged cry of dire warning, the challenge to America, if we were not to be overwhelmed in
one way or another, was seen to be immense, calling for
a great thrust forward with vast energy and inevitable
sacrifice. The meaning of the Rockefeller report, which
was published in full, was hardly less plain.

Yet one clearly sensed again the old drift of inaction.
We had been rudely awakened by the *sputniks*. But we
seemed to prefer to go back to sleep. In the words of the
familiar hymn:

> Earth might be fair and all men glad and wise . . .
> Would man but wake from out his haunted sleep.

There could be no doubt that it was a haunted sleep,
for beneath the old familiar surface there was the sense
of forces moving beyond the control of anyone in authority. In seeking to avoid a summit conference, we seemed to
be choosing nothing but the old perilous drift of the cold
war. In the Middle East we seemed to be drifting toward
new disasters. There was consolation in the fact that on the
last day of January an American satellite went into orbit.

But this had come to seem a small triumph against the doubt of our own purposes and destiny. While the words out of Washington had the old reassuring sound, even when they were uttered by the President they failed to carry the weight of conviction. He was gradually fading from view.

"Shadow and Substance"

Hugh Haynie in the Greensboro *Daily News*   December 4, 1957

Thirteen

The Afterimage

As in other years, the Eisenhowers went in early February to Milestone, the Humphrey plantation in Georgia. This had been a magic restorative in the past—the place itself and, even more important, the temperament of the host, with his easy, confident outlook. But their visit this time reflected the profound changes that had taken place.

When the *Columbine* arrived at Thomasville, there was snow on the ground. For a week the weather was windy and blustery, and the President stayed close to the fire playing bridge with the Humphreys and the Ellis Slaters. Reporters who had gone down with him wrote about how the famous Eisenhower luck had changed. In other years it had been sunny and warm and the men had each day gone out for quail.

Toward the end of the stay, an incident occurred that illustrated the alteration in the public attitude toward the Eisenhowers. Reporters learned that the President intended to fly back to Washington by way of Phoenix, Arizona, so that he could take his wife to the Elizabeth Arden beauty resort there. On being closely questioned about the 3,000-mile flight, Hagerty lost his temper. It was, he said, nobody's business where the President chose to fly his own plane.

This could scarcely have occurred a year before, and it would have been considered almost lese majesty in the

275

first term. If the President knew of the criticism, he ignored it and flew to Phoenix, where he managed to get in a round of golf before returning overnight to Washington. While other presidents have known the pinpricks of such criticism of their private acts, Eisenhower had until that point been almost completely immune. Even when the sum total of the gifts made to him for his Gettysburg farm had been revealed, amounting to more than $40,000 in everything from tractors to blooded cattle, the public seemed to accept it as though this were part of the tribute due a hero. Asked about the attack on Eisenhower for taking his wife 3,000 miles to a beauty resort in a government plane, Harry Truman came to his defense, saying that a president had a right to shield his private life and that of members of his family from the public gaze, and that to attack him through his wife was grossly unfair.

Although this trivial incident may have caught the public attention, being the type of "extravagance" readily comprehended, far more important was the fact that during his fortnight at Milestone no pretense was made that the President was taking part in any of the decisions of state. No reports of consultation by telephone with Dulles and others in Washington were forthcoming. Hagerty simply had no news to give out, and reporters saw the President only once, as he was finally able to start out with Humphrey for a morning of quail shooting. And again a small incident, the fact that in the photographs taken on the occasion the President was holding his gun improperly, became news to emphasize the changed attitude.

His withdrawal from view for that fortnight seemed to mark a kind of divide in opinion. Publications such as *Time* that had up to that point treated him as though he had been a holy relic burst forth in criticism. It was as though he now stood out of the line of vision against a sunset sky, his shadow still large across the earth, but a shadow nevertheless. The aura of the hero, the man of boundless good will, the man in whom we had all wanted to believe, was there, but it was an afterimage; the glow fainter and far less compelling.

At his first press conference after his return to Washington the question arose once more that had all along been perhaps most troubling and persistent. How much did the President know of what went on in his administration? In his absence a festering scandal involving the Federal Communications Commission had grown out of a House investigation into the independent agencies. This had a strong family resemblance to the "mess in Washington" that the Republican crusaders had sworn in 1952 to exorcise. In the course of the investigation it developed that Sherman Adams had written two letters to Murray Chotiner, Nixon's campaign manager in 1952, saying that he had taken up with the Civil Aeronautics Board a matter in which one of Chotiner's clients was interested. Asked about these letters the President replied:

Well, you are bringing up a thing I have not heard of; but I will say this: There is a number of cases that come under the CAB that the White House must act on. Any time that they refer or have anything to do with the foreign routes that CAB has authorized, or refused to authorize, then the President himself is required to make the final judgment. And, very naturally, my staff would want to get any additional information that I need. So, I would assume it is so on that case.

This was quite beside the point, since the case in question involved a nonscheduled domestic airline and was in no way concerned with a foreign route. The reporter started to put another question on the same subject when the President, visibly displaying his annoyance, said, "I don't want anything more about that."

Trivial though this matter happened to be, it was a mir-

"Well, Men, What'll We Refrain from Doing Now?"

Herblock in the Washington *Post*, 1958   April 28, 1958

ror of larger doubts and uncertainties. A man preoccupied with the awful problems of a time in which the fate of the whole human race hung in uncertain balance might understandably have overlooked such a fly speck. But whether he had any firmer knowledge of the details of the problem of survival in the nuclear age was a question raised by a disturbing revelation that came at about the same time. At issue was the question of negotiation with the Russians over disarmament and the singling out of a proposed suspension of nuclear testing as a first step in such negotiation. Involved, it is scarcely necessary to add, were choices so weighted with meaning for the future as to be almost beyond ordinary human understanding.

In June of 1957 the President had seemed about to come around to the view of his adviser on disarmament, Harold Stassen, that consideration of agreement on a controlled experiment in limiting the tests could be separated from the other elements of a complex American proposal put forward on an all-or-nothing basis. At this point the chairman of the Atomic Energy Commission, Lewis Strauss, intervened. He took with him to the White House for a talk with the President two physicists, Dr. Teller, popularly known as the father of the hydrogen bomb, and Ernest Lawrence. Their views in opposition to any cessation of testing, however temporary, were well known, and having seen the President they broadcast these views to the world with the White House steps as a sounding board. The President then wavered, subsequently rejecting the Stassen position and finally dispensing with Stassen himself.

The Atomic Energy Commission had in September of 1957 conducted an underground nuclear explosion. The first reports on the outcome of this test were taken as confirming the contention of Teller and those arguing against any suspension that tests could be conducted secretly and that therefore no trust could be put in any system of inspection and control. This was the kind of persuasion undoubtedly brought to bear on the President to harden his attitude. The Commission announced that the shock waves of the explosion had not been felt beyond a range of 250 miles. But a little inquiry brought to light the truth, which was that stations of the Coast and Geodetic Survey had recorded the test explosion at an Alaska station 2,300 miles distant and at other points in the continental United States more than a thousand miles from the site. Confronted with these findings, the Commission explained it had made an "inadvertent" error.

Did the President understand the means by which he had been brought to change his views on the issue of nuclear testing? Did he have any knowledge at all of the episode and its significance? Another scientist, Harrison Brown, a geochemist at the California Institute of Technology, delivering the Gideon Seymour Lecture at the University of Minnesota, spoke of "the iron wall of secrecy" shutting out all but a privileged few from the knowledge on which survival could depend. The President seemed unaware of this wall or indifferent to it and the fact that he himself might be shut off by it from information on which an independent judgment could be formed.

At a press conference in late April his remarks revealed something of his attitude toward information: "I do not believe," he said, "that any individual . . . can do the best job by just sitting at a desk and putting his face in a bunch of papers. Actually, the job when you think of the interlocking staffs and associates that have to take and analyze all the details over every question that comes to the presidency, he ought to be trying to keep his mind free of inconsequential details . . . so that he can make clearer and better judgments."

Outwardly he was so little changed; the same erect frame, the same firm, smooth face with a slightly pinkish glow, the smile not quite so ready or so spontaneous, yet the familiar trademark. Faithful to ceremony, he was photographed regularly attending church with members of his family. Here was the exemplar, the man of good will who had believed that he could transcend the strident discord of politics and bring harmony by good will itself.

If he were disillusioned one would never know it from him except as his seeming indifference to the office he held became more and more evident. This was a phenomenon that puzzled and distressed many who had been most admiring in the past. The *Wall Street Journal* in a long and remarkably frank editorial on "The President's Leadership" suggested that the growing sense of public uneasiness came from the feeling "that there has been nobody in Washington running the show." One evidence of this, according to the editorial, was the way in which members of Congress and administration officials alike were turning to Nixon for both political guidance and direction on government policy. Nixon, it was pointed out, had become more and more a center of authority with the marked alteration in the President's role.

Others were hard put to explain the alteration and the open attacks on the President that went with it. He seemed to be more isolated from the outside world, more insulated in the shell of the White House. All presidents in modern times have had to break out of this shell or reconcile themselves to their insulation. Eisenhower had ceased to try, or so it appeared to even his charitable critics. To an even greater degree he was alone with the few friends out of business whom he liked and trusted. The guest list for the state dinner for Queen Elizabeth II was largely comprised, outside the inevitable officialdom, of these cronies, with no representation of the arts, letters, science, or any field of endeavor other than business. This exclusion seemed shocking, since it was an official occasion of the first magnitude in honor of the ruler of America's principal ally. The members of his administration saw the President rarely and then only on official appointment obtained often with great difficulty.

His commitment to politics, to the office, to the responsibilities of leadership was visibly slackening. Given in the first instance reluctantly and under duress, as he believed, it was being allowed to lapse. In mid-March the President addressed a conference of Republican women who had come to Washington for a series of pep talks on the forthcoming congressional elections. As the cautious Associated Press noted, the President's speech consisted for the most part of familiar reassurances that the recession would end and that there was no cause for concern. "This recovery effort of the American people will be successful," the President said, rejecting the "make-work approach with its vast, slow-moving projects." This was at a time when the number of jobless was officially reported at 5,200,000, and if involuntary part-time work were included the total was closer to 6,000,000.

Where was a program on which the party could unite to wage an election campaign in the fall? One reply was foreign aid and renewal of the reciprocal-trade agreements act. The President had spoken strongly in behalf of both measures, but unfortunately a large number of Republicans in Congress, perhaps a majority, were in favor of greatly reducing foreign aid and emasculating the trade agreements act. Senator Andrew Schoeppel of Kansas, chairman of the Republican senatorial campaign committee, announced that if candidates for office found these issues embarrassing in their own states they were free to ignore them. This was interpreted by the Democrats as an invitation to Republican office seekers to turn their backs on the President if it suited their convenience, and they asked what would happen to the measure on which such a high priority had been placed if Republicans were told that they might desert their leader should it be expedient to do so.

The recession had in any event made it more difficult to obtain approval for reciprocal-trade and foreign economic assistance. Why should we vote help for people outside the country, so the argument went, when Americans are without jobs? Powerful interests, such as in the domestic lead and zinc industry, both mineowners and miners, were pressing for higher tariffs either through special concessions or by a revision of the reciprocal-trade act that would weaken the authority of the President to hold tariffs down. At stake in this instance was the good will of immediate neighbors of the United States—Canada, Mexico, and Peru—for whom the sale of minerals was one of the few sources of dollar earnings. If they were shut off from this source then they would perforce curtail their dollar purchases. In this way a process of constriction threatened to spread and deepen the recession.

The President asked Eric Johnston, the head of the Motion Picture Association of America, to direct a full-scale publicity campaign for the foreign-economic program. One result was a great rally in Washington at which Eisenhower, Truman, Stevenson, Dulles, Acheson, and many others called on Congress to approve the program of nearly $4,000,000,000 the President had requested. This was impressive as a demonstration of support at the highest level. But was it a substitute for the kind of hard political bargaining to which other presidents have resorted when a program they considered vital to the nation was in jeopardy? Again and again the President had said he would recommend measures to Congress, which then had the responsibility to pass them or reject them. But in the

troubled air the question arose once more as to whether
this luxury of detachment was one which the occupant
of the White House could afford.

The same detachment was evident in the President's
approach to his role as party leader and the November
election. He indicated that he would not support candidates who declined to back his program. He had, however, done little of a positive nature to advance the cause
of "modern Republicanism." While certain of the troglodytes on the extreme right for whom the President felt
the greatest repugnance, such as Senator Jenner of Indiana, were withdrawing, this appeared to be a tactical withdrawal in preparation for a later struggle to control the
party. And there were few signs that more moderate Republicans were either in the incubation or the hatching
stage ready to come forward and fill in the vacancies.
When they spoke frankly in private, Republican leaders
confessed their dismay at facing an election under these
circumstances.

Elections, however, come and go with constitutional
regularity, and parties rise and fall. Far more important,
with the expectation of a meeting with the Russians at the
summit, was the President's role as leader and spokesman
not alone for the United States, but for the West. Would
he go to such a conference with the confidence of the peoples of the West and with the vigor and resolution necessary to negotiate with such hard, shrewd negotiators as
Khrushchev and Company?

The Gallup poll announced on March 21 showed that
he had dropped five more points to fifty-two per cent, the
lowest standing ever recorded in his popularity score. According to Dr. Gallup, this was equivalent to the low point
that Franklin Roosevelt had reached in his twelve years in
the presidency. Without benefit of polls, the word from
Western Europe, and particularly from Great Britain,

"I've a Good Mind to Start Talking Back!"
Hugh Haynie in the Greensboro *Daily News*   April 21, 1958

"The Melancholy Days Are Come—"
Hugh Haynie in the Greensboro *Daily News*
October 28, 1957

where he had once been held in such high esteem, was that his prestige had all but vanished. No longer was the full measure of blame for American rigidity and uncertainty, as seen in European eyes, put on Dulles. The President had defaulted on his responsibilities, and, whether the reason was his infirmity or his indifference, Europe was no longer in a trusting or even, for that matter, a forgiving mood.

The attitude toward the President and his administration in the United States was one of unease and embarrassment even. He appeared more and more as a prisoner of his office, a captive of his own indecisiveness, a captive of the hero-worshiping public, a captive of the agonizing dilemma of an era of nuclear annihilation in which man's old savage instincts lay close to the fragile surface of law and order. There were those who contended that since he had nearly three more years in the office it was wrong to say anything that would further damage the President's reputation. But surely the future of the nation in relation to the office and its transcendent importance, the rigidities and the incongruities of the power of the presidency and the resources for exercising that power, deserved to be discussed however much the discussion might reflect on the man who happened to occupy the office. If this was to conclude in a personal tragedy, it was also a national tragedy, because the American people had romantically, impetuously, frivolously almost, invested so much of the future in a dream of the past.

Epilogue

Weak President, Strong President

It is only in the long perspective that the real substance and lasting consequences of Dwight Eisenhower's role in America's history will be apparent. It is not too early, though, to make some preliminary observations. If his public record had ended with his military career, it seems safe to assume that a high place would be secure for him. But he went on to become President of the United States in a time when this office was never of greater moment for the country and the world. General Grant is remembered for his successes as a general at least as much as for his failures as a president, but Eisenhower's performance in the presidency will count much more heavily in the final summing up. At the same time, his record casts new light on the office itself.

The office of president, with all its powers and its limitations, has been the subject of a debate that has gone on almost from the beginning of the American form of government. Theoretical discussion of the presidency can hardly be detached from a consideration of the men who have occupied it. The inherent difficulties of the office, its limitations as against its powers, are overcome by a strong president. A weak president resigns himself to the narrow boundaries prescribed for the office while authority drains away through all the chinks of a structure rigid in its inception and shaken over the years by the massive weight put upon it. This judgment of weak and strong, convenient and popularly accepted, is one way of tagging the presidents with readily identifiable labels. But it ignores the evidence accumulated in ever-increasing volume in recent decades that the office itself in a time of recurring crisis makes exactions difficult or impossible to meet.

The thesis of strong and weak presidents, by way of interpreting the American past, may have sufficed before 1914. Just a century ago we had a perfect example of the weak president in James Buchanan, who failed utterly to come to grips with the growing conflict over slavery and the rights of the states. As he delayed and compromised and looked the other way, the nation drifted toward a civil war that might conceivably have been averted if a strong stand had been taken in time. Buchanan was followed by Lincoln, who in order to save the Union had to strain the powers of the presidency almost to the breaking point as commander in chief during the four years of civil war. Lincoln was a strong president. Theodore Roosevelt at the turn of the century was a strong president, asserting America's authority far beyond the ocean boundaries.

But it is in the twentieth century that the simple and convenient categories seem to falsify history. Woodrow Wilson was surely a strong president. The program of reform carried out in his first term was a far-reaching recognition of America's rapid industrialization. But under this strong president the country drifted ever closer to the orbit of the European war. Until he was forced to do so by events, Wilson was unable or unwilling to set a course in accord with America's own interest that might have put the warring powers on notice as early as 1915 of our ultimate determination.

There were, to be sure, many reasons besides the inherent difficulties of the office of the presidency why this should have been so. One was the deep division in the country, political, ethnic, emotional, over the issue of the war. But when it came to the peace at the end of the war and adherence to the League of Nations, of which Wilson had been the architect, the strong president failed to master the dichotomy of the system. By repudiating the League of Nations, the Senate prepared the way for so much that was to happen in the future: the tragedy of the long stagnation between the wars and then the catastrophe of World War II itself.

One may argue that the defects of personality of the ailing Wilson brought about the debacle. But surely it is obvious that the system itself puts a premium on personality. It makes it imperative in times of stress and strain that the president by the very force of his personality triumph over the handicaps of an office that suffers under so many inhibiting restraints while at the same time the burden upon it is each year increased. In this way, with a growing concentration on the personality of the man, the nature of the office has been magnified in recent times to an extraordinary degree.

Franklin Roosevelt was a strong president who followed a weak president. Herbert Hoover had stood helplessly by while the Depression deepened toward disaster. As Roosevelt sought through one improvisation after another to end the economic crisis, all the facets of his remarkable personality were brought into play. By his political skill, his showmanship, his great intuition, his mastery of the media of communication he tried to reconcile the powers of the executive and the powers of Congress in order to end the massive unemployment and bring the economy back to normal. But what he asked of Congress was more often than not too little and too late, and on Capitol Hill it was subjected to further delays and reductions. He was faced with the fact that almost invariably Congress looks upon a strong president as a natural enemy who must be subdued.

There can be no doubt that Roosevelt understood what the rise of Hitler meant to Europe and the world. Yet in his 1936 campaign he said next to nothing about the peril threatening the world of which America was a part with the Nazi and Fascist dictatorships. This was a strong president, and yet not until September of 1937 did he venture to speak of his country's responsibility and duty in view of the drift toward war. His speech in Chicago calling for a quarantine of the aggressors drew a violent reaction both in and out of his party. Although the Democrats had large majorities in Congress, and he had won the greatest victory in the history of the presidency, he never again, except by indirection, tried to bring the American people to confront the peril that was steadily growing both in Europe and in Asia. The preparations to meet that danger were also taken for the most part by indirection, with military measures camouflaged as relief projects.

Here once again one may argue that political necessity, in the face of seemingly irreconcilable divisions in the country, dictated Roosevelt's caution. But the division of powers between the executive and legislature, which time after time has made them seem like hostile nations maintaining only the most tenuous and wary relationship, accentuates and aggravates the divisions in the country and the lack of coherence and discipline within the two parties.

The assessment, as between the man and the system, can be debated endlessly, and the conclusion is very likely to be subjective. In the instance of Eisenhower the powers of the presidency have been greatly diminished. Taking a detached view of his own role, the President has been unwilling or unable to exercise many of those powers. Declining in both authority and prestige, the office has resembled much more nearly what it was in the late nineteenth century, when a ceremonial president was content to let the tides of economic destiny have their way. Because of his repeated illnesses, the President has delegated perhaps more authority than any other man to occupy the White House. He has done this in part by default and in part because of his own belief and conditioning in the chain-of-command system of the Army. The paradox, in view of his indifferent and hesitant approach to the powers of his office, is that the popular image, one of the important factors in his rise to great national popularity, was that of a strong man sweeping all before him as the triumphant commander of the allied armies in Europe.

It is here that the magnification of the office, to which Roosevelt contributed so much with the glitter of his personality, is seen in sharp perspective. After the glamour of FDR and the cult of personality that adhered to him, it was for a time, at least, something of a relief to have Harry Truman in the White House. In the popular interpretation he was just a plain, ordinary American, proving that any American boy could be president, and his popularity in the polls rose to a high point. But this did not last for long. Soon many of his fellow citizens were discovering that he was a small man, not big enough for the presidency, "just a politician." In contrast, Eisenhower was above politics, he was a big man, he stood for something. The desire, one might say the necessity, was for a new personality inflated by one device and another to fit the new dimensions of war and crisis, the dimensions of the big man, the leader. With his self-deprecation, his determined modesty, Adlai Stevenson ran counter to the popular desire.

While the office itself has suffered a serious erosion of power in Eisenhower's tenure of the White House, the magnification of the personality is still in evidence, rather like the tune of a song that persists long after the words have been forgotten. For his failure to use the powers of the office, Eisenhower, in the interpretation of weak and strong, must be put down as a weak president. But any assessment has also to take into account the fact that he brought to the office so little preparation for what is surely the most difficult and demanding position in the world today. The unreasoning expectations were so high in the light of a towering reputation that had little or nothing to do with politics or government.

What manner of man then can fill the office? This is the question we ask ourselves with 1960 in view. Put alongside the vast inflation of both the office and the personality of its incumbent that has taken place, the candidates in each party are one by one dismissed. No, X will not do, too young, too immature. Y? Certainly not; he is unstable and you cannot trust his judgment in a crisis. Z? Yes, he is honest, but limited, stupid even. Thus are the names ticked off in a long litany of discontent.

Of one candidate we have seen enough to gain an idea of what sort of president he would be. Vice-President Nixon has been working with the energy of two or three men and the zeal of at least ten to make up for some of the deficiencies of the White House. In so doing he has put himself forward as a kind of deputy president, although he has had to follow a wary course lest he seem to be trying to usurp power.

Where the President has wavered or seemed reluctant to act, Nixon has pressed for action. This has been true particularly of measures to end the recession and bring about a business upturn. In collaboration with some of the younger, activist members of the cabinet, the Vice-President worked up a catalogue of remedies to be applied as quickly as possible. As president it is quite evident he would use all the resources of government with little regard for the ideological prejudices of the right wing of his party. At every opportunity he has pushed the cause of foreign aid and reciprocal trade.

One can be sure that as president he would employ all the public-relations opportunities of the office to the fullest. For Eisenhower the press conference once a week has been an ordeal to be avoided whenever possible. Nixon could be expected to go back to a twice weekly conference, and he would make frequent use of the free television and radio time that is available to a president to explain his policies and inform the country on the state of the nation. Here, too, the contrast with Eisenhower would be sharp.

In short, Nixon might be a strong president. These judgments cannot be reached in advance of events, but he would certainly be an active one. The question that remains is whether this is a new Nixon or whether the same motivating force of brash, unmitigated ambition is still dominant. At the Gridiron dinner in March 1958, a character representing the Vice-President was made to say, "Yes, this is the new Nixon—everything new except the ambition." For many who remember the campaigns against Jerry Voorhis and Helen Gahagan Douglas in California and the famous good-cloth-coat–Checkers telecast in the 1952 campaign the image of the ruthless opportunist will not be overlaid by the portrait of the responsible statesman.

But even those who refuse to let the bitterness of the past be erased by the stress on constraint and constructive policy, and part of this, it must be noted, is due to a skillful public-relations approach, cannot deny that Nixon is preparing himself for the presidency as few men have ever done. He told a friend that he was reading Arnold Toynbee's full seven-volume essay in the philosophy of history. But because he knew so little about world history he

"Let's See—What'll I Wear Today?"
Herblock in the Washington *Post*, 1956

February 15, 1956

wanted advice on another history fairly extended and yet
without the intrusion of a philosophic bias. Is this maturity or is it merely a sort of cultural Operation Boot-
straps? Maturity is the imponderable, and the chief ingre-
dients in the presidency are courage and integrity. Only
the test, if it should come, can determine whether the
brash young man has grown up to the responsibilities of
Toynbee's time of troubles on an unparalleled world scale.

As to the impossible office itself, it is an interesting reflection on the American character that while we have
talked a great deal about what might be done to remedy
some of its more obvious defects, little actually has been
done. This must be put down as one of President Eisenhower's most conspicuous failures, for he surely, more than
most presidents, has had reason to know how impossible
are the demands of the office. His own lack of knowledge
and experience has in fact served to illuminate how overwhelming are its exactions on the time, the talents, and the
temperament of the individual who occupies the White
House.

From the administration, in the face of an obvious and
urgent need, has come little more than the vague suggestion of consideration for establishing administrative assistants: three vice-presidents, deputy presidents, in effect—
one for foreign affairs, one for domestic administration,
including supervision of the array of independent agencies, and one for the ceremonial and public side of the
office. Yet even this has never been put forward in the
form of proposed legislation, and there has even been a
reluctance to discuss it, as though it were somehow a confession of the President's inadequacy. To have brought
forward for discussion a relatively modest proposal to for-
malize and legalize the lifting of at least a part of the
burden, even if this had ultimately failed of passage,
would have been a service to the country. And in the

aftermath of the President's heart attack, when the public was keenly aware of the burdens and pressures of the presidency, such a proposal might have met with great favor.

The indefatigable Adams has done as much as he could. But a great deal of what he did was extracurricular, without benefit of legal sanction, and therefore his position has been awkward and anomalous. He has been accountable neither to Congress nor to the public, and so, very much as in the instance of Harry Hopkins, who performed some of the same services for Roosevelt during the war, he has had great power which he has used by indirection. As a consequence, he has come under increasing attack. One can only assume that both Adams and his chief felt that it was the better part of valor to pursue a discreet course that could be masked by the claims of the executive to privacy of executive action. But this was scarcely a service to future presidents who must try, whether strong or weak, to fill the specifications of an office created in the eighteenth century and overborne by the burdens of the mid-twentieth century.

In the same way, nothing has been done to try to cure the anomaly of the vice-presidency, which continues to be a kind of half-horse half-alligator betwixt and between the executive and the legislative branches. Committed by the Constitution to preside over the Senate, a nominal and minor duty, the vice-president cannot be a deputy president. Would it not have been a service to the country if the administration had put forward a Constitutional amendment aimed at curing this anomaly? If only for purposes of discussion, and there are strong arguments for maintaining the vice-presidency as it is, such an amendment would have brought a greater public awareness of how outmoded and outgrown the relationship between the president and the vice-president must appear against a background of continuing crisis.

With respect to one of the principal uncertainties, the administration did make a cautious move. The Attorney General sent to Congress a proposal to define the terms under which a president might delegate his powers to the vice-president in the event of his own incapacity and when, if he were again able, he might have these powers restored to him. This met with stubborn resistance from Sam Rayburn, the Speaker of the House, who has long exercised arbitrary authority over the course of legislation. While the proposal produced some discussion of the hazards involved in failing to clarify the ambiguous language of the Constitution on presidential disability, the matter was dropped. Yet the hazard is as great as ever despite the personal agreement entered into by Nixon and Eisenhower. In the illness of Woodrow Wilson, when, except for the routine function of government, the executive branch existed in a state of suspended animation, this was clear enough. We may not always have presidents who are strong, vigorous, healthy, and yet the office as constituted, with its exactions on a single individual, demands nothing less than that.

One may ask a further question, and that is whether a reform of the office, no matter how carefully worked out to modify the burden and to insure greater flexibility, is in itself a warranty against the disaster of a weak president in a time of crisis, a president in office, short of the impossible process of impeachment, for four years. As Buchanan's procrastination and evasion became more apparent in the face of the gathering storm over slavery and secession, John Sherman of Ohio, then a representative and later a senator, said: "Timidity controls the executive power. The President listens to, and is controlled by

"Shouldn't You Sort of Be Out Front?"

Hugh Haynie in the Greensboro *Daily News*

April 11, 1956

threats. . . . The Constitution provided against every probable vacancy in the office of President but did not provide for utter imbecility." Sidney Hyman has shown in the Christian Gauss Lectures at Princeton how fateful was the drift:

In the year 1856, every American leader of the first rank except for James Buchanan had been bloodied up in the bitter fight over the Kansas-Nebraska bill. The nation itself was sick of political strife over the slavery issue and of the politicians who were in the forefront of that strife. As for James Buchanan, however, it had been his good fortune in the immediately preceding years to be out of the country and in England where he served as the American minister. Since his person was free of all the rancors clinging to the other leading politicians, the Democrats brought him back from England, nominated him for President and engineered his election on the ground that he was the one man best equipped to restore peace and union in the nation.

In the White House, Buchanan was faithful to the campaign image which gave him the keys to the place. Social ceremony in his administration reached new refinements of elegance. A great religious revival movement, with the President as its head, swept the country—as if religion was an effective substitute for politics. Soon, also, Buchanan came to be known as the Parlor President. He built a hot house to the rear of the executive mansion where he grew flowers and grapes for the White House table—a hot house that stood until Franklin D. Roosevelt tore it down as a needless extravagance.

The months and years dropped away in this decorous fashion. Certainly no one could complain that Buchanan had lowered the dignity of the presidency. But the time came when his Southern Secretary of War shipped Federal arms to Southern arsenals where they could be seized by prospective secessionists. His Southern Secretary of the Navy sent the Federal fleet on a cruise away from Southern ports where they might stop their seizure by prospective secessionists. Presumably President Buchanan could excuse his oversight of these matters by saying they had not yet reached his desk. For they were, indeed, performed while he seemed to be concentrating on grapes. But when the danger of secession shrieked so loudly that even the President could not ignore it, he offered a legal opinion that he had no power to "coerce" the rebellious states. All he could do was to "conciliate" them.

It was not that President Buchanan did anything bad. He simply did nothing. He may have felt that the forces he confronted were beyond control, the rivers of passion and hatred rushing on irresistibly toward a sea of blood.

In our dismay in the aftermath of the *sputniks* and of Little Rock we called on the President to unify and inspire the country, and the commonest judgment was that he failed. But what an inordinate task it was—a task for a man with a sense of mission such as Eisenhower, the compromiser, the reconciler, has never had. He began by believing that he could unify the country. Yet in his years in the White House the differences—the differences that transcend the conventional political boundaries—have if anything been accentuated. Whoever follows after will have to reassert the authority that has been permitted to decline. He will find that he must go against a common assumption that we can afford to permit authority to wander about the horizon like a lost ghost. It is an unenviable prospect, and we shall be more fortunate than we deserve if we find the man who has at the same time sufficient strength and sufficient restraint to fill an office that has grown so amazingly in the scope of the demands made on it and so little in the resources available to it.

Index

DATE DUE

NOV 4 '68			
GAYLORD			PRINTED IN U.S.A.